Produced by Gensler Research
New York, NY
www.gensler.com/research
research@gensler.com

Published by ORO Editions
Publishers of Architecture, Art, and Design
www.oroeditions.com
info@oroeditions.com

˙10 9 8 7 6 5 4 3 2 1 First Edition

ISBN: 978-1-939621-41-2

Library of Congress data available upon request.

Color Separations and Printing: ORO Group LLC
Printed in China

International Distribution: www.oroeditions.com/distribution

ORO Editions makes a continuous effort to minimize the overall
carbon footprint of its publications. As part of this goal, ORO
Editions, in association with Global ReLeaf, arranges to plant
trees to replace those used in the manufacturing of the paper
produced for its books. Global ReLeaf is an international
campaign run by American Forests, one of the world's oldest
nonprofit conservation organizations. Global ReLeaf is American
Forests' education and action program that helps individuals,
organizations, agencies, and corporations improve the local and
global environment by planting and caring for trees.

Gensler

Research

Catalogue Vol.2

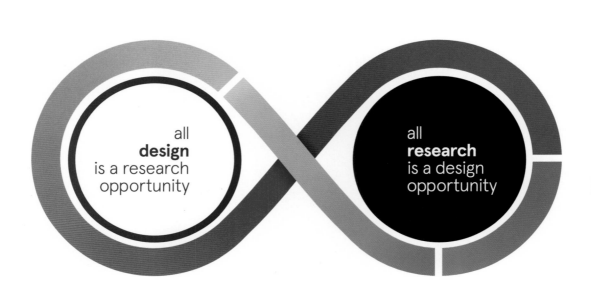

Why We Research at Gensler

Our design philosophy is centered on enhancing the human experience. As a firm and community, we are committed to making a positive impact on how people live and work in our modern world. To truly enhance the lives of people, our design approach is informed by insight, observation, and research. We call this the design/research cycle.

As our lives are molded by remarkable flux and transformational change—driven by technological innovation, globalization, climate change, and shifting demographics—our projects are becoming more nuanced and complex than ever. It's clear to us that design solutions for this new world cannot be based on yesterday's models. Great design today directly addresses the transformational forces shaping our world with elegant, empirical solutions that enhance human experience and chart a new path forward.

That's where our research comes in. Our people are taking on the toughest questions of our day, applying research findings to real-world challenges and creating positive impact for our clients and communities. Not only do the insights we uncover shape the innovative outcomes of our large projects like Shanghai Tower; they also inform our approach to every project we touch, from a retail store to a law firm design.

This catalogue documents our research efforts, summarizing 41 projects completed by teams across the globe. Similar to our first catalogue, each entry is organized around a simple framework that outlines what each team did, the context, the results, and what's next. Also similar, this catalogue leverages creative information graphics to capture the issues and findings in a rich, multilayered representation—a celebration not only of research, but of the power of design. We hope you find it informative and thought-provoking.

Diane Hoskins, FAIA, IIDA
Co-CEO

Andy Cohen, FAIA, IIDA
Co-CEO

Contents

01–05

Evolving Cities

06–08

Cultural Transformation

09–13

Engagement & Experience

14–16

Organizational Strategy

Appendix

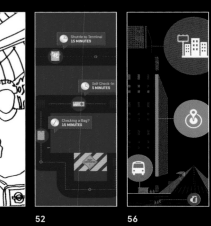

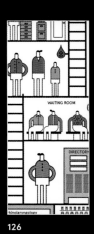

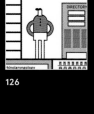
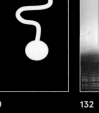

1980s
New financing vehicles are developed, which allow backing from a wider array of sources – including the newly developed commercial backed-mortgage security

1985
LA Times reports that of downtown LA's properties are foreign investments – a large portion backed by Japanese investors

1980s
LA City institutes an Artist in Residence program – encourages more initial live-work reuse in the downtown core on a small experimental scale

1947-1990

aving the privat

Attorney open plan

rategy room

Evolving Cities

As the migration toward urban centers continues, the way we design our cities must evolve to accommodate increasing populations, shifting expectations, new technologies, and a growing understanding that globalization must be balanced with local, community-centric design solutions.

Evolving Cities:

Building Performance

Hack the City

What is the best way to improve our buildings and cities?

Existing, underutilized infrastructure permeates our cities. Transforming these buildings can unlock untapped opportunity, helping better meet local, community, and business needs.

WHAT WE DID

Building on Gensler's prior "Hackable Buildings" research, we developed speculative design proposals to improve our various local neighborhoods and cities via creative design intervention. To achieve this, we also developed an event-based exhibit format to gather innovative, cross-disciplinary feedback and hyper-local data directly from community members and stakeholders, which helped to refine our ideas and ensure relevance.

By conducting these design explorations and events in multiple cities, we were able to develop locale-specific design solutions, while exploring broader demands and trends in commercial development. Our goal is to use this process of engaging civic leaders and local stakeholders to improve and contextualize design solutions, and expand the scope and understanding of how design can positively impact cities.

THE CONTEXT

Mobility and technology are changing the way we live and work. Our lifestyles are becoming more urban, driving a shift in expectations of the type, or even amount, of space we expect to have in which to live, work, and play. Rising prices in many cities are compounding the issue, shifting focus toward adaptive reuse of existing buildings and other under-utilized infrastructure to make best use of the space and resources available. As a result, the challenge for architects, developers, and building owners in the future may increasingly be how to "hack" the buildings we already have, instead of how to build the next cool thing.

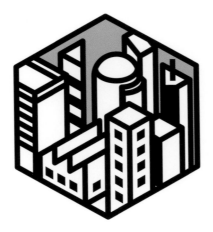

Hack cities, not just buildings.

We must think beyond the interior and exterior design of individual buildings to focus on how they fit into the fabric of an urban neighborhood or district. Successful development serves this macro picture by integrating with nearby housing, transit, retail, dining, and educational institutions. Change may occur at the building scale, but impact should be felt well beyond.

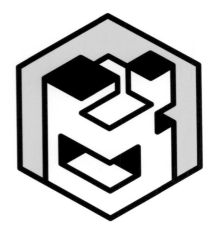

Celebrate existing infrastructure.

We observe a growing interest in "authentic" existing buildings in many cities. A hackable approach can preserve an older building's character while improving performance and usability for modern tenants.

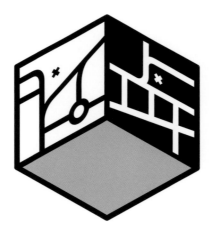

Learn from other cities.

Opportunities and challenges must be identified at the local scale, but similar questions are often being tackled in other neighborhoods and cities as well. Integrate global knowledge and best practices into the design and development process.

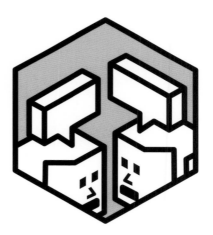

Engage the public.

Issues of authenticity, context, and history are nuanced and cannot be approached in a top-down manner. Engaging public and civic stakeholders in the process of hacking our buildings and cities is an opportunity to integrate with the community and better uncover opportunities, insights, and successful strategies.

THE RESULTS

We gathered and documented our research to create a website (www.hackablecities.com) through which we, and the broader public, can engage with our research and ideas on a city-specific level, as well as begin to draw broader connections across geographies. This exercise highlighted some unexpected connections and similarity of issues between cities, and the digital platform has become a tool for dialogue.

The role of entrepreneurship in urban development, the influence of a thriving technology sector and workforce, and questions of placemaking and "stitching" together a disconnected urban fabric emerged as common themes across many of the cities explored. Questions around the right scale of development and the types of intervention needed were also frequent— in several projects, our teams chose not to focus on a specific building to hack, instead focusing on an entire block or district.

Perspectives

"Baltimore's emergent entrepreneurial landscape is rapidly evolving. Biotechnology, education, and social enterprise are cross-pollinating, creating a hotbed of activity some are calling the 'Next Economy.' By providing a space that fosters cross-sector collaboration, we can tackle some of Baltimore's most complex challenges and opportunities, widening the region's social and economic potential."

– *Building from Strength: Creating Opportunities in Greater Baltimore's Next Economy,* Jennifer Vey, The Brookings Institution

WHAT'S NEXT

Our current efforts are focused on further developing tools and processes to engage the public around the idea of hackable buildings and cities. Gensler has spent the past few years exploring this idea among our designers and clients, but we want to open it up to new and broader perspectives. We want feedback from end-users, developers, city leaders, community members, and other stakeholders on what they think a hacked building, space, or city can be. We want to motivate people and the community to activate vacant spaces, promote neighborhood development, and encourage creative entrepreneurship.

Hackable Buildings, Hackable Cities Event, Baltimore, MD

Manhattan's Next Hot Neighborhood

Can policy change revitalize Manhattan's Midtown East?

WHAT WE DID

We partnered with Cornell University to investigate the development of a new set of urban policy recommendations for the "up-zoning" of Manhattan's Midtown East neighborhood. Our goal is to encourage building renovation and neighborhood redevelopment in an area of Manhattan that is currently undervalued despite robust existing, and upcoming, transit connections.

This research builds upon a prior proposal to change zoning laws in Midtown East put forward by the Bloomberg administration in 2013, which is being reconsidered by the current administration. Our ideas also build on prior Gensler research and design exploration around "Hackable Buildings," which focused on the potential to transform existing buildings to meet new uses and tenant expectations via creative design intervention.

THE CONTEXT

Midtown East has the potential to be a model central business district. Despite the multiple problems that the area has today—an antiquated office building stock with an average age of 70 years and 78 percent of buildings 50 years old or more, alongside pedestrian network challenges, overcrowded transit, a lack of open space, and a dearth of capital investment for renovations and upgrades—its future can be bright if the right actions are taken.

Its proximity to Grand Central Terminal, a major local and regional transportation hub and architectural landmark, makes the area particularly ripe for development. The in-progress "East Side Access" project, which promises easier commuting from Long Island and Queens via Grand Central, and the eventual addition of a new Second Avenue Subway both represent significant opportunities for the area. And proximity to major development projects focused on the technology and biotech industries—from Cornell Tech on Roosevelt Island to the NYU Alexandria Center for Life Science—makes the area poised for future interest from similar tenants.

A key challenge for the area is that the existing buildings are largely old, but not the type of historic or loft buildings currently drawing premium rents from tenants in the creative and technology industries. These buildings are often challenged by low slab-to-slab heights, tight column spacing, and small windows—all traits typical to their age, and a roadblock to traditional renovation schemes focused on the more open, flexible workplaces prevalent today.

Midtown East Building Statistics

Acres of land

173

Buildings

400

Employees working in Midtown East

245,000

Commercial businesses

8,000

Office space (sf)

70,000,000

Pedestrian congestion
■ Amount of space vs. ■ Volume of use

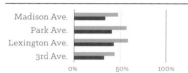

Madison Ave.
Park Ave.
Lexington Ave.
3rd Ave.

0%   50%   100%

Buildings 50+ years old	Avg. building age	Avg. FAR	Open space
78%	**70**	**11.2**	**0.1%**

Understanding Floor Area Ratio (FAR) and Density in Urban Context

A building's Floor Area Ratio, or FAR, is calculated by dividing a building's usable floor area by the total area of the building lot.

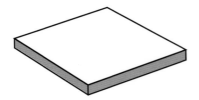

FAR = 1.0
10,000 sf building covering 100% of lot

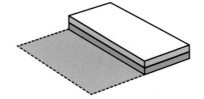

FAR = 1.0
10,000 sf building covering 50% of lot

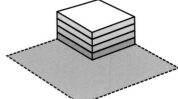

FAR = 1.0
10,000 sf building covering 25% of lot

THE RESULTS

Despite the challenges of Midtown East's existing building stock, **it is not financially feasible to demolish and rebuild every building in Midtown East.** Instead, we must find new ways to incentivize the revitalization of the existing buildings in this area to achieve transformational change in a manner that is more economically and environmentally sustainable. Often development is spurred by the use and transfer of unused Floor Area Ratio (FAR)—building area or "air rights" allowed by code but not used by an existing building—to adjacent buildings.

The district's current zoning laws are too restrictive for this to happen at the scale and pace necessary.
A prevalence of smaller buildings makes the assembly and redevelopment of large parcels extremely challenging, which in turn makes the opportunities for large-scale redevelopment projects, to which current zoning and development policies and practices are tailored, few and far between. At the building scale, redevelopment often requires dramatic intervention that can reduce usable space—for example, removing floors or adding atria to increase ceiling heights or natural light—which can mean lost revenue and even greater unused FAR.

The result is a significant amount of development opportunity within Midtown East in the form of this unused FAR. **We propose a modified zoning and FAR transfer strategy for Midtown East,** which would provide excellent opportunities for companies that need creative space with easy access to transportation and amenities. This would also enable building owners to renovate parts of existing floor plates to create more open spaces, implement smart and playful design to existing buildings, and increase program/usage diversity through strategic programming.

WHAT'S NEXT

Now is the time to create policies and incentives that will help Midtown East evolve into a vibrant district reflective of the significant location and transportation benefits that it already holds. We hope to use this research to open discussions with the city's policy makers, building owners, and developers to make that happen.

PERSPECTIVES

"**Although Midtown East historically has been one of the most sought after office markets in the New York region, the average age of its office buildings is 70 years old. Much of East Midtown's office building stock has low floor-to-ceiling heights and numerous interior columns that fail to meet the standards of corporate tenants. Without new office buildings that meet modern standards, the area's competitiveness as a premier business district will be compromised.**"

– *East Midtown Rezoning Overview*, NYC Department of City Planning

WHAT THIS MEANS

Allow building owners and developers to transfer FAR to nonadjacent properties within their portfolio. The ability to transfer recovered or unused FAR to nonadjacent properties has precedence in NYC policies that designate "special districts" to free development opportunities, often while preserving historic landmarks. This strategy is currently in place for the Grand Central Subdistrict, and is also in use at Hudson Yards.

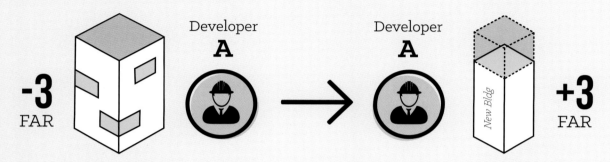

Create a FAR marketplace through which air rights can be aggregated, bought, and sold. This would expand incentives at the level of individual buildings; unused air rights and/or FAR "recovered" through building renovation or repositioning could be sold in an open marketplace. The city would also directly benefit through taxation of transactions.

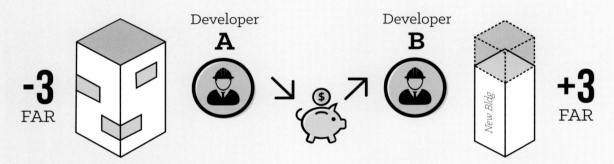

Provide incentives to developers willing to renovate existing buildings and the public realm. Creating policies that prioritize building renovation not only is more sustainable and more feasible at a district level, but also offers opportunities to incentivize public realm improvements. Tax incentives or bonus FAR in exchange for infrastructure and public realm improvements should be pursued.

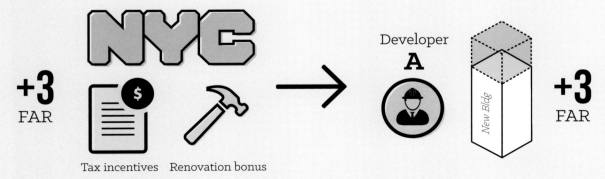

Tax incentives   Renovation bonus

Curating the Right Mix

How should we design mixed-use spaces to connect the urban landscape and elevate the human experience?

Unprecedented urban growth is compromising China's public spaces; we must place higher value on cultural, human-scale "spaces in-between."

WHAT WE DID

We investigated the economic impact and characteristics of mixed-use spaces in Chinese cities, building on prior exploratory research into the optimal design of mixed-use developments and "spaces in-between." In this phase, we focused on a series of eight case studies of mixed-use projects in China and used Jones Lang LaSalle data on rental rates and other factors as a basis for analysis. We also conducted a survey among 72 developers and design industry professionals to discover the most important aspects of these mixed-use spaces from their perspective.

THE CONTEXT

Chinese cities are under tremendous pressure. In 2015, there were 1.4 billion people living in China, making it the world's most populous nation, accounting for one-fifth of the planet's population. And, this vast population is quickly shifting from rural to urban centers—300 million people have migrated to Chinese cities in the last 20 years. While these popular movements coincide with general economic growth and prosperity in Chinese cities, we also see two notable, unintended consequences:

Geographic and cultural fragmentation. Between 1981 and 2008, nearly 600 million Chinese citizens were lifted from poverty. But as they migrated to cities for greater employment opportunities, many Chinese residents left their families and communities behind. The result is cities full of people with few interpersonal connections, searching for new communities while also trying to retain their identities and recover lost cultures and traditions.

Loss of human scale. The significant increase in urban populations has led to massive housing development in Chinese cities. Sometimes occupying entire city blocks, these giant buildings have had a dramatic impact on the scale and experience of Chinese cities, and the way residents interact with the environment.

This is a unique time in China's development, and as designers, it is our responsibility to work with developers, government, and citizens to ensure a sense of community, ownership, and empowerment among residents of Chinese cities.

◆ **Xintiandi** is seen as one of the most successful mixed-use developments in China. It was able to preserve several blocks of traditional Shikumen architecture, built on a human scale with traditional motifs, and connect it to the nearby man-made Taiping Lake and Park. Art and event programming throughout the Shikumen district and park promote gathering and socializing among residents, while alleys, indoor plazas, and proximity to subway lines keep Xintiandi well-connected.

◆ **Sanlitun** is a unique, two-site mixed-use project focused on retail, leisure, and hospitality, located within a busy office and residential hub. While Sanlitun employs many of the strategies of Xintiandi, its local Hutong architecture is slightly different in style, and connects spaces through open courtyards rather than alleys. Open plazas feature trees and fountains, and serve as venues for public sculpture exhibits and other cultural events. Multilevel pedestrian walkways ensure connectivity between destinations.

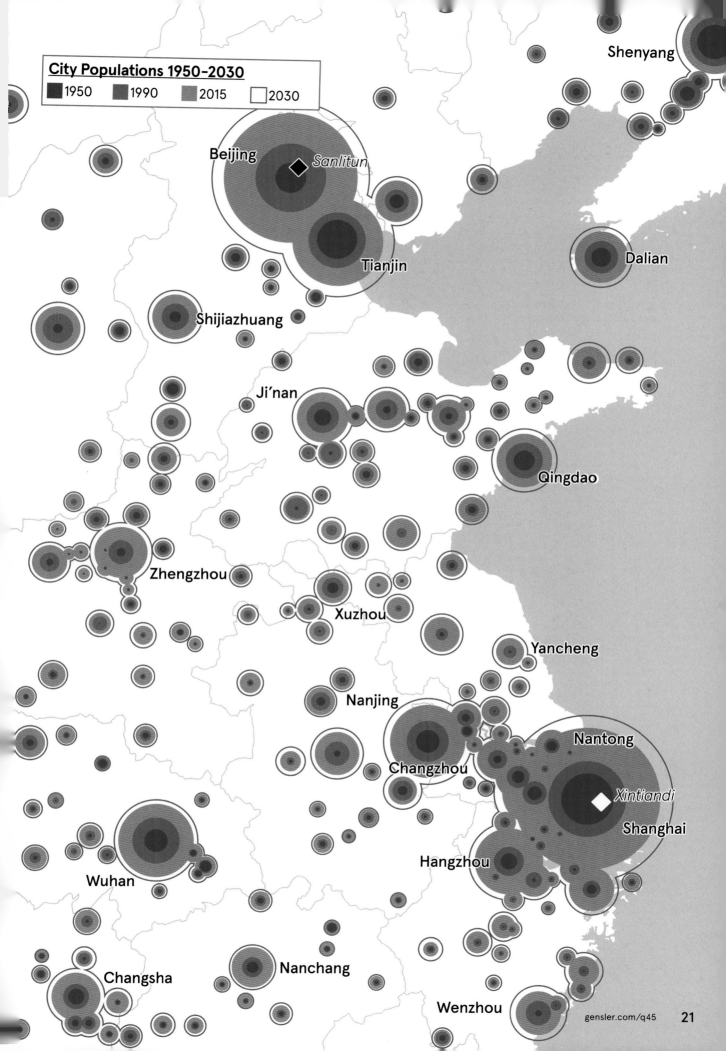

City Populations 1950-2030

■ 1950 ■ 1990 ■ 2015 □ 2030

Beijing ◆ *Sanlitun*

Tianjin

Shijiazhuang

Shenyang

Dalian

Ji'nan

Qingdao

Zhengzhou

Xuzhou

Yancheng

Nanjing

Nantong

Changzhou

◇ *Xintiandi*

Shanghai

Hangzhou

Wuhan

Changsha

Nanchang

Wenzhou

THE RESULTS

Mixed-use spaces have become one of the most prevalent types of new development in contemporary China. Given their scale, these projects have significant impact on the image and function of their neighborhoods and cities—with potential to improve and elevate the human experience, or further erode the urban experience based on their success or failure. Traditionally, decisions on the form and function of these developments focus on qualities such as tenant needs, programmatic elements, aesthetics, and infrastructure, as well as vehicular and pedestrian circulation.

While these are all tangible aspects of successful design, **we believe that we can deliver greater value and better spaces by also accounting for the less tangible aspects of the spaces that connect destinations within urban spaces.** The interstitial spaces between buildings—plazas, courtyards, passageways, sidewalks, parks—are where nuanced activities and social interactions occur. These spaces in-between can be the glue that holds a city and its people together. The design and activation of these spaces is key to unlocking the full performance potential of urban mixed-use projects.

In our first phase of research, we identified **six key aspects of well-designed spaces in-between that framed our efforts: nature, art, culture, human scale, connectivity, and community.** The responses to our survey of developers offered additional insights and confirmed their importance. While the 72 professionals surveyed considered all six factors important to successful projects, integration with nature and the human scale were considered most important (82 percent and 74 percent ranked them as important, respectively), quickly followed by cultural connection and community (both ranked by 69 percent of respondents).

These findings are also supported by our case study and data explorations. Analysis of JLL real estate data showed that **projects that leveraged the experiential measures identified in our research also proved to have better traditional performance** (lower vacancy and higher rental rates, for example). Two case studies in particular—one in the neighborhood of Xintiandi in Shanghai, and another in the neighborhood of Sanlitun in Beijing—proved useful. As successful developments, both were good proving grounds; in Xintiandi, 20 percent of the overall development was devoted to nature, 8 percent to historic cultural districts, and 3 percent to outdoor art space. In Sanlitun, an impressive 41 percent of the district was devoted to nature.

Data represents the percent of survey respondents who consider each element important to spaces in-between.

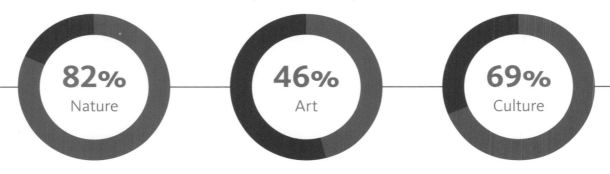

82% Nature   **46%** Art   **69%** Culture

RESPECT INTANGIBLES TO MAXIMIZE PROJECT PERFORMANCE.

The in-between elements of the built environment are what create the connective fabric of a city's character and soul—and they are also key to the success and financial performance of mixed-use projects. Though the elements of these projects are often intangible in nature, we have shown through case studies that their inclusion leads to tangible performance benefits.

CREATE A DYNAMIC MIX OF SPACE TYPES AND EXPERIENCES.

Cross-pollination of the various elements identified as successful to spaces in-between is an opportunity to improve performance and create a differentiated urban experience. Each element delivers experiential value on its own, but the designed interaction between elements—spanning art, nature, scale, culture, connectivity, and community—is where the greatest opportunity to improve performance lies.

PERSPECTIVES

"Well-conceived public art can also confer ongoing visibility, publicity, and brand identification to a development."

– "How Public Art Affects Real Estate Values,"
Butler Burgher Group

WHAT'S NEXT

This research is a continuation of a previous project that first established the importance of spaces in-between among investors, developers, and property advisors. What is most exciting is that the application of this research is relevant across many different project types and scales.

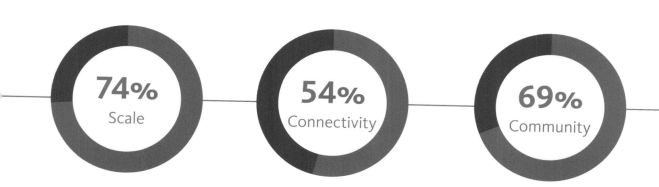

74% Scale   **54%** Connectivity   **69%** Community

ART NATURE PROMENADE STADIUM MUSEUMS HOSPITAL STRUCTURE PLAZA INDUSTRY SPORTS COMMUNITY

Impact through Design

Can architecture and design be part of a global climate change strategy?

**UPPER OCEAN
HEAT IS RISING**

**GLACIER VOLUME
IS SHRINKING**

WHAT WE DID

We reviewed and analyzed published data on the building sector's contribution to climate change, and audited Gensler's building portfolio to understand overall project performance and develop specific sustainability benchmarks. We used data-informed statistical models to measure energy savings, greenhouse gas emissions, and aggregate water savings for projects that were designed to high–performance standards, versus the national Commercial Buildings Energy Consumption Survey (CBECS) baseline. We used these results to estimate the impact the global buildings sector could have in mitigating climate change, and identify additional steps architects can take to positively impact its effects.

THE CONTEXT

Climate change threatens our ability—and the ability of future generations—to live in a peaceful and prosperous world. According to NASA reports, the earth's surface has warmed significantly since 1880. Most of this warming has occurred since the 1970s, with the 20 warmest years on record having occurred since 1981, and 10 of the warmest years occurring in the past 12. Additionally, the National Centers for Environmental Information (NCEI) reports that global upper ocean heat is rising, snow cover is retreating, glacier volume is shrinking, and climate extremes and storm intensities are increasing.

The global buildings sector is responsible for more than one–third of global energy use and CO2 emissions. The International Energy Agency (IEA) estimates buildings must drop total emissions by 77 percent by 2050 to cap global temperature rise at 2° Celsius, the best-case scenario for planetary surface temperature rise. We believe that it is important to elevate the conversation about the connections between climate change and the built environment, and we are focusing our attention on the power of design to create dynamic new models of energy usage, urban density, potable water conservation, and sustainable economies.

CLIMATE EXTREMES AND STORM INTENSITIES ARE INCREASING

SNOW COVER IS RETREATING

THE BUILT ENVIRONMENT HAS A SIGNIFICANT IMPACT ON THE PLANET AND HUMAN HEALTH, GIVING ARCHITECTS AND DESIGNERS A TREMENDOUS OPPORTUNITY TO PROTECT OUR CLIMATE AND CREATE A HEALTHIER WORLD.

THE RESULTS

Sustainable building design solutions are already having an enormous impact.

In 2014, Gensler's new building projects alone spanned 820 million square feet and were designed to use approximately 81.1 kBtus of energy per square foot per year—a 32 percent improvement over the U.S. national average. For the same period, Gensler's commercial interiors portfolio spanned 469 million square feet and was designed to use approximately 0.82 watts per square foot for lighting—a 23 percent improvement over the U.S. national average. At that scale, these energy savings represent a significant reduction in greenhouse gas emissions by designing buildings to exceed code requirements.

The next generation of high-performance buildings can do even better.

If we designed every project at the efficiency achieved by those performing in the top 20 percent of our portfolio, we could double our impact and achieve a net reduction of approximately 8 million metric tons of CO2 emissions a year. Compounded annually until 2030, this would equal more than 102 million tons of CO2 saved from the atmosphere. Over 15 years, the emissions savings would be equal to permanently removing 6 percent of U.S. power plants from the grid.

Green building strategies are proven economic drivers.

The green building industry has shown encouraging growth, reaching a reported $260 billion globally in 2013. It is predicted that as much as $1 trillion will be spent on sustainable retrofits for existing buildings over the next 10 years. Even with this growth, green buildings continue to make up a small fraction of the total building stock in highly industrialized, wealthy nations.

Measurable impact requires a higher standard and broader scale.

Architectural designers, planners, and engineers around the world need to deliver effective solutions to climate change–related phenomenon to ensure we are doing everything in our power to reduce energy demand, improve water savings, and reduce greenhouse gas emissions stemming from the built environment.

To achieve this, we must pursue design partnerships with engineers and clients who share and advance our commitment to reducing operational energy demand supported by our designs. We must design and specify building materials that consume less energy, beginning when and where they are made, and continuing through maintenance and the full building life cycle. We identified six key strategies we believe can make a significant impact:

1. **ENERGY REDUCTION**
   Initiate energy conversations with clients at the onset of the design process, document client energy targets, and track those targets to stay honest.

2. **INNOVATIVE PARTNERSHIPS**
   Form industry-leading teams of engineers and consultants who are able to execute energy models and simulations, and leverage these models for decision making.

3. **MATERIAL SELECTION**
   Before choosing materials, analyze their life cycle and embodied energy to inform discussions with clients, and encourage the selection of sustainable materials.

4. **INFORMED COMMISSIONING**
   Coach clients to commission their projects and building systems appropriately to align with building operations and energy-use targets.

5. **INCLUSIVE DECISION MAKING**
   Encourage building operators to be stakeholders in the design process to build understanding and awareness of energy goals, and ensure operators have the tools needed to track those goals.

6. **POST-OCCUPANCY EVALUATION**
   Promote post-occupancy evaluations for all projects. These conversations are another opportunity to work with building owners and occupiers to fine-tune and calibrate projects for the highest performance.

We will be working closely with our clients in the coming years to evaluate their global real estate portfolios and develop strategies for meeting their own sustainability and climate change impact goals. We have affirmed our commitment to limiting global temperature rise to under 2° Celsius by signing the Paris Pledge for Action, a critical step on the path to solving climate change. We pledge our support to ensuring that the level of ambition set by the agreement is met or exceeded.

"THERE'S ONE ISSUE THAT WILL DEFINE THE CONTOURS OF THIS CENTURY MORE DRAMATICALLY THAN ANY OTHER, AND THAT IS THE URGENT THREAT OF A CHANGING CLIMATE."

– **BARACK OBAMA, PRESIDENT,** UNITED STATES OF AMERICA

DECREASE GREENHOUSE GAS EMISSIONS

DECREASE ENERGY DEMAND

IMPROVE WATER SAVINGS

02

Evolving Cities:

Community Engagement

Downtown Tech Boom

What can other cities learn from San Francisco's urban tech migration?

WHAT WE DID

We investigated the strategies employed by companies moving or establishing downtown offices as a way of attracting tech talent, focusing on San Francisco as a case study. We began by interviewing various members of the local business community, followed by secondary research and case studies exploring various situations in which a technology company invested in a downtown location or headquarters. We used these case stories as a lens through which to understand what strategies spurred successful integration with the city and neighborhood, and which strategies created challenges or tensions worth considering as other companies pursue similar moves.

MONTREAL 20
VANCOUVER 18
SEATTLE 8
TORONTO 17
BOSTON 4
SAN FRANCISCO 1
CHICAGO 7
NEW YORK CITY 2
LOS ANGELES 3
AUSTIN 14
SÃO PAULO 12

2015 TOP TECH ECOSYSTEMS

Compass, a San Francisco–based benchmarking software company (compass.co/blog.compass.co), has published a 2015 Global Startup Ecosystem Ranking Report that identifies the top 20 startup "ecosystems" in the world.

THE CONTEXT

Not too long ago, discussions with technology companies in the Bay Area were largely focused on how to bring elements of urban living into the Silicon Valley. This trend has flipped—today, we more typically see suburban organizations exploring or executing moves into the city. Tech companies founded in San Francisco have seen tremendous growth, while companies located in the South Bay are considering satellite offices in the city in search of the young talent that resoundingly prefers urban living and working.

These moves have not been without their challenges. Local and national news continues to focus heavily on a growing tension brought about by the surplus of young tech workers moving into the city and driving up housing prices. And while the influx of a young, affluent population should bring benefits to local businesses, the traditional amenities strategy many companies brought with them from the suburbs—providing everything in the building to keep employees happy and working—stood in the way of many of the potential benefits to local neighborhoods.

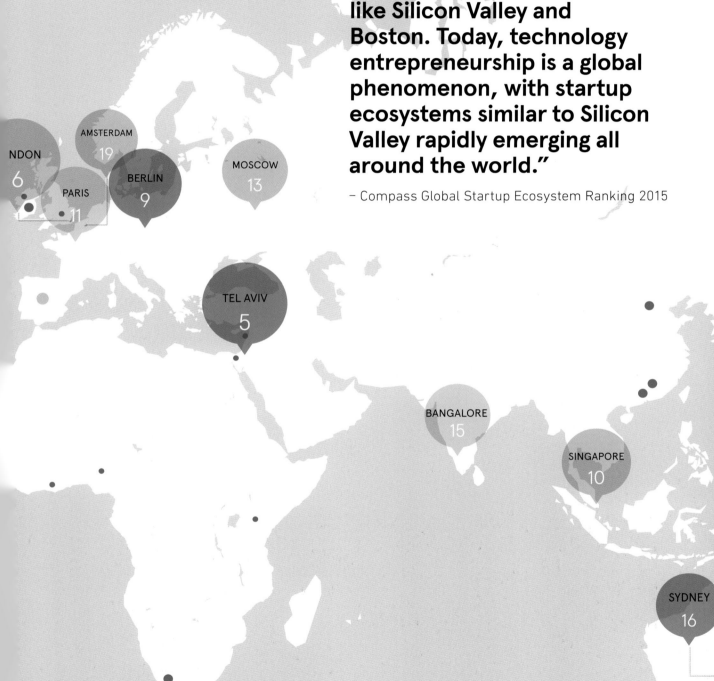

"Twenty years ago, almost all tech startups were created in startup ecosystems like Silicon Valley and Boston. Today, technology entrepreneurship is a global phenomenon, with startup ecosystems similar to Silicon Valley rapidly emerging all around the world."

– Compass Global Startup Ecosystem Ranking 2015

NDON
6

AMSTERDAM
19

PARIS
11

BERLIN
9

MOSCOW
13

TEL AVIV
5

BANGALORE
15

SINGAPORE
10

SYDNEY
16

As the urban migration of technology companies continues, and as many other industries look to technology companies as the vanguard of workplace strategy, it's worth stepping back to reflect on lessons learned with the San Francisco technology community as a case study.

FOLLOW THE TALENT

San Francisco is increasingly being used as a lure for tech talent as more and more companies consider opening up satellite locations in the city. Policies about who gets to work from the satellite locations vary by company, and many are still exploring the optimal relationship between urban and suburban locations, but the message is clear—the young employees that companies are looking to attract prefer urban locations, and companies are following suit if they want the best people.

TECH EMPLOYMENT IN SAN FRANCISCO IS AT AN ALL-TIME HIGH, REACHING 65,300 IN THE FOURTH QUARTER OF 2015,
UP FROM 56,700 A YEAR EARLIER, 36,639 AT THE END OF 2011, AND 32,500 IN THE BEGINNING OF 2001 AT THE HEIGHT OF THE DOT-COM BUBBLE.

SOURCES: State of California Employment Development Department and New York State Department of Labor

SAN FRANCISCO TECH EMPLOYMENT

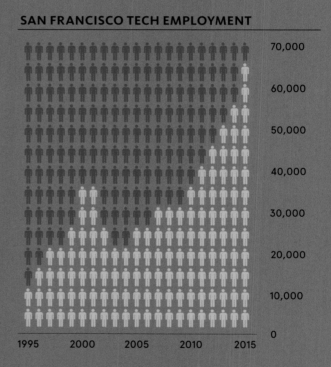

70,000
60,000
50,000
40,000
30,000
20,000
10,000
0

1995   2000   2005   2010   2015

WHAT THIS MEANS

POSITIVE URBAN DISRUPTION

The opportunities for companies to create meaningful change and regeneration in the urban realm is huge—but so are the potential pitfalls. Change should happen in partnership with the community, and preserve not displace local culture and people.

CREATE A POROUS WORKPLACE

Insular suburban workplace models don't translate to urban areas. Inclusive experiences that encourage employees to engage with the community, and vice versa, are more respectful and more successful.

NEIGHBORHOOD INTEGRATION

San Francisco's "Mid-Market" area has seen the greatest influx of companies in recent years, often driven by tax breaks in return for improvement engagement with the local community.

Companies have done this through various methods, many proving successful, including community service and education programs. Design strategies that offer a service to the public—making workspaces available to host not-for-profit or local events, creating shared amenities—have also been proved successful.

CHALLENGES OF INSULARITY

There has been a learning curve, however—not all strategies proved successful. Companies providing a bevy of in-office amenities that keep employees in the building have hurt local businesses even as property values rise, driving displacement and tension. Companies that provide food vouchers for use in local businesses and create spaces shared between their employees and the larger community—whether cowork space, event space, retail space—have fared better.

NEW YORK CITY TECH EMPLOYMENT

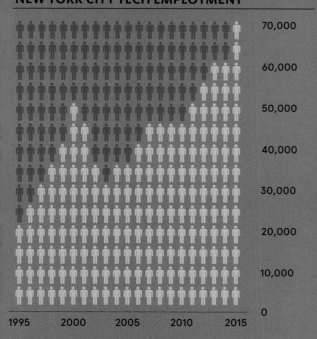

LOS ANGELES TECH EMPLOYMENT

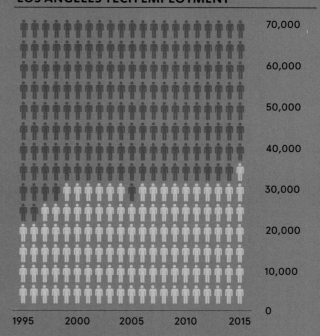

LEARN FROM OTHER CITIES

The dramatic shift of tech companies toward San Francisco is a lesson to other cities for what change is possible, and where tension can arise. As cities from London and New York to Seattle, Austin, and Seoul support a growing tech market, these lessons will prove invaluable.

WHAT'S NEXT

As work, and life, continue to shift toward cities across the globe, we hope to expand this discussion beyond San Francisco to engage other cities in similar dialogues.

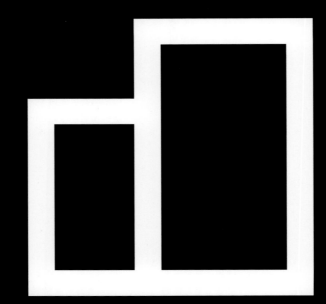

Social Architecture 2.0

Letter to the editor, excerpt, originally published on architecturalrecord.com

• • • • • •

At the same time that we are witnessing a resurgence of socially oriented design, there has been another equally significant trend toward research and evidence-based design in architecture. Research has gained momentum as a path to question and move past old assumptions at the core of traditional design solutions. With the dramatic pace of change—global, economic, climatic, and technological—every project must address a host of issues that were non-extant five or 10 years ago. The standard solution just doesn't fit current challenges. Research allows architects to go to the driving issues underlying complex problems and ask, Why?

The intersection of socially engaged architecture and research-informed design is potentially a defining opportunity for our profession today. One that could produce a new era of impact and leadership from a community of architects armed with knowledge, information, research, and data that uncovers real levers of change. Just as modernism, postmodernism, and deconstructivism defined the role and the public image of the 20th-century architect, we are poised to alter the way we approach the profession in line with the emerging social, economic, and political conditions of the 21st century.

The importance of research combined with the pursuit of socially engaged design cannot be overstated. As history has shown, uninformed design solutions, no matter how genuine the good will, can do more harm than good. In the 1960s we saw a similar trend toward socially engaged architecture in both the U.S. and Europe, and in hindsight, many social projects designed during that time, while well intended and idealistic, did not result in effective solutions. Not only did they not produce lasting positive impacts, many created more problems than they solved. This dynamic was exemplified in many urban renewal and mass housing projects.

Likewise, in the 1970s, the well-intended response to the global oil crisis through a singular focus on glazing and engineering systems produced a generation of unhealthful buildings and office parks.

Unlike the 1960s and 1970s, today we have access to an enormous amount of information and data allowing us to see our projects through a broader lens. Through research, big data, building partnerships, and design leadership, we can bring new levels of innovative design to our communities, creating more socially impactful, empowering solutions.

I want to challenge today's architects not to mimic the past efforts of social architecture. Big issues like economic opportunity, equality, climate, and health are very visible problems, but they emerge as the result of complex drivers. We don't need to be idealists, we need to be realists. That means being a global citizen and recognizing that all projects carry an inherent social impact that will help to shape the lives and experiences of the people living in the communities where they are located. Armed with this understanding, architects should see getting involved with projects—whether they are considered "commercial" or "social"—that have a critical role to play in the future of a neighborhood, city, or country as the defining opportunities for our profession today.

Through the use of research, data, and leadership we can bring new levels of innovative design to these opportunities and create healthier and economically sustainable communities. Creating places that bring vitality and enhance the human experience is an open invitation to every architect.

• • • • • •

– By Diane Hoskins, FAIA, IIDA, Co-CEO, Gensler

Alignment for Impact

What's the business case for community engagement?

As part of a comprehensive real estate strategy, community engagement is critical to building support for development, achieving social impact, and improving business and community outcomes.

WHAT WE DID

We audited best practices for community engagement across a spectrum of industries, including design and construction. Our goal was to measure its importance—and effectiveness—as part of an integrated design process. We surveyed a cross section of professionals involved in community-related work to understand how community engagement fits into their design process today, and what advantages that engagement brings —from achieving social impact or meeting corporate social responsibility goals, to improved business or community outcomes.

We also interviewed design professionals, not-for-profit organizations, community development groups, and academic institutions to seek a wider range of precedents and experience with community engagement. Our findings focused on a comparative analysis of engagement strategies, and the identification of best practices and recommendations.

THE CONTEXT

Design and construction projects, by their very nature, bring immense opportunity to positively impact their communities and provide far-reaching benefits. As individuals, organizations, and businesses today continue to place significant value in social responsibility, engaging the community in these projects is an opportunity not only to gather important insight directly from a project's end-users, but also to improve acceptance, commitment, and overall project success. Today, however, **community engagement is too often treated as a nice-to-have**—and when it happens, it is too often part of a pro bono strategy to assuage community stakeholders.

Economic Impact

Infrastructure

Workforce

Economy

Research & Development

Environmental Impact

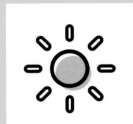

Outdoor Space

Sustainable Design

Life Cycle & Use

Access & Mobility

Social Impact

Education

Arts & Culture

Well-Being

Vacancy, Safety & Security

You are not here merely to make a living. You are here in order to enable the world to live more amply, with greater vision, with a finer spirit of hope and achievement. You are here to enrich the world, and you impoverish yourself if you forget that errand.

– Woodrow Wilson

Better engagement can promote meaningful, impactful design.

THE RESULTS

Community engagement can provide significant economic, environmental, and social impact, and should be considered an integral part of the design and development process. By integrating engagement strategies into the goals of every design project, we can begin to better align the built environment with business and community outcomes. To achieve this, design services must evolve to include a broader range of stakeholders in collaborative decision making.

The potential to leverage community engagement has not been fully recognized or incorporated in the design process. Our research uncovered significant, burgeoning interest, as well as a range of engagement toolkits and best practices geared toward social impact across the industry. Better engagement can promote meaningful, impactful design by broadening the dialogue to include key stakeholders, ultimately revealing mutually beneficial or unrecognized design opportunities.

Engaging the community improves decision making. By aligning diverse stakeholder and user voices, designers and clients can make more informed decisions to align project goals, community needs, and user expectations. This information proves relevant at all stages of real estate development, from master planning to move-in, and is critical to identifying areas in the community that hold the greatest opportunity for intervention.

Involvement in the design process also improves acceptance. Designing with the community, rather than for it, makes end-users and stakeholders more likely to feel ownership of, and connection to, a final product. Particularly for projects where the users or customers represent a broader community, involvement can deliver significant returns in terms of ultimate project success.

We must draw on our diverse skillsets to identify and maximize social impact benefits.

Communicate the value of engagement.
The importance of community engagement, and its ability to improve project outcomes, must be better communicated to our clients and industry. The more we engage the community, and document its impact on our project work, the better.

Create a diverse stakeholder group.
Engaging a diverse set of stakeholders enables a robust, informed design solution. For the community, the result is a product better aligned with their needs and interests; for the client, acceptance and alignment with community goals improves overall chances of success.

Use input to target investment.
Soliciting and documenting community input informs decision making and helps identify opportunities for maximum impact. Use this information to align resources to optimize community benefit through design and real estate investments.

We must draw on our diverse skillsets as architects, designers, planners, and strategists to identify and maximize social impact benefits related to real estate investments. This requires developing and expanding multidisciplinary capabilities to strategically advise clients and communities about real estate and the built environment, and continuing to pilot social impact tools and methods.

Making Global Business Work

What makes for a successful government relations campaign in emerging markets?

WHAT WE DID

We reviewed existing studies and conducted over 100 interviews with industry experts, government officials, and Gensler leaders from around the globe to understand the approaches that multinational firms employ in developing and executing their government relations strategies. Through these interviews, we identified best practices for developing government relations programs in emerging markets. We also surfaced challenges and opportunities that companies encounter in specific countries. This data provides strategic knowledge of how global firms are successfully engaging and navigating government relations.

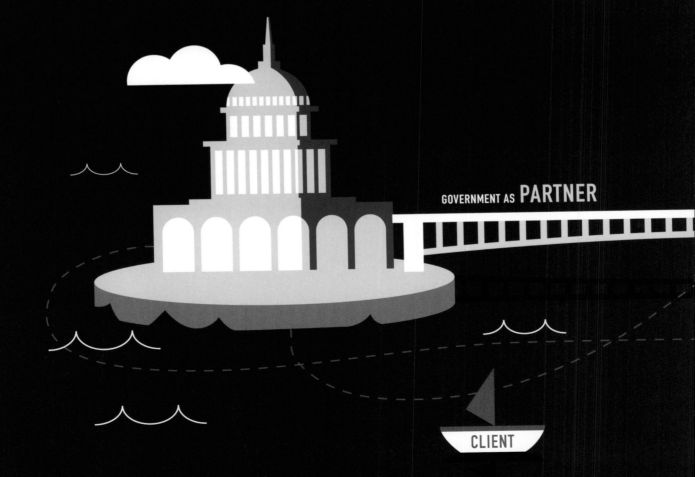

GOVERNMENT AS **PARTNER**

CLIENT

There is a pressing need to understand how businesses are successfully interacting with governments as clients, partners, and regulators—and for good reason. Government is more likely to affect a company's economic value than any other group of stakeholders except clients. As multinational companies continue to expand overseas, they are facing increasing complexity in how their business and clients' businesses operate.

Whether in a heavily regulated industry like financial services or less regulated ones like retail, companies seek to mitigate risk and avoid undue scrutiny from government regulators. For example, companies cite the government's role in passing and enforcing taxation and regulations as the main hurdle to overcome when engaging with the public sector. Managing government relations can help companies stay on top of these challenges.

The opportunity goes far beyond risk mitigation, however. At a time when public finances are under pressure, governments are seeking to tackle large-scale problems, access new sources of foreign investment, and utilize private sector expertise. As a result, private companies ranging in industries from technology and finance to healthcare and education are increasingly working with the public sector to help achieve policy and organizational goals.

Companies are also partnering with governments to work together on large-scale projects. From improving infrastructure to renovating or building hospitals, public and private sector groups are collaborating to achieve mutually beneficial results. In these public-private partnerships (PPPs), the private company often bears additional risk and management responsibility, while helping governments operate more efficiently and execute projects on time and within budget.

Understanding your company's relations with governments as a client, partner, or regulator is critical to doing business globally.

REGULATOR

THE RESULTS

You can't be successful in emerging markets unless you're aware of and prepared for government involvement in your business. The spread of economic power around the world is making it harder to reach consensus on a single approach to doing business globally. Bilateral and regional deal making are increasingly common, and these more local arrangements will remain largely market-based. Yet for business, this continuing shift away from a single set of rules will inevitably make it more challenging to seize opportunities globally.

Companies with successful government relations develop and continuously refine a proactive, market-specific strategy for each country in which they work. Before a company enters a market, a network or stakeholder map can help it target influential members of the government who may be key decision makers or

detractors. With this information, the company can take a targeted approach to cultivating relationships with specific political entities, economic players, and thought leaders. Partnering with industry or trade groups can also help the company learn the political landscape and cultivate relations with local regulators and government officials.

Understanding government interests goes a long way. Alignment with local interests, and a genuine concern for tackling pressing local needs via volunteerism, pro bono cases, or public impact work, help to align with public goals and foster long-term public-private partnerships. Government relations in one country also affect those in others; pay attention to political or historical ties that can influence business across national borders, particularly in high-profile business agreements.

PERSPECTIVES

"It is very important for companies to develop government relations at all levels while times are good, so companies can get the appropriate assistance when challenges later arise."

– Senior Counselor, Global Public Affairs Firm

"If you are a global organization with a strategic plan beyond doubling offices, you inevitably have to consider government relations."

– Director of Public Policy, Global Cloud Computing Company

WHAT'S NEXT

The dynamic and unpredictable global economy calls for new levels of leadership, advocacy, and creativity from multinational firms and governments. Companies with successful external relations recognize that future business projections rely on better understanding and embracing how they engage with governments as clients, partners, and regulators.

We continue to gather best practices from various industries on how they are engaging governments around the world. We are also conducting a pilot study on select countries and developing a framework to understand how companies tailor their government relations programs to local challenges. This knowledge helps every company develop appropriate engagement strategies as they work in today's global society.

WHAT THIS MEANS

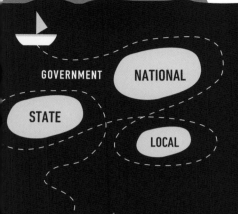

GOVERNMENT

NATIONAL

STATE

LOCAL

1 **Engage governments at the local, state, and national levels.** Given the cyclical nature of politics with parties, leadership, and personnel constantly in flux, companies should develop relations with contacts at the top, middle, and lower echelons of government. For example, one global accounting firm employs local talent who have close personal relationships with government officials and can work together with expat team members to advocate for the company's domestic and broader interests. They also reach out to local business associations and their home government officials to help advocate for the company.

2 **Embrace opportunities to grow the business and increase access to new or evolving markets.** As countries seek foreign investment and expertise to grow their local economies and strengthen domestic industries, many are creating special economic investment zones and seeking private sector partners. For example, a large oil and gas company invested heavily in China and formed a joint venture with state-owned enterprises, sharing their expertise on carbon capture and storage. Through this relationship, the company gained greater market access and political support to continue operating in the country.

3 **Closely monitor state influence in business.** Government influence can vary from country to country as political objectives may drive business decisions more than purely economic objectives. In many countries, state influence in business is widespread throughout the public and private sectors. State-owned enterprises, for example, are often an important instrument in a government's toolbox. Some governments use ownership as a form of supervision and a way to maintain control of industries crucial to economic performance and national security.

4 **Form localized government relations teams.** Partner local hires with expats to strike the right balance in knowledge on how to navigate local governments with business expertise and a global perspective. As government relations need to be localized, so too do companies' teams who have personal relationships and understand cultural nuances for doing business in each country. Companies utilize the on-the-ground knowledge of these local teams to advise a global government relations strategy group and review issues that may impact the organization overall. CEO-level engagement is later called upon when working with high-level stakeholders such as government ministers.

GOVERNMENT RELATIONS TOOLKIT

5 **Build a customized government relations toolkit.** Company processes range from tracking community plans and investments to identifying client relationship owners for each government organization. Government relations tools include developing an issues-monitoring dashboard and reporting structure, planning thought leadership events, updating internal customer relationship management systems, and compiling a portfolio of community impact and government projects.

Evolving Cities:

Transportation

Rethinking Public Transit

Can we improve the public transit user experience?

We examined the current London "Underground" experience by identifying typical user profiles, creating a comprehensive journey map, and analysing upcoming trends in operations, retail, and technology that might impact user experience. We then conducted a survey to find the spaces used/liked most by commuters, which helped to identify areas with the greatest opportunity.

In partnership with a group of collaborators, we identified key sections of the commuter journey with the greatest opportunity for impact. Using the London Underground as a case study, our ultimate goal is to identify both locally applicable solutions and scalable ideas that can become a prototype for other transport modes and other cities.

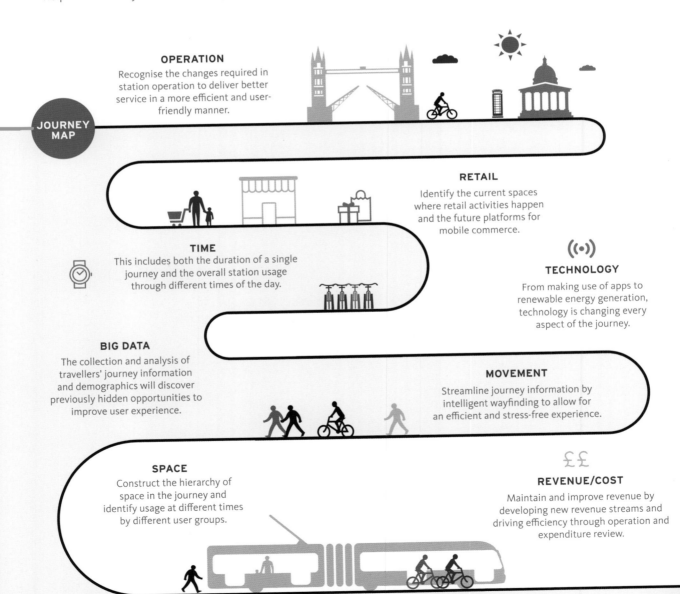

JOURNEY MAP

OPERATION
Recognise the changes required in station operation to deliver better service in a more efficient and user-friendly manner.

RETAIL
Identify the current spaces where retail activities happen and the future platforms for mobile commerce.

TIME
This includes both the duration of a single journey and the overall station usage through different times of the day.

TECHNOLOGY
From making use of apps to renewable energy generation, technology is changing every aspect of the journey.

BIG DATA
The collection and analysis of travellers' journey information and demographics will discover previously hidden opportunities to improve user experience.

MOVEMENT
Streamline journey information by intelligent wayfinding to allow for an efficient and stress-free experience.

SPACE
Construct the hierarchy of space in the journey and identify usage at different times by different user groups.

REVENUE/COST
Maintain and improve revenue by developing new revenue streams and driving efficiency through operation and expenditure review.

THE CONTEXT

As cities grow, commuters are traveling longer distances, making the user experience more critical now than ever. An increase in ridership means more tracks and stations need to be built and maintained. To achieve this without constantly increasing ticket fares, operators need an expanded set of revenue sources.

With over 1.3 billion commuters every year, the London Underground is a prime example of the need and opportunity to leverage new strategies to improve public transportation's user experience. Recent conjecture about 24/7 operation, beginning with 24-hour weekend operation in 2015/16, and its broader economic effects also informed our study.

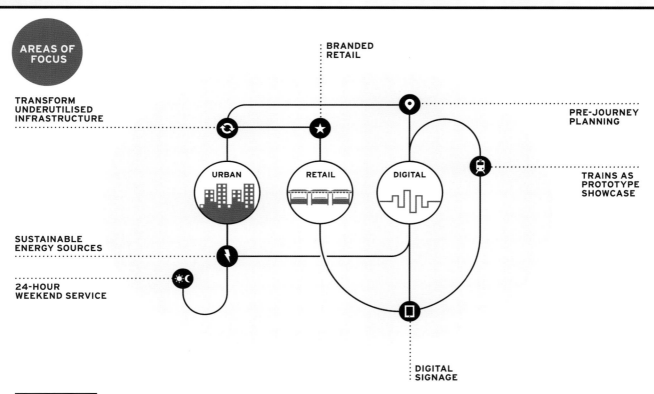

AREAS OF FOCUS

BRANDED RETAIL

TRANSFORM UNDERUTILISED INFRASTRUCTURE

PRE-JOURNEY PLANNING

URBAN

RETAIL

DIGITAL

TRAINS AS PROTOTYPE SHOWCASE

SUSTAINABLE ENERGY SOURCES

24-HOUR WEEKEND SERVICE

DIGITAL SIGNAGE

THE RESULTS

We focused our research on three main areas of interest for the improvement of the transit experience. **Urban** solutions focus on leveraging and improving existing city infrastructure and transportation patterns, and meeting diverse user needs. **Retail** solutions explore opportunities for integrated commercial and retail elements to generate added revenue for transit improvement and expand opportunities to meet diverse user needs. **Digital** solutions focus on using new technology to create new opportunities for customer communication and brand integration.

Building on these categories, we then identified a more detailed set of opportunities for exploration, including pre-journey planning, sustainable energy sources, branded retail opportunities, using trains as prototypes for user input, expanding to 24-hour weekend service, integrating digital signage, and the transformation of underutilised infrastructure. A particular focus on infrastructure transformation led to the development of our "London Underline" design proposal to convert abandoned subway lines into pedestrian and bicycle paths.

TRAVELLER TYPES

WEEKDAY COMMUTERS are focused on reducing their commute time.

TOURISTS want to know about events that are happening in the area and how to get there.

OFFPEAK TRAVELLERS want their trip to be convenient.

NIGHT ADVENTURERS are focused on having a safe and easy journey.

The London Underline

The London Underline is Gensler's speculative design proposal to convert disused subway tunnels into the world's first self-sustainable subterranean pedestrian and cycle path network. The project was awarded Best Conceptual Project in the 2015 London Planning Awards and received the 2015 Gensler Design Excellence Awards (GDEA) People's Choice award.

UTILISING PREEXISTING & UNUSED STATIONS

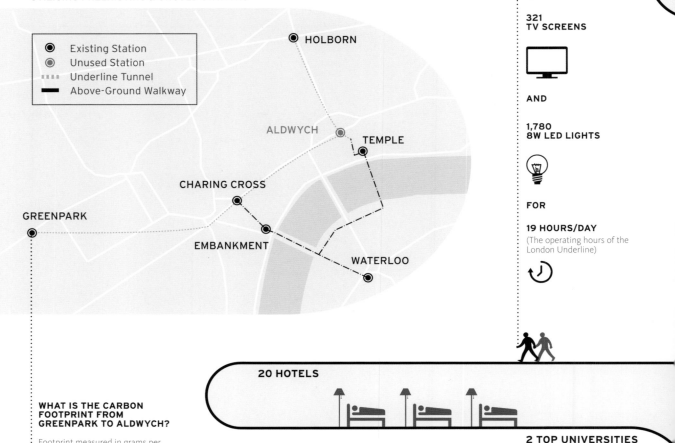

Legend:
- ◉ Existing Station
- ◎ Unused Station
- ···· Underline Tunnel
- ▬ Above-Ground Walkway

Stations shown on map: HOLBORN, ALDWYCH, TEMPLE, CHARING CROSS, EMBANKMENT, WATERLOO, GREENPARK

WHAT COULD A DAY'S KINETIC ENERGY POWER?

One-half million people/day from the six stations shown could generate power for:

↓

321 TV SCREENS

AND

1,780 8W LED LIGHTS

FOR

19 HOURS/DAY
(The operating hours of the London Underline)

20 HOTELS

2 TOP UNIVERSITIES

WHAT IS THE CARBON FOOTPRINT FROM GREENPARK TO ALDWYCH?

Footprint measured in grams per kilometer (g/km) travelled

 205 G/KM VS. **2310 G/KM**

WHAT THIS MEANS

THE OPPORTUNITY, AND TECHNOLOGY, TO CREATE A 21st-CENTURY TRANSIT EXPERIENCE EXISTS.

For the city of London, and other cities struggling with similar issues around the world, the question will be how best to prioritise funds and explore new revenue opportunities to make change happen. We believe that branded retail, digital signage, and the transformation of underutilised infrastructure offer the most significant near-term opportunity.

THE FULL TRANSIT EXPERIENCE MUST BE CONSIDERED IN TANDEM.

Understanding the user experience and decision making process before and after using public transportation informs smart planning. Alternative transportation modes—buses, cycling, trains—should also be considered to understand how ridership and experience on one influences the others.

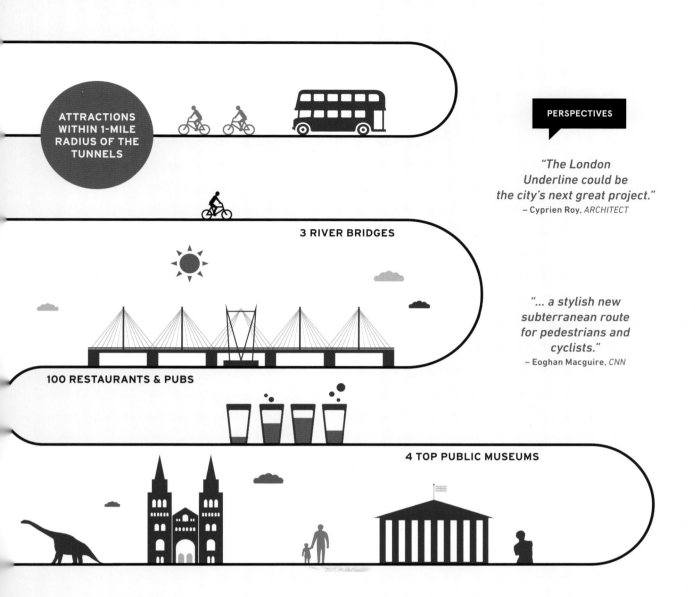

ATTRACTIONS WITHIN 1-MILE RADIUS OF THE TUNNELS

3 RIVER BRIDGES

100 RESTAURANTS & PUBS

4 TOP PUBLIC MUSEUMS

WHAT'S NEXT

As we continue our research, our goal is to "export" our London-based findings to help other cities and regions engage in similar discussions relative to local context. These discussions will help to develop design proposals and trends specific to each city, and allow us to look more closely at feasibility and specific requirements for these trends to materialise in those markets.

NEW TRANSPORT STRATEGIES REQUIRE CROSS-DISCIPLINE COLLABORATION.

This research integrates design expertise across project types including transportation, retail, digital media, and branding. The sharing of ideas between practices and professionals with differing experience allows for broader, more innovative solutions.

NEW OPPORTUNITIES FOR TRANSPORT CAN CAPTURE THE PUBLIC'S ATTENTION.

The work focused particular attention on opportunities to better leverage existing infrastructure. This resulted in a concept design for the London Underline, which catapulted the project into the public realm, and created unprecedented interest in the proposal across the world.

Airports without Waiting?

An investigation into what's next for airport design

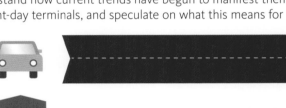

WHAT WE DID

We reviewed existing white papers, surveys, and studies in three key areas of interest for the future of airport terminals: the passenger experience, changing revenue models, and sustainability. A significant amount of research is currently focused on the impact new technology has on the travel experience, and is largely published by technology companies. However, gaps exist in wider research on how this technology boom affects the architecture of the near-future terminal. We sought to interpret existing data and predictions from a design perspective to understand the effect on airports, while also expanding our investigation to address the terminal and travel experience more holistically.

A primary focus of our investigation relates to large regional or hub terminals with significant amenity and processing space. Gensler's recently completed and in-progress terminal design projects of this type served as case stories for our investigation. We used these projects to understand how current trends have begun to manifest themselves in present-day terminals, and speculate on what this means for the future.

Air travel today...

> **Keeping passengers moving is key for tomorrow's airport—waiting will be a thing of the past.**

THE CONTEXT

The aviation industry is highly dynamic and competitive, and as the globalization of business and culture continue apace, air travel is increasingly essential to the global economy. The aviation industry is also ripe for change and innovation—the significant CO2 impacts of air travel and volatile fuel costs make sustainability a key concern for the future, while the stress and frustration often induced by travel highlight the importance of a new and improved passenger experience.

Communities today expect more out of their local airport than transportation access—they want a responsible neighbor that conserves energy, water, and material resources, while minimizing pollution and waste.

Alongside these issues, the business of air travel is changing as well. An evolving aircraft fleet mix, satellite-based air traffic control systems, and innovations in biometric and self-service technology are changing airport infrastructure needs, passenger flow, and baggage processing. New revenue models are greatly diminishing the importance of aeronautical revenue derived from airline tenants, displaced by other sources such as retail, customized passenger services, and mobile advertising to take up the slack in an "end-to-end" passenger experience.

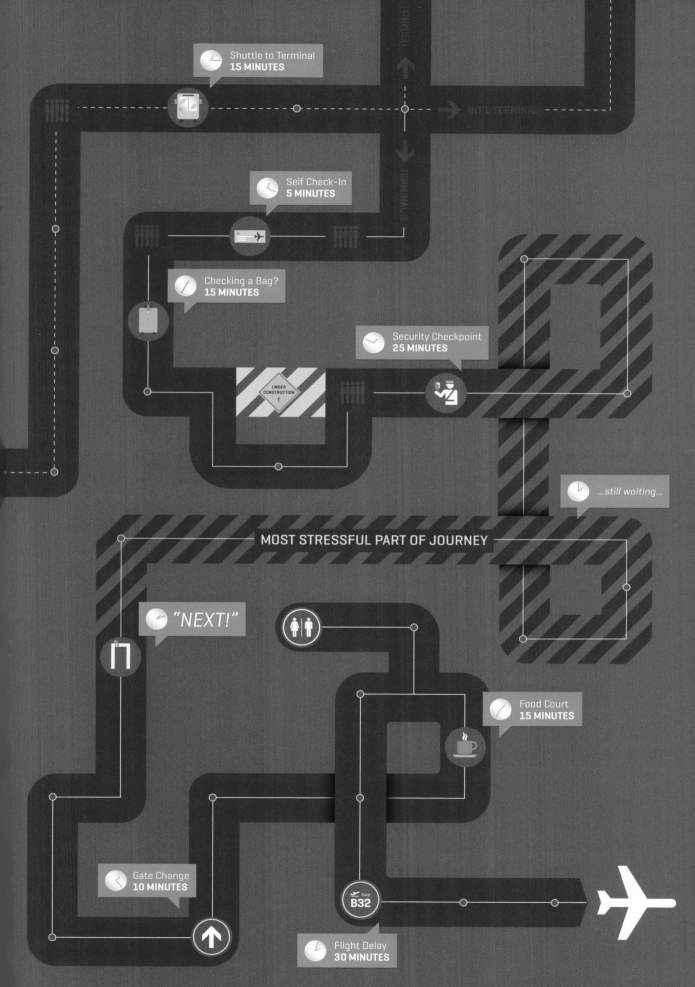

COMPRESSED
THE "NON-PROCESS"—INVISIBLE & SEAMLESS

MOBILE TICKETING
Anytime, anywhere on mobile devices

AUTOMATIC CHECK-IN
NFC detection allows for automatic check-in

SELF BAG DROP
RFID luggage tracking

PASSIVE SCREENING
Face and baggage portal screening

 **5 MINUTES**

THE RESULTS

The present-day airport is about **waiting**. Wait to park. Wait to check-in. Wait to be screened. Wait to board. The near-future airport will be about **moving**. Passengers will experience a personalized journey through the airport, with increasingly seamless transitions and blurred lines between terminal spaces as security becomes "invisible" and services become tech-enabled and individualized.

This shift will be realized through secure near field communications technology, allowing passengers to use a Near Field Communications (NFC)–enabled phone as a boarding pass to automatically open security, airline lounge, and boarding gates. The shift has already begun—"self" bag tagging and "self" boarding have been implemented in 115 instances around the world according to the International Air Transport Association (IATA).

Personal mobile technology is also complicating the debate on who "owns" the passenger, with both airport and airlines exploring individualized advertising to and communication with passengers in search of new revenue sources. In 2015, 78 percent of airlines planned to tailor content they provide via their direct distribution channels and by data mining passenger profiles.

Recent surveys show 61 percent of passengers are open to direct, mobile advertisements if they are relevant and have some level of control. Passenger surveys also reflect the need to de-stress the travel experience and the importance of nontraditional design features: 31 percent of passengers cited an outdoor park area as the most wanted airport amenity.

Not only will the experience of the airport change, but the terminal building itself must change. To meet community and sustainability expectations, smart buildings must become genius buildings. The near-future airport campus will utilize an "all of the above" sustainability strategy, harvesting its own energy and water, recycling its own waste, and growing its own aviation fuel. As airports seek to increase capacity within physical expansion constraints, many may move toward a 24/7 model—though the opportunity for increased capacity will have to be weighed against nighttime noise impacts and limited demand for late-night/early-morning departure times. Ultimately, the near-future terminal building will be a sophisticated machine, continually adjusting systems based on millions of real-time weather and passenger movement data points.

PERSPECTIVES

22%

higher sales per enplanement were reported for Terminal 2 compared to othe domestic terminals within SFO, through a program focused on higher-quality, local, sustainable, healthy choices.

EXPANDED
"ME TIME"—SPEND, WORK, RELAX

DWELL TIME
Luxification, crafted, localization

30+ MINUTES

SELF BOARDING
Device detection in pocket capability

Experiences shift to local, craft, deluxe

The localization and "luxification" of the airport environment will increase as airlines and airports compete for dwell-time revenue, incorporating nontraditional design elements such as biophilia and well-being focused amenities that reduce stress and give passengers a grounded sense of place.

Traditional space boundaries disappear

Aircraft gates, customer service, and back-of-house areas will be designed to allow for ultimate flexibility, eliminating long-term leases and expensive custom fit-outs. Digital tenant branding will define spaces on an as-needed basis, changing with the touch on a keypad.

Processing space becomes amenity space

Traditional airport spaces will recede to the background. Remote check-in will minimize the ticketing hall, portal security screenings will eliminate the centralized security checkpoint, and call-to-gate technology will blur the boundary between retail and departure lounge spaces.

The "non-process" changes everything

What if there were no queues at ticketing, security, immigration, or the boarding gate? Biometric, self-service, and personal mobile technology will reduce waiting, allowing passengers more time to work, eat, and shop.

WHAT'S NEXT

The near-future airport is already beginning to emerge via progressive, experience-focused terminal designs in new and renovated terminals around the world. Design strategies focused on passenger comfort and well-being have already gained traction and are showing success, as measured by both passenger satisfaction and terminal revenue. As personal and airport technology continue to improve, terminals must continue to embrace opportunities to employ strategies and solutions that emphasize ease of movement, passenger experience, and sustainability.

We researched and conceptualized strategies for improving navigational infrastructure for the 2020 Tokyo Summer Olympics that can be used by the city long after the games conclude. We conducted the research in three parts: 1) an investigation of successful wayfinding systems from previous Olympic events and third-party research; 2) a survey of 70 residents and foreigners on their perspectives of Tokyo's current navigational infrastructure; and 3) developing conceptual navigational systems in various scales for use during and after the games.

THE CONTEXT

In 2020, Tokyo is set to host the Summer Olympics for the second time in its history. As the largest city in the world, the city offers a highly complex transportation and navigation infrastructure. The number of foreign visitors is expected to increase dramatically during and after the games, with some estimating by as much as 300 percent. This dramatic influx of foreigners necessitates an upgraded wayfinding and navigation system to enhance the visitor experience in the city, in particular for those who do not speak or read Japanese.

This goal fits with broader plans for the future of the city. The Tokyo Metropolitan Government has set a plan in motion, "Creating the Future: The Long-Term Vision for Tokyo," that envisions a city that can be easily navigated by multilingual visitors. The government's aspirations go well beyond wayfinding—they also hope to become a city that is resilient from natural and man-made disasters and acts of terrorism, including measures for disaster preparedness, counterterrorism, and hospitality. **We believe an improved urban navigation and communications system can address goals not only of greater hospitality and navigation, but also can improve the city's overall resilience and preparedness.**

THE RESULTS

More than 80 percent of our survey respondents reported that foreign visitors to Tokyo find the city's navigation system challenging due to poor signage and a shortage of information in their native languages. **Tokyo needs to implement a city-wide, multiscaled strategy for wayfinding that eases the user experience.**

For confused travelers, offering navigational information in multiple scales can ease anxiety and instill a sense of confidence as they navigate a new city. For residents, multiscaled wayfinding allows the public to keep informed when city and regional announcements are broadcast to the system.

We propose design interventions across five distinct scales within the existing built environment:

XS (personal scale)
S (pedestrian scale)
M (street scale)
L (district scale)
XL (city scale)

Each scale can serve dual purposes: to provide a simple and clear navigation and information source during the Olympic Games, and to improve resilience after the games by providing vital information during emergency evacuations. By connecting across scales, navigational infrastructure has the potential to provide a seamless experience, reducing stress for those who need information anytime and anywhere.

PERSONAL SCALE

USE MOBILE DEVICES TO PROVIDE REAL-TIME TRANSLATIONS, DIRECTIONS.

Create a multi-language navigation "app" that Tokyo residents and Olympic visitors can download that feeds interactive information to their smartphones and tablets. This could potentially integrate augmented reality, real-time information, and translation of users' surroundings, powered by an icon-based, intuitive search engine. Rather than changing existing signage to be multilingual, this navigation system could instead change the way users read them.

STREET SCALE

REPURPOSE BUS STOPS AS COMMUNICATION HUBS.

Bus stops have long been a place for public advertising, and can be enhanced as a public utility to provide free Wi-Fi. During the Olympics, bus stops can be repurposed as small public viewing spots, broadcasting live events from nearby stadiums. They can also provide interactive maps for locating event details and planning transportation routes. In the case of a large-scale emergency, the large digital screens can be transformed to display evacuation routes.

PEDESTRIAN SCALE

MAKE VENDING MACHINES WAYFINDING AND DISASTER RELIEF TOOLS.

Japan has the highest ratio of vending machines to landmass in the world, with more than 5.5 million machines nationwide. Together, they can hold three days' worth of water and other beverages for the entire population of Japan. During the Olympics, high-tech vending machines with digital displays can serve as dual-purpose information centers for the games and as a source for free Wi-Fi. When the games end, they can serve as community message boards and communicate real-time disaster relief information when necessary, while also dispensing emergency kits, food, and water for residents and visitors.

PERSPECTIVES

Tokyo received over 10 million foreign visitors in 2013, and expects this number to rise dramatically leading up to and after the Olympic Games. The government aims to increase foreign visitors to 20 million by 2020, and 30 million by 2030.

– "Olympic Games expected to provide economic stimulus," *Japan Times*

DISTRICT SCALE

INTEGRATE DIGITAL DISPLAYS INTO BUILDING FAÇADES, CONVENIENCE STORES.

Digital displays installed on key building façades are capable of transmitting general information to the public, such as weather and traffic updates. They can also sync with mobile devices to provide directions to featured content, working across the scales described previously. Convenience stores in particular are an opportunity—Japan has more than 50,000 convenience stores, mainly concentrated in Tokyo, that could become an integral part of an enhanced navigational infrastructure.

CITY SCALE

INSTALL SUPER-GRAPHICS AT MAJOR INTERSECTIONS TO BROADCAST TO THE MASSES.

Oversize graphic billboards and digital displays are common throughout Tokyo. During the Olympics, they can become major public viewing spaces. For example, more than 500,000 people cross the famous Shibuya Crossing every day, resulting in millions of impressions per day for its surrounding displays. In the case of a major regional emergency, large-scale digital signage— including those at Shibuya Crossing—can become a critical place to provide disaster relief information quickly to a broader audience.

WHAT'S NEXT

We continue to explore methods for implementing a comprehensive wayfinding system across Tokyo. Our first step will be to use a test area within the city to evaluate feasibility and usability of our proposed strategies.

Evolving Cities:
Emerging Metrics

62 **Measuring Urban Experience**

Project Name: From Data to Place, A Tool for Gathering Qualitative Data about the Urban Realm
Research Team: Carlos Cubillos, Carolyn Sponza, Rizki Arsiananta, Nina Charnotskaia, Jaymes Dunsmore, Susan Hickey, Hanin Khasru, Mariusz Klemens, Celine Larkin, Midori Mizuhara, Joshua Vitulli

Measuring Urban Experience

How can we quantify the quality and authenticity of our urban spaces?

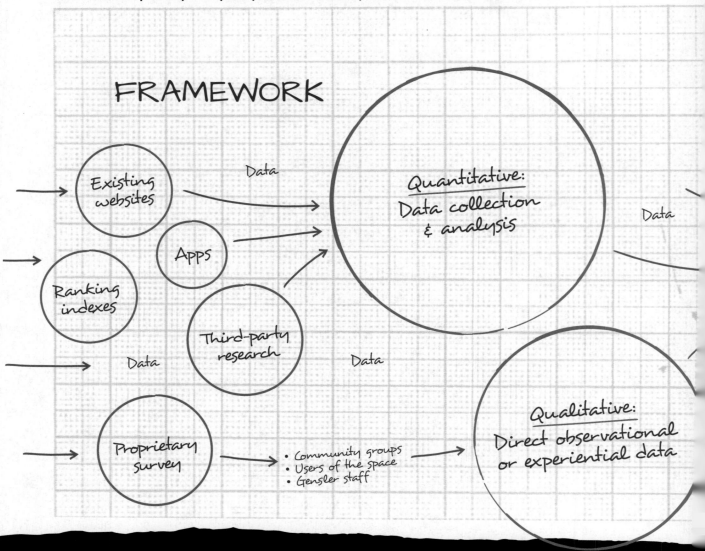

FRAMEWORK

Existing websites

Data

Apps

Ranking indexes

Third-party research

Data

Proprietary survey

Data

Quantitative: Data collection & analysis

Data

- Community groups
- Users of the space
- Gensler staff

Qualitative: Direct observational or experiential data

WHAT WE DID

We developed a framework for evaluating the myriad factors that contribute to successful urban environments. It combines quantitative data—walking distance to open space, access to transit, for example—with qualitative input, such as comfort, culture, or design quality. Quantitative data is sourced from existing websites, apps, ranking indexes, and third-party research projects focused on evaluation of vibrant, successful urban environments. Qualitative data is gathered via a proprietary site survey designed by our team to capture the experiential aspects of the environment via community group, user, and designer input.

THE CONTEXT

As publicly accessible data is becoming more widely available, there has been an increase in attempts to measure and compare the success of cities, neighborhoods, and other subsets of urban space. Many of these initiatives are limited, however, by focusing on one aspect of the urban experience, such as pedestrian safety at intersections or traffic congestion. Only a handful attempt to identify the overall quality of place, at the neighborhood and site scale. This proves particularly challenging as both quantitative data and qualitative input are needed to truly measure urban experience.

5 Data Categories

	Categories	Subcategories	
1	Ambient Comfort	□ Wind comfort □ Daylight □ Temperature & humidity control	□ Sound/noise □ Air quality/odor □ Light levels
2	Amenities	□ Quality of amenities and services □ Percentage of public amenities and services □ Quantity of amenities and services that promote 24-hour activity □ Quantity of amenities and services that provide 4-season activity	
3	Built Form	□ Relationship of buildings □ Sidewalk widths □ Open space accessibility □ Open space quantity □ Open space size □ Open space distance □ Distance to parking □ Building setbacks	□ Accessible entrances □ Building transparency □ Quantity of street intersections □ Width of sidewalk buffer □ Availability of appropriate seating □ Amount of seating □ Landscape provision
4	Mobility	□ Bicycle access □ Transit availability	
5	Safety	□ Incidence of crime □ Site contamination	□ School attendance □ Number of police stations

THE RESULTS

We propose a framework that measures the success of urban areas across five different categories identified through our review of existing ratings and measurement systems: **ambient comfort, amenities, built form, mobility, and safety.** Quantitative data is pulled in a systematic manner via a set of vetted sources to ensure consistency across projects, paired with general demographic information for each site to give a larger context to the data. Qualitative data is then gathered in the same five categories via our team's survey and observational work, the combination of which allows for more direct conclusions to be made in each of these areas.

Our framework is designed to work in three different capacities: first as a tool to assist Gensler's clients and developers during their **site selection** process; second, as a way to organize the **site analysis** process, typically during the early stages of planning; and third, as a tool for performing **post-occupancy analyses** for clients seeking to understand the impact of urban interventions or considering the repositioning of existing assets. We also developed an instructional guide to support the adoption of this framework in the planning and design of buildings and public spaces.

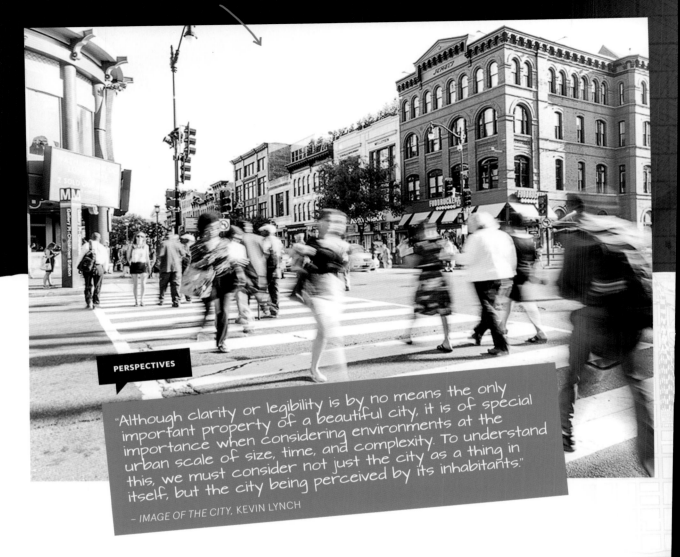

PERSPECTIVES

"Although clarity or legibility is by no means the only important property of a beautiful city, it is of special importance when considering environments at the urban scale of size, time, and complexity. To understand this, we must consider not just the city as a thing in itself, but the city being perceived by its inhabitants."

– *IMAGE OF THE CITY*, KEVIN LYNCH

WHAT THIS MEANS

Big data is an important tool, but so is individual perspective.

Early in our process, we explored the potential of collecting qualitative data from publicly available databases such as Yelp! or Trip Advisor. However, without a full understanding of what was influencing the data, such as the time of day the entry was made or the users' familiarity with the location, this data proved to be more anecdotal than demonstrable. The survey we developed to capture experiential aspects of place seeks to gather this data instead.

Scoring systems are not finite.

Uniform ranking systems could not adequately consider the unique characteristics of the environments being scored. To capture these subjective considerations, we instead document each category of quantitative data against the qualitative feedback for each site. For post-occupancy projects, this allows property owners or developers to identify specific areas of improvement and establish design goals relative to each.

One public space does not fit all.

There is no universal ideal when it comes to creating public space. For instance, maximizing access to sunlight is desirable with the cool temperatures and tall buildings in Chicago's Loop area, while shade is at a premium during hot days in Los Angeles' Pershing Square. Our framework layers the diverse cultural and social uses of public spaces across the world into its considerations.

LOS ANGELES

1. Ambient Comfort

Wind comfort	●	○	○	○	○
Daylight	○	○	○	●	○

❌ In Los Angeles, an abundance of sunlight may have a negative impact on comfort—shade is at a premium instead.

Sound/noise	○	○	●	○	○
Air quality/odor	○	○	●	○	○

CHICAGO

1. Ambient Comfort

Wind comfort	●	○	○	○	○
Daylight	○	○	○	○	●

✅ Chicago may have a higher tolerance for direct sunlight given cool temperatures and tall buildings.

Sound/noise	○	○	●	○	○
Air quality/odor	○	○	●	○	○

📍 Location of Measurement ○ 1/2-Mile Radius from Location ⊘ Positive/Negative Tolerance 🔖 Amenities

WHAT'S NEXT

After initial testing, we now seek to deploy our system more widely and gather aggregate information for deeper analysis. This would allow us to identify correlations between specific physical aspects of space and user perceptions of these places, and test our assumptions or existing tenets of design against real-world data.

For instance, our inclination as designers may tell us that 15-foot-wide sidewalks are appropriate for a business district, but feedback from the experiential survey may tell us this would not accommodate actual foot traffic at a particular site.

05

Evolving Cities:
Technology

Fuel Cells Now

What role will fuel cells play in our alternative energy future?

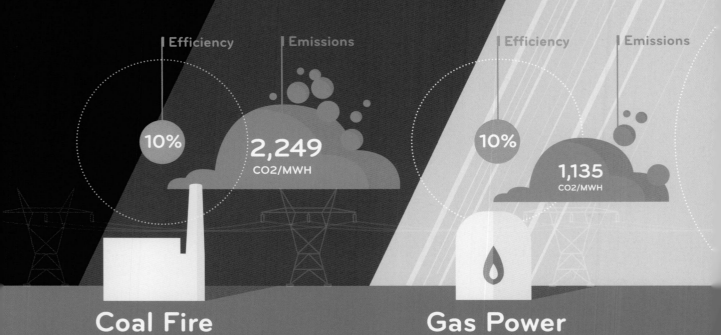

| Efficiency | Emissions | | Efficiency | Emissions |

10%   **2,249** CO2/MWH   **10%**   **1,135** CO2/MWH

Coal Fire Plant

Gas Power Plant

USAGE OF WATER

147 Million GAL / Year Per MW Generation Capacity

58 Million GAL / Year Per MW Generation Capacity

MORE DETAILS

LB CO2 / MWH
2,249

GAL H2O / MWH
16,052 WITHDRAWN | 692 CONSUMED

ELECTRICAL EFFICIENCY AT SOURCE
34%

SITE-TO-SOURCE CONVERSION FACTOR
3.317

Coal currently produces approximately **23% of the world's electricity** and accounts for over **40% of global carbon emissions.**

LB CO2 / MWH
1,135

GAL H2O / MWH
6,484 WITHDRAWN | 172 CONSUMED

ELECTRICAL EFFICIENCY AT SOURCE
34%

SITE-TO-SOURCE CONVERSION FACTOR
3.317

Natural gas burns much cleaner than coal. **What if there were a way to drastically improve its utilization and further reduce carbon emissions?**

WHAT WE DID

We conducted a yearlong research project on the potential application, and benefits, of using fuel cells in buildings. Our goal was to get an understanding of how, when, and where this technology is being deployed in the building industry today, and to speculate on the next generation of a high-performance built environment that could incorporate this technology.

We studied aspects of environmental, economic, and policy considerations as well as the current and projected state of fuel cell technology. We presented these findings at a roundtable discussion in March 2015, hosted in San Francisco, alongside presentations by industry experts to inform our broader findings and implications.

Fuel cells are ready for prime time. They are more resilient, efficient, and environmentally friendly than several other energy generation sources.

As costs fall, adoption will increase with benefits ranging from water conservation to long-term cost savings.

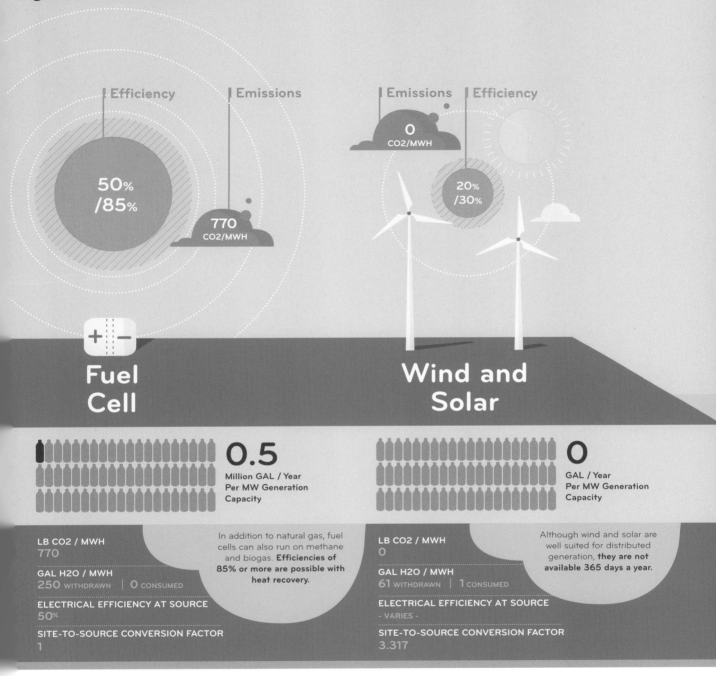

| Efficiency | Emissions
| Emissions | Efficiency

50%
/85%

770
CO2/MWH

0
CO2/MWH

20%
/30%

Fuel Cell

Wind and Solar

0.5
Million GAL / Year
Per MW Generation
Capacity

0
GAL / Year
Per MW Generation
Capacity

LB CO2 / MWH
770

GAL H2O / MWH
250 WITHDRAWN | 0 CONSUMED

ELECTRICAL EFFICIENCY AT SOURCE
50%

SITE-TO-SOURCE CONVERSION FACTOR
1

In addition to natural gas, fuel cells can also run on methane and biogas. **Efficiencies of 85% or more are possible with heat recovery.**

LB CO2 / MWH
0

GAL H2O / MWH
61 WITHDRAWN | 1 CONSUMED

ELECTRICAL EFFICIENCY AT SOURCE
- VARIES -

SITE-TO-SOURCE CONVERSION FACTOR
3.317

Although wind and solar are well suited for distributed generation, **they are not available 365 days a year.**

THE CONTEXT

Fuel cells are electrochemical energy conversion devices that generate electricity by combining positively charged hydrogen ions and oxygen. They were invented in 1838 and first used commercially by NASA for space probes, satellites, and capsules. Clean energy legislation, incentives, and policy are making fuel cells more accessible today, which has contributed to an accelerating demand and utilization of the technology in the past five years. The Department of Energy (DOE) anticipates that fuel cells will become economically viable for mass-market adoption around 2030, based on similar cost/kilowatt trends observed for solar cells and wind turbines in the past.

THE RESULTS

Reliability, efficiency, and sustainability are among the key advantages of fuel cell technology compared to other energy sources. Further, fuel cells are well suited for on-site energy generation, which provides benefits such as heat recovery potential and minimization of transmission losses.

Reliability: Fuel cells have been demonstrated to be 10x more reliable than power from the grid, and function with fewer moving parts to break over time. They can allow buildings to go "off grid" and potentially eliminate other backup power systems that are often more hazardous.

Efficiency: Conventional coal, petroleum, and natural gas power plants produce electricity at efficiencies between 27 and 42 percent, with "real" efficiency (after transmission and distribution losses are accounted for) between 10 and 15 percent. Fuel cells in production today achieve approximately 50 percent electrical efficiency, and that can increase to over 85 percent when utilized in conjunction with heat recovery.

Sustainability: Increased efficiency means fuel cell systems require dramatically less fuel to produce a similar amount of power. They do not involve the combustion of fuel, so reduce nitrogen oxide, sulfur oxide, and particulate-matter emissions to negligible levels, while simplifying carbon sequestration. An even greater boon comes from a drastic reduction of fresh-water consumption for power generation.

WHAT THIS MEANS

We see additional benefits specific to the application of fuel cells in the built environment. Fuel cells not only are more reliable, efficient, and sustainable, but also a) are more **modular and scalable** than other power generation sources, suitable for application in stand-alone facilities as well as at the utility; b) generate very **little noise and no vibrations,** making them suitable for on-site installation without neighborhood/community impact; and c) offer the potential for direct current (DC) power output on-site, **reducing conversion losses** and providing additional efficiency/environmental benefits.

Water is also a key opportunity. While much attention has been given to the use of fossil fuels and the production of CO_2 in the generation of electricity, few realize the impact power generation has on the world's fresh-water supply. In 2010, an estimated 161 billion gallons of water per day, over 45 percent of all water used in the United States, was used in conjunction with power generation. **Fuel cells can eliminate or drastically reduce this draw on our fresh-water supply,** requiring little to no water to produce a megawatt of power.

Grid infrastructure also takes up millions of acres of real estate for power transmission lines, substations, and power plants. With an increased adoption of distributed generation (generating power at the point of use) not only is it possible to substantially reduce transmission losses, but it may be possible to free up valuable land for development, agriculture, or to give back to nature. **Fuel cells are an ideal technology to utilize for distributed generation.**

Additional advantages are available, depending on building type, that range from heat capture to enhanced fuel utilization efficiency, which support environmental impact reduction goals for corporations and commercial office buildings. Understanding the current energy utilization levels of different building types alongside opportunities specific to fuel cell application helps to identify areas for potential application today, as well as in the future as the technology continues to evolve and become more accessible.

Chart below indicates the magnitude of the potential impacts fuel cells could have for different project types. Areas in dark green offer the greatest opportunity.

BENEFITS ACROSS BUILDING TYPES	Data Centers	Higher Education Campuses	Hospitals	Corporate HQ and Campuses	Retail
Environmental					
Reliability and Availability					
Modular and Scalable					
Silent Operation					
Heat Recovery Potential					

PERSPECTIVES

"In 2014, the fuel cell industry grew by almost $1 billion, reaching $2.2 billion in sales, up from $1.3 billion in 2013."

– Fuel Cells Technology Market Report 2014,
U.S. Department of Energy

WHAT'S NEXT

Fuel cells are anticipated to follow a similar technology adoption trajectory as solar and wind generation, with policy and market forces driving down the cost of installation to a price point comparable to diesel generation and micro turbines by 2030. While the "first" cost of a fuel cell system today is estimated at $8,000/kilowatt (with an average payback of 20 years), a future cost of $2,000/kilowatt is projected, reducing average payback to three years and vastly increasing applicability.

POLICY & TRIGGERS

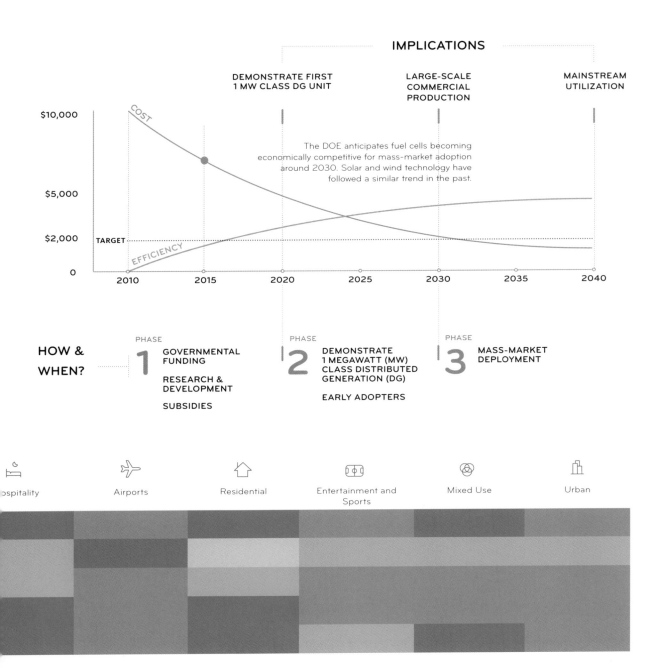

Technology | Mobile Unmanned Printing Platform (MUPP) in Flight, Los Angeles, CA

3D Printing Takes Flight

Can we build a fully mobile 3D printer, not limited by the X, Y, or Z axis?

WHAT WE DID

We undertook a multiyear prototyping project with a goal of creating a 3D printer that could generate objects of any size and in remote locations. The concept behind the research is astonishingly simple: free the printhead from its container and attach it to an aerial vehicle. The impact is potentially vast—if the objects created by 3D printers are not limited in size by the dimensions of the printer, the applications expand dramatically.

We began our research by conducting an extensive third-party audit of successful 3D printing and robotic platforms. With this information, we set out to design and fabricate our own proprietary 3D printer and modify an off-the-shelf hexacopter (an unmanned aerial vehicle, or UAV) to carry it. Our goal was to explore this advanced technology and discover new ways it could be utilized for the creation of architecture for both commercial and humanitarian purposes.

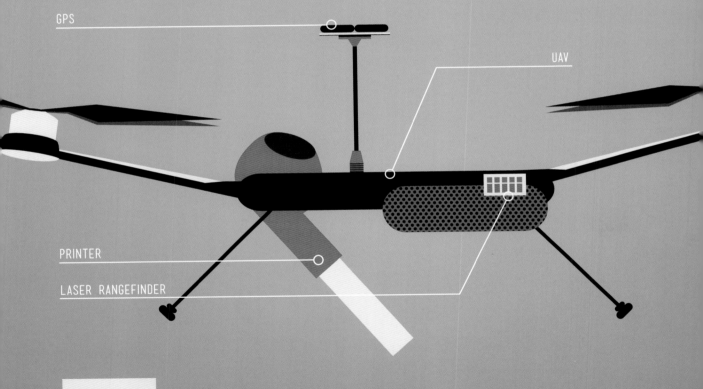

GPS

UAV

PRINTER

LASER RANGEFINDER

PERSPECTIVES

A running joke during the course of our research was regarding how often we made mistakes or experienced setbacks and failures. Our motto became, "we learn how to do things wrong."

"Success is the ability to go from one failure to another with no loss of enthusiasm."

– Winston Churchill

> "Progress is made by trial and failure; the failures are generally a hundred times more numerous than the successes; yet they are usually left unchronicled."
>
> – William Ramsay

THE CONTEXT

Three-dimensional printing provides endless opportunities to revolutionize everyday life, and as the costs continue to fall, those opportunities are becoming increasingly more accessible. Thanks in part to our research, discussions about using mobile 3D printing technology to create structures are taking place in various sectors across the globe.

In parallel, UAV technology continues to make significant advances, improving in both quality and price. The combination of these technologies provides a key opportunity for using 3D technology to improve the processes we use to construct and manage our built environment.

We could revolutionize the way we construct and repair buildings, and even respond to natural disasters, by freeing the 3D printer from the confines of its container.

① FREE THE PRINTHEAD

② ATTACH TO AERIAL VEHICLE

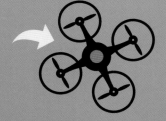

③ BUILD TIME!

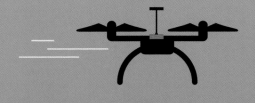

THE RESULTS

We developed a functioning prototype **Mobile Unmanned Printing Platform (MUPP)**, including an extruder (the component of the printer that deposits materials into layers), built from the ground up, and optimized for use on a hexacopter through an iterative, rapid prototyping process. Each component is parametrically controlled and can be adapted to different-size copters or to accommodate different materials in a matter of minutes.

We designed the feeder with an open top to allow for liquid material to be refilled during flight. When activated, a custom-made auger moves material through the conveyor and out the nozzle. The location and quantity of material output is controlled by toggling when the auger rotates. For our initial testing, we developed a lightweight, rapid-setting concrete that sets within 15 minutes. This ensures the material can be layered on top of itself without slumping.

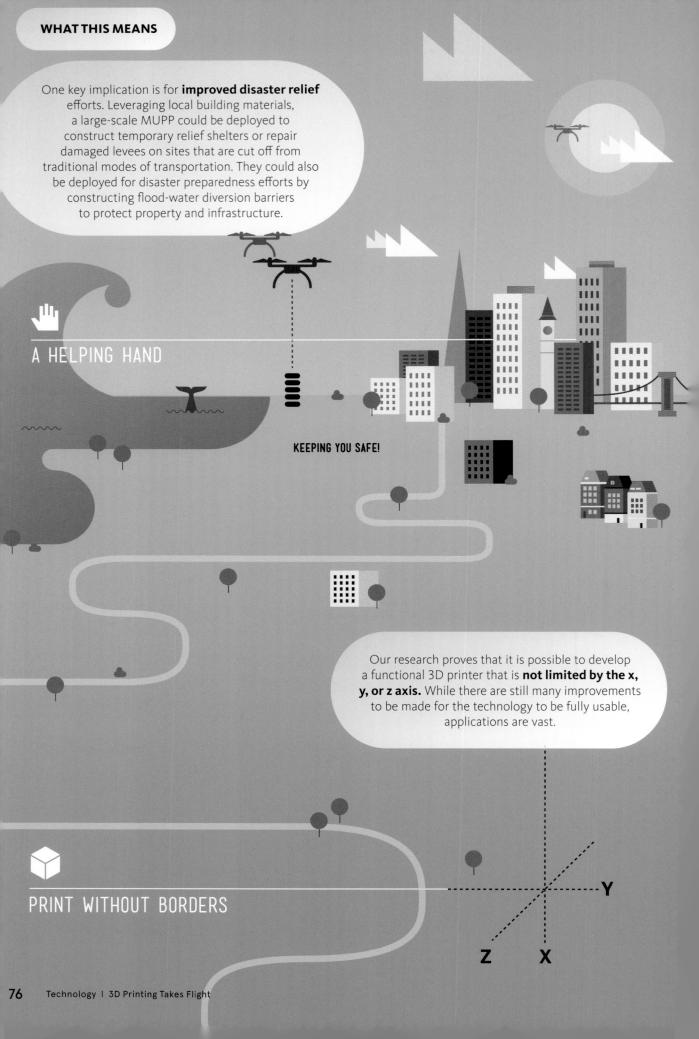

WHAT THIS MEANS

One key implication is for **improved disaster relief** efforts. Leveraging local building materials, a large-scale MUPP could be deployed to construct temporary relief shelters or repair damaged levees on sites that are cut off from traditional modes of transportation. They could also be deployed for disaster preparedness efforts by constructing flood-water diversion barriers to protect property and infrastructure.

A HELPING HAND

KEEPING YOU SAFE!

Our research proves that it is possible to develop a functional 3D printer that is **not limited by the x, y, or z axis.** While there are still many improvements to be made for the technology to be fully usable, applications are vast.

PRINT WITHOUT BORDERS

Y

Z X

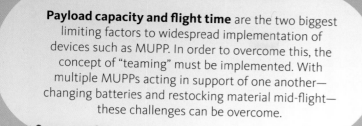

Payload capacity and flight time are the two biggest limiting factors to widespread implementation of devices such as MUPP. In order to overcome this, the concept of "teaming" must be implemented. With multiple MUPPs acting in support of one another—changing batteries and restocking material mid-flight—these challenges can be overcome.

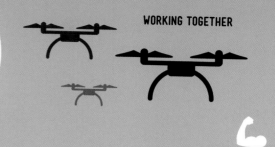

WORKING TOGETHER

STRENGTH IN NUMBERS

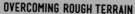

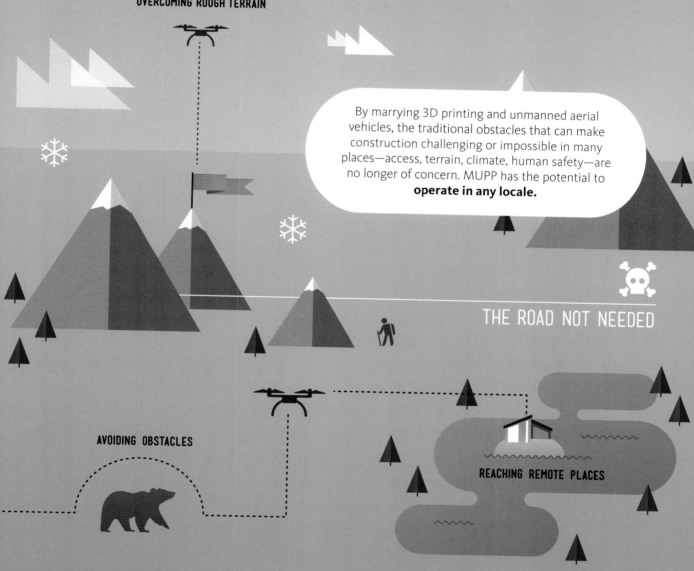

OVERCOMING ROUGH TERRAIN

By marrying 3D printing and unmanned aerial vehicles, the traditional obstacles that can make construction challenging or impossible in many places—access, terrain, climate, human safety—are no longer of concern. MUPP has the potential to **operate in any locale.**

THE ROAD NOT NEEDED

AVOIDING OBSTACLES

REACHING REMOTE PLACES

WHAT'S NEXT

To better assist us in developing partnerships with outside entities and rapidly advance the technology, we have developed a website (www.printerswithoutborders.com) to illustrate our research process and document the evolution of the MUPP prototype. Questions remain as to how this technology can be utilized by the architecture, engineering, and construction industries,

and what other applications may exist that are currently unexplored. We continue to theorize how devices like MUPP can impact everyday life; not just about how it could be more efficient doing what we can already do, but by uncovering entirely new functions that would be impossible without it.

The Prefab City

Can the traditional construction process be replaced by modern manufacturing techniques?

WHAT WE DID

We explored modular construction trends and technology to understand their potential impact on the architecture, design, and construction industry. In the first phase of our research, we documented existing prefabricated (prefab) construction methodologies and applications. We conducted site visits and interviews with manufacturers to understand the current state of the industry; and collaborated with schools and leading manufacturers to understand the financial, ecological, and regulatory dimensions of manufacturing for prefab construction. In the second phase of our research, we identified potential new markets and uses for emerging prefab technologies.

THE CONTEXT

Current construction techniques do not reflect new innovations and technology in manufacturing and construction. We are building now in largely the same way we built in the past. We believe this is a missed opportunity, and take lessons from the consumer products industry as inspiration. Consumer products companies excel at maximizing efficient manufacturing techniques, often predicting new methods before consumer demand requires it. In contrast, the construction industry has long struggled to apply new methods and technologies industry-wide.

THE FIVE KEY PILLARS FOR SUCCESS

1. **Automatic/Robotic production**

2. **Global standards and connected regions**

3. **Tiered supply chain**

4. **Global mass manufacturing and trading**

5. **Universal infrastructure and mass customization**

THE RESULTS

Today, prefab construction methods only marginally leverage the benefits of modern manufacturing processes. We believe the construction industry can move beyond fabricated/off-site construction toward "true" manufacturing of the built environment. We documented our research in a publication, *Architecture for Manufacturing and Assembly (AfMA),* which is our proposed roadmap for achieving the full potential of manufacturing for construction. The publication summarizes the technical aspects of prefabricated construction, and provides guidelines for architects and engineers in the planning, design, manufacturing, transportation, and installation of prefab construction projects.

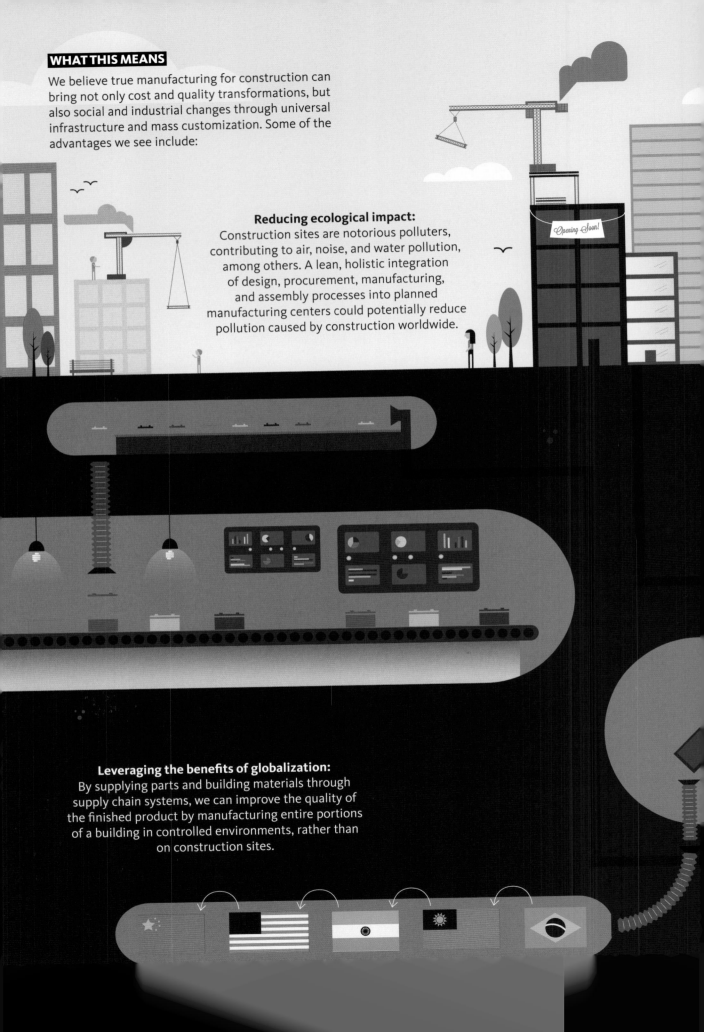

WHAT THIS MEANS

We believe true manufacturing for construction can bring not only cost and quality transformations, but also social and industrial changes through universal infrastructure and mass customization. Some of the advantages we see include:

Reducing ecological impact:
Construction sites are notorious polluters, contributing to air, noise, and water pollution, among others. A lean, holistic integration of design, procurement, manufacturing, and assembly processes into planned manufacturing centers could potentially reduce pollution caused by construction worldwide.

Opening Soon!

Leveraging the benefits of globalization:
By supplying parts and building materials through supply chain systems, we can improve the quality of the finished product by manufacturing entire portions of a building in controlled environments, rather than on construction sites.

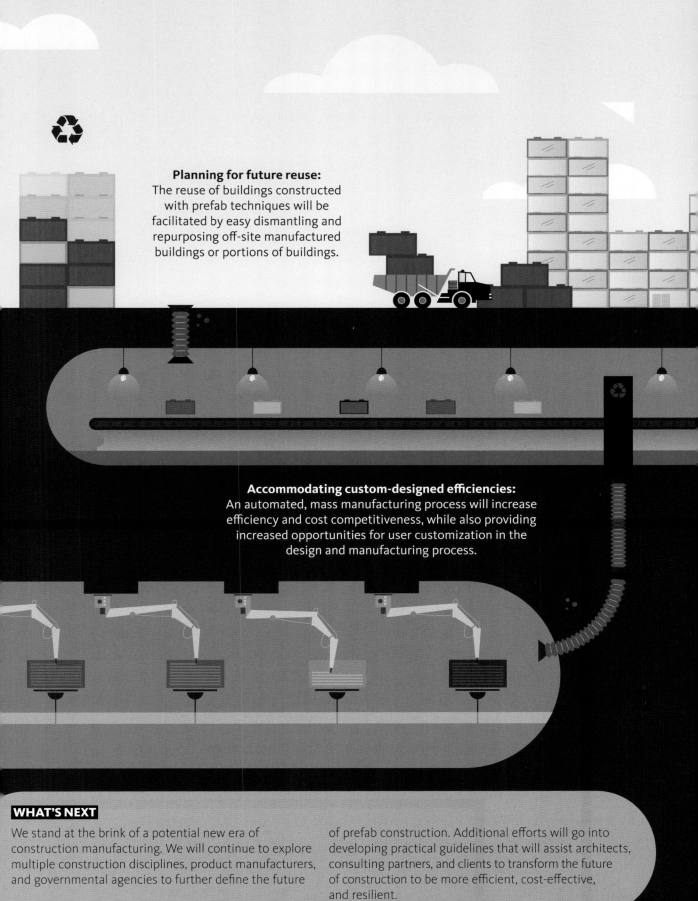

Planning for future reuse:
The reuse of buildings constructed with prefab techniques will be facilitated by easy dismantling and repurposing off-site manufactured buildings or portions of buildings.

Accommodating custom-designed efficiencies:
An automated, mass manufacturing process will increase efficiency and cost competitiveness, while also providing increased opportunities for user customization in the design and manufacturing process.

WHAT'S NEXT

We stand at the brink of a potential new era of construction manufacturing. We will continue to explore multiple construction disciplines, product manufacturers, and governmental agencies to further define the future of prefab construction. Additional efforts will go into developing practical guidelines that will assist architects, consulting partners, and clients to transform the future of construction to be more efficient, cost-effective, and resilient.

Cultural Transformation

The institutions that form the bedrock of our neighborhoods and communities are being reconsidered, shifting the ways we learn, how we stay healthy, and how we connect with and experience art and culture.

Cultural Transformation:
The Student Experience

he Post-Book ibrarian?

stigating how library leaders see the future of their institutions

eld a series of roundtables convening library
ers from institutions across the U.S. and U.K. to
ss their plans and visions for the evolution of
libraries to meet the shifting needs of students
schools. We followed the roundtables with a survey
ther further input from participants, and received
onses from 45 library leaders of both public and
te institutions.

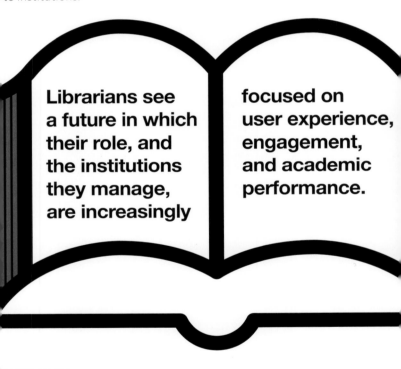

Librarians see a future in which their role, and the institutions they manage, are increasingly focused on user experience, engagement, and academic performance.

CONTEXT

y of the questions facing today's libraries—and librarians
volve around a central premise: **Will the rising
of electronic sources and online readership
ce the need to house and access physical
ks?** If so, does the physical to digital shift have
e implications as libraries plan for the future? A key
lenge as we tackle these questions—which speak
ot only the space but the idea of the library—is
for many, the library has become a proxy for
ger set of questions facing higher education. Should
tutions ride the wave of digital education and the
h-hyped but as-yet-unproved benefits therein?

Or is a focus on de
support in-person
more aligned with
institutions, and the
suite of services an
spaces and innova
attention on the d
investigation, and a
are at the core of o
holistic perspective
academic library.

In the future...

We asked library leaders about the future of their role, as well as the resources and user experience at their facilities. Results represent weighted rankings, with the highest-ranked items at the top.

...What is ideal user experience?

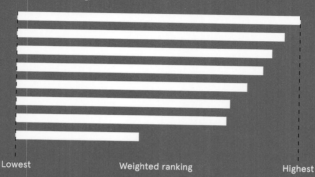

- Flexible and evolving
- Vibrant, inspiring, stimulating
- Collaborative
- Sense of place
- Intimate yet social
- Quiet and focused
- Culturally unique
- Not a building

Lowest — Weighted ranking — Highest

...What resources are most important?

- Digital resources
- Collaborative space
- Quiet space
- Integrated technology
- Instructional space
- New services / systems
- Books / stacks on-site
- Public space

Lowest — Weighted ranking — Highest

...What is the librarians' role?

- Digital curator
- Connector
- Innovator / change agent
- Outreach to users
- Archivist / preservationist
- Chief information officer
- Distance educator
- Planner / marketer / fundraiser

Lowest — Weighted ranking — Highest

PERSPECTIVES

"In the past three years, 62.6 percent of academic libraries reported repurposing space for group study, student success areas (writing/tutoring centers), quiet study space, technology learning spaces, and additional seating."

– *The State of America's Libraries 2015*, **American Library Association**

THE RESULTS

Roundtable participants stressed the wide variety of roles and services that libraries currently provide and must continue to provide in the future. They also noted the challenge of creating a single conception of the library, emphasizing cultural and programmatic differences between facilities, as well as variations in usage by space, floor, and time of year.

The continued shift toward digital and online resources was top-of-mind for participants. Many expressed excitement at the potential evolution of their libraries and roles in light of these shifts, but also concerns that students were not fully equipped to effectively find information online while maintaining rigor and quality of information. When asked directly about their roles, participants noted the changing skillset and possibly even educational background of tomorrow's library leader.

Survey respondents echoed these findings, underscoring a perceived departure from the traditional conception of the library leader. When asked about the future role of the librarian, respondents noted connection and engagement as key components of their jobs. The factors they considered most important to the library of the future included digital resources and collaborative space, followed by quiet space; books and stacks on-site fell well toward the bottom of the list. When asked to describe the ideal experience in the future library, flexibility, inspiration, stimulation, and collaboration top the librarian's list, above quiet, focused space.

Not all responses suggested wholesale change, however. When asked how library space is likely to be used in the future, respondents noted the importance of flexibility and supporting diversity of uses, but still focused on access to information and academic pursuits. Experimentation and event or community space do not appear to be a priority. And when asked how they measure success, librarians ranked student engagement and learning outcomes at the top. **Whatever the library of the future becomes, it must continue to be a space directly focused on student learning.**

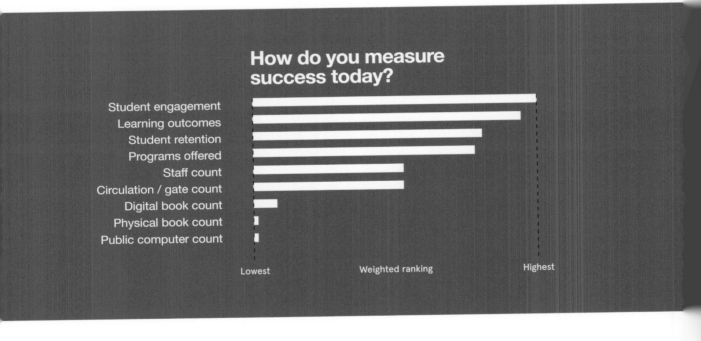

How do you measure success today?

Student engagement	
Learning outcomes	
Student retention	
Programs offered	
Staff count	
Circulation / gate count	
Digital book count	
Physical book count	
Public computer count	

Lowest   Weighted ranking   Highest

WHAT'S NEXT

Our research confirms the vital importance of libraries to student and faculty life, but the future of these storied institutions is still very much in a state of flux. Defining the right spaces and services is a question that must be tailored to each campus and student population, unified by a drive to connect students to knowledge and resources—and help improve their learning experience and outcomes.

The student voice must play a growing role in this conversation, particularly as librarians seek to measure their success based on engagement and academic achievement. And alongside a willingness to evolve the physical and digital presence of the library to better meet student needs, it is equally imperative to know and celebrate what aspects of the library are currently working and don't need to change.

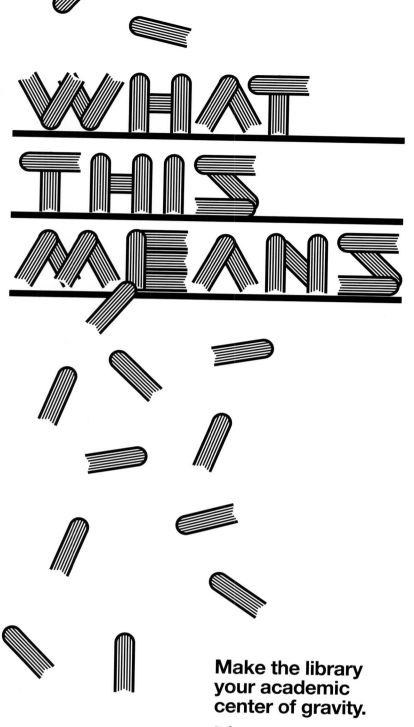

WHAT THIS MEANS

Create a seamless user experience, online and off.

As libraries embrace a wider programming and resource range, ease of navigation and use grows in importance. Librarians have a key role to play, much of which may happen behind the scenes to create a seamless user experience that students can navigate on their own. And as student engagement happens as much online as in-person, creating a unified experience across all platforms and spaces is a key concern for the future.

Make the library your academic center of gravity.

Refocus attention on the purpose and power of the academic library: a place for academic reflection and intellectual pursuit, and a central piece of a university's intellectual life. Create libraries that serve as students' and faculties' gateway to knowledge in all of its forms, and live up to its symbolic role at the heart of the college campus.

Consider librarians as facilitators of experience.

In the new library ecosystem, librarians and library staff must help students navigate the emerging mix of library services and spaces to maximum effect. Developing new strategies to engage students when and where they seek services will be necessary to achieve success.

Libraries Are for Studying

How do students envision the present and future academic library?

Students value the academic library as a bastion of quiet and a prime place to complete individual work, and see this core purpose continuing into the future.

Libraries serve a critical role in the on-campus experiences of today's student—as they have for generations. Often iconic buildings in prominent campus locations, a college's library system expresses a commitment to academics and a promise to parents that they're sending their students to a quality institution. But the value goes far beyond the symbolic. Libraries continue to serve highly practical campus roles as well: as places to study, to find quiet, and to access resources—even if those resources are as much pixels as paper.

As colleges seek to keep their campuses relevant in the wake of a changing educational landscape, libraries often take center stage. The library, for many, conjures images of books, stacks, and card catalogs—physical objects that seem outdated as resources and collections shift toward the digital realm. Library buildings, as a result, have become a key focus as institutions seek to update campus facilities to align with new students and study habits.

But in discussions ostensibly focused on supporting the student's ability to study and learn, a direct representation of the student voice is often absent. As a result, assumptions about the shifting needs and behaviors of today's student—based on their status as "digital natives" and an assumed shift toward digital tools, multitasking, and "always-on" communication— often prove misplaced.

WHAT WE DID

We conducted an online, panel-based survey among a sample of 1,200+ college students across the U.S. to understand the study habits and preferences of today's students, how the library is supporting those needs, and how they see the library evolving in the future.

This builds on prior Gensler survey research documenting overall student behavior and campus needs, observational research of libraries to document usage patterns and uncover opportunities for improvement, and a series of library leader roundtables. Our goal was to capture the student voice and to understand the library spaces, services, and experiences that best support learning and the evolution of the library.

TOP-RANKED LIBRARY QUALITIES

1 QUIET AND FOCUSED

2 SENSE OF PLACE FOR INDIVIDUAL SCHOLARSHIP

3 INTIMATE YET SOCIAL

4 INSPIRING

PREFERRED PLACES TO:

 STUDY/WORK ALONE   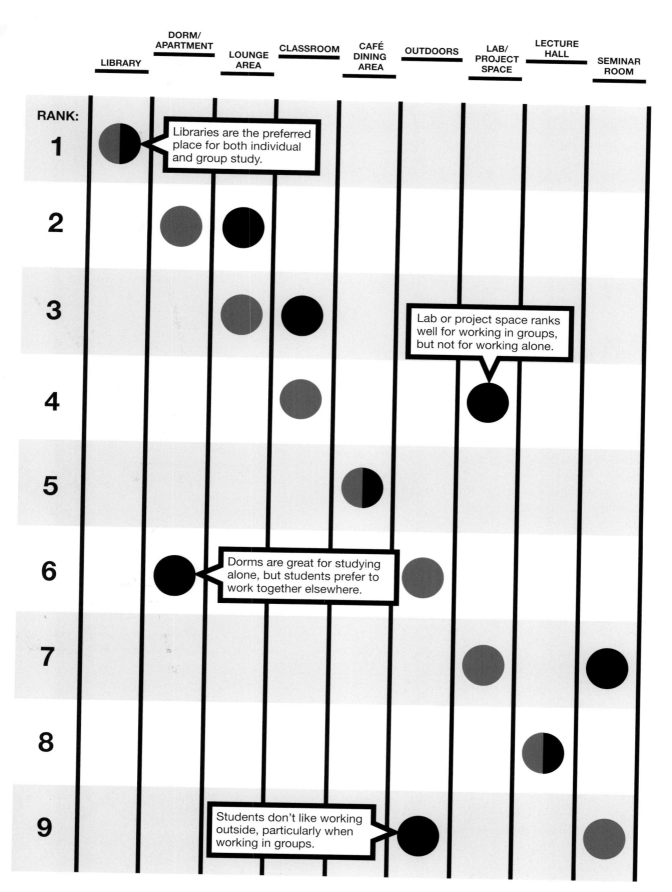 WORK IN A GROUP

LIBRARY   DORM/APARTMENT   LOUNGE AREA   CLASSROOM   CAFÉ DINING AREA   OUTDOORS   LAB/PROJECT SPACE   LECTURE HALL   SEMINAR ROOM

RANK:

1 — Libraries are the preferred place for both individual and group study.

2

3 — Lab or project space ranks well for working in groups, but not for working alone.

4

5

6 — Dorms are great for studying alone, but students prefer to work together elsewhere.

7

8

9 — Students don't like working outside, particularly when working in groups.

THE RESULTS

Despite a continued narrative around the perceived irrelevance of the library in an age of digital resources, **students see the library as an essential part of their college experience, and see this role continuing as they look to the future.** While students report the library as a preferred space for both individual and group activities, their conception of the ideal library skews toward the solitary. Their top-ranked library qualities center around space to complete focused, individual work, and when asked what resources are most important to libraries today, "quiet space for students" ranks first. When asked about the future, the rising importance of digital resources and connectivity becomes clear, while quiet space shows its continued importance.

This conception fits with how students are spending their time—they spend on average 13.5 hours/week studying or working alone on campus, compared to only 4.3 hours/week engaged in collaborative or group work—and aligns with findings from prior Gensler research. Individual work dominates the library experience as well: when asked what activities they visit the library for, studying/working alone tops the list, followed by group work and access to digital resources. Students' preference for individual work is also supported by the behavior of the highest performers—"A" students report more time studying alone than average, though this added study time appears to be outside the library.

TIME SPENT STUDYING

Average hours per week, by studying mode and student performance level.

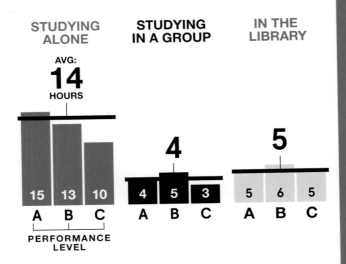

STUDYING ALONE

AVG: **14** HOURS

15	13	10
A	B	C

STUDYING IN A GROUP

4

4	5	3
A	B	C

IN THE LIBRARY

5

5	6	5
A	B	C

PERFORMANCE LEVEL

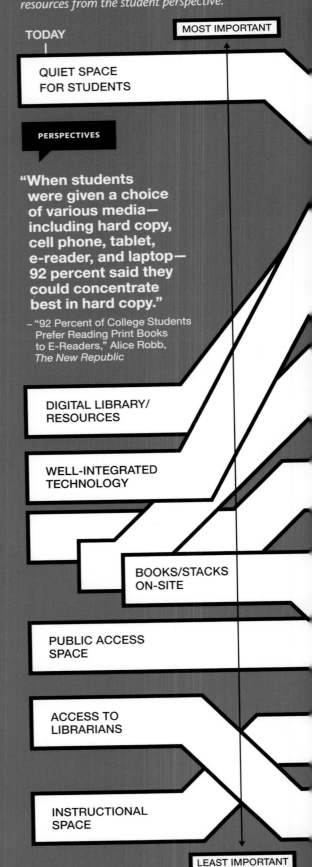

MOST IMPORTANT LIBRARY RESOURCES OF TODAY AND TOMORROW:

Rankings show relative importance of library resources from the student perspective.

TODAY

MOST IMPORTANT

QUIET SPACE FOR STUDENTS

PERSPECTIVES

"When students were given a choice of various media— including hard copy, cell phone, tablet, e-reader, and laptop— 92 percent said they could concentrate best in hard copy."

– "92 Percent of College Students Prefer Reading Print Books to E-Readers," Alice Robb, *The New Republic*

DIGITAL LIBRARY/ RESOURCES

WELL-INTEGRATED TECHNOLOGY

BOOKS/STACKS ON-SITE

PUBLIC ACCESS SPACE

ACCESS TO LIBRARIANS

INSTRUCTIONAL SPACE

LEAST IMPORTANT

WHAT THIS MEANS

Focus on pragmatic, individual student needs.

Students seek out the library for both focused and collaborative work, and to access digital and print resources. Prioritize areas in support of these activities to best support student need.

Don't sacrifice quiet in pursuit of collaboration.

Libraries must deliver spaces to support both individual and group work, but these goals can be in conflict if not managed correctly. Consider delineating group-focused activities and spaces from areas devoted to quiet work to maintain an appropriate atmosphere and noise level.

Integrate technology as a companion to analog tools.

Students appear to be reliant on both analog and technological tools to complete their work—both must be supported for space to be effective. When students were asked what resources will be most important to the library of the future, the responses of quiet space, digital resources, and integrated technology top their list.

WHAT'S NEXT

Students express a clear preference for completing individual work at the library, but it's not the only place they're working alone—nor is it the only place they go to collaborate or access digital resources. Yet something both physical and symbolic about library space appeals to students seeking to study and connect. As libraries consider their future, expanding their culture and reaching beyond their walls, both physically and virtually, is an opportunity to make an even greater impact.

Smart, flexible approaches to technology are also a key opportunity—and challenge. Integrated technology and digital access will continue to grow in importance, but how to best integrate tech differs by institution and student profile. An expanding suite of personal technology and a BYOD (Bring Your Own Device) culture means many facilities may prioritize accommodating students' personal devices over continually purchasing and integrating the newest technologies.

A Student View of Academic Libraries

Article excerpt, originally published in Gensler Dialogue 27

While much of their content is web accessible, libraries endure on the campus. New Gensler research looks at their current and future use.

University and college students put in three times more hours studying on their own than studying with peers, according to a recent survey of 1,200 U.S. students, analyzed in Gensler's *Student Perspectives on the Library*. The survey also confirms that extra study time correlates with better grades. Interestingly, while the "A" students put in the most hours, they use the library less than the "B" students. This suggests that the top performers are best able to screen out distraction. Whatever their performance level, students report that they prefer to study in the library. The main reason they give for this is straightforward: libraries offer places where they can focus, and focus makes their study time more effective.

The power of proximity

Given this preference, it's surprising that two-thirds of students' study time happens elsewhere. Their living situations may play a role: for individual study, students in dorms and campus housing prefer their own quarters slightly more than the library—with a slight gain in performance. Gensler's research on student living confirms this, says David Broz: "Students expect to find a live/work environment at on-campus dorms and housing. This often reflects study habits they established in high school."

Students' study time also relates to where and how they live. Those living on campus spend the most time studying alone and the most time studying collaboratively. Those living within walking distance of campus also study slightly more than average, while those commuting to campus spend the least time on each activity. This suggests that commuters lack options about where to study, compared with their on-campus and near-campus peers. Providing more options that address their unique needs may be an important direction for libraries in the future.

· · · · · ·

Implications for the future

Academic libraries can benefit from a better understanding of how and why students use them. What they value, beyond the libraries' book collections, are the ways that focused study and research are supported. "The competition for great study spaces on campus is fierce," says Gensler's Melissa Mizell. UC Berkeley's Moffitt Library, which her team is renovating, accentuates libraries' third-place aspect: "the vibe, the slight din, the social component, being near others yet able to focus."

Commuting students and those struggling academically are the most in need of libraries and their services, but are not currently the library's heaviest users. To serve them better, libraries will have to give them more targeted attention in the future. One approach to consider is to provide places where commuters can easily access a variety of study settings and resources; another is to put in place a network of outreach facilities tailored to the special needs of lower-performing students.

Academic libraries will continue to evolve around core study and access needs. In this role, they will have to balance the energy of gathering with the need to support focused work. But they will also need to invest in new facilities that close the gap with students who aren't being served by the current model. Adding spokes to the hub and integrating the digital more seamlessly are among the potential strategies.

– By Mark Thaler, AIA, Senior Associate, Gensler

Remaking Student Living

Can we enhance student living environments to better respond to the needs of today's students?

WHAT WE DID

We conducted a three-year study focused on student life on university campuses, and the role of the residence hall in fostering student success. In the first phase of our research, we examined the study habits of high school seniors using surveys, focus groups, and one-on-one interviews to document their preferred methods of learning before attending university.

We then conducted surveys, focus groups, and meetings with university students and administrators to understand challenges that current college students face regarding studying and focusing specific to their living situations. Ultimately, we used this information to identify areas for improvement, measure students' perceptions of the on-campus living experience, and understand the challenges faced by facilities and building managers as solutions are developed.

Students have strong differences in learning styles and social styles. The ability for an environment to adapt to those styles is ripe for improvement. One size does not fit all.

VISUAL
Learning by seeing

AUDITORY
Learning by listening

KINESTHETIC
Learning by doing

A **transition in focus** occurs as student engagement shifts from socialization to academic study throughout the course of the semester.

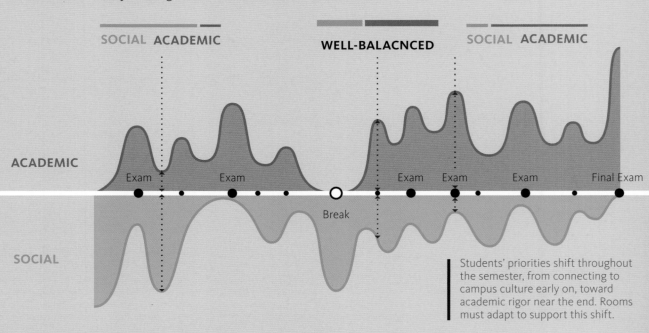

SOCIAL **ACADEMIC**

WELL-BALACNCED

SOCIAL **ACADEMIC**

ACADEMIC

Exam   Exam   Break   Exam Exam   Exam   Final Exam

SOCIAL

Students' priorities shift throughout the semester, from connecting to campus culture early on, toward academic rigor near the end. Rooms must adapt to support this shift.

Today's student residences are based on assumptions around how students live, and learn, that are decades old. On-campus living spaces must have the ability to adapt easily and frequently to accommodate the spectrum of ways students learn, and socialize, today.

THE CONTEXT

For most university students, moving to college—and into the dorms—offers a new sense of independence and personal responsibility. On-campus residences embody a culture that is uniquely social, encouraging casual interactions in an environment focused both on learning and socializing. But with the exception of the amenity-rich, suite-style student residences that began to emerge in the 1990s, the design of most dormitories does not reflect this cultural and social experience. The dorms that most first-year students enter today have seen little change since their parents attended college in the 1970s: cell-block rooms with two beds, two desks, two dressers, and two shelves.

Are today's digital native students—along with their unique, technology-driven study habits and social preferences—able to make the most of the spaces they're given? Gensler's prior research into student study habits identified a key problem—great study spaces are hard to find on campus. Sixty-eight percent of students reported a preference for quiet space, while only 39 percent reported that the space where they studied recently was actually quiet. **And, while the library was their first choice for quiet study time, most students were not satisfied with its acoustics, availability of space, or hours of operation. Their other preferred learning space? The dormitory.**

THE RESULTS

Our research suggests that the residence hall is an overlooked and underutilized asset in an integrated campus network, one that could bridge common gaps in student needs. **The academic potential of the student residence is too often overshadowed by its real estate efficiency and social amenities.** Residence halls should transform living spaces into something more academically productive, socially dynamic, and culturally rich. Great dorms have the potential to make the student experience more successful, memorable, meaningful, and satisfying.

We also identified key attributes that a successful student living environment must embody. For one, students have strong differences in learning styles and social styles. These not only differ between individuals, but also evolve as priorities shift from acclimating to campus culture and making connections, to the academic rigor near the end of a semester. **Rooms must be adaptable to support this variety in work styles, priorities, and activities—one size does not fit all.**

The residence hall also proves to be an essential component for students' informal learning and personal growth. Well-being and student success happen when social and academic needs are managed in tandem, which can be a challenge for many students in their first time away from home. The residence hall can benefit from spaces that help students balance the new demands of college and foster a culture of choice, contemplation, and individuality.

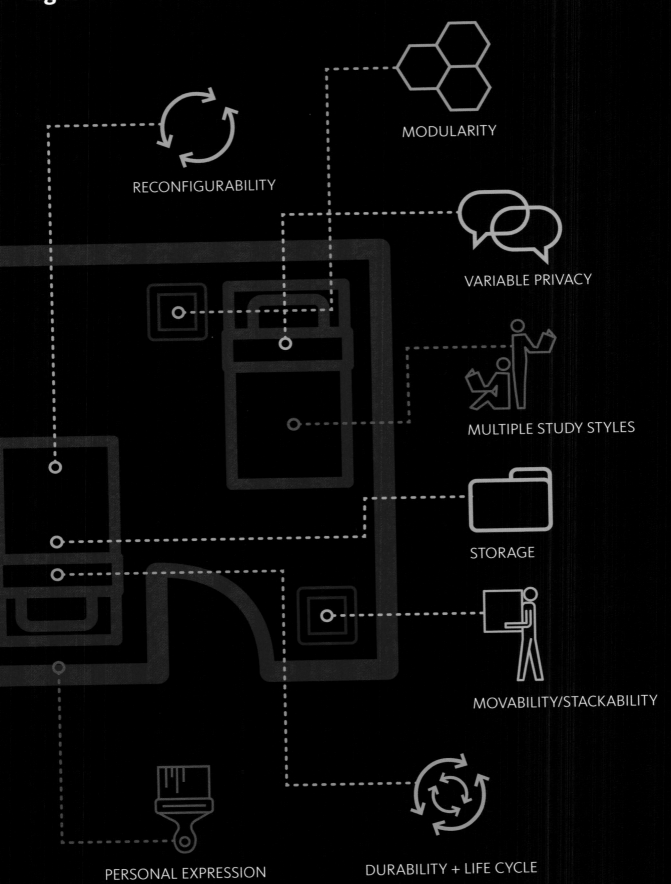

CASUAL, FLEXIBLE, AND ADAPTABLE:

Eight Considerations for Rethinking Student Housing Furniture

MODULARITY

RECONFIGURABILITY

VARIABLE PRIVACY

MULTIPLE STUDY STYLES

STORAGE

MOVABILITY/STACKABILITY

PERSONAL EXPRESSION

DURABILITY + LIFE CYCLE

Allow students to "make their mark." The dorm room is a place for them to simultaneously express their unique identity, while becoming a part of a larger campus culture. Students want to actively participate in the arrangement and configuration of their space.

Create simple and logical storage solutions. Most students won't choose to be organized, but intuitive, effective design of the environment and furniture in the residence hall room can nudge students toward using their space more effectively. This can, in turn, have a positive impact on student behavior and learning outcomes.

Provide transitional spaces. Students need spaces that allow them to transition from social to private modes based on their individual personality type and learning style, often oscillating between these needs multiple times in a given day or week. This need to shift from social to private space increases over the progression of the semester.

Build flexibility into living and learning environments. Casual and adaptable furniture solutions create spaces that can be tailored to changing needs daily, weekly, and throughout the semester. Students love to study in casual lounging postures in semi-casual environments, giving them the ability to take breaks or snack periodically.

Break the mold of traditional dormitory furniture. The academic landscape is changing rapidly—furniture solutions need to follow suit. Students often need to pull away from the hectic pace of campus life and seek out places for quiet focus work. Residence hall furniture has the opportunity to provide a customizable, functional solution to meet this need, bridging academic performance and residence hall life.

PERSPECTIVES

"...institutions of higher learning are looking for student housing designs that create greater opportunities for students to interact with each other, thereby fostering a closer sense of community."

– "6 Trends Steering Today's College Residence Halls,"
Building Design + Construction

WHAT'S NEXT

By looking at the intersections of the built environment, academic success, and user satisfaction, we hope to better understand the opportunities presented by the residence environment. Our team is currently designing and prototyping a collection of residence hall furniture for today's students—a generation of young people who are tech-savvy, academically focused, and socially connected.

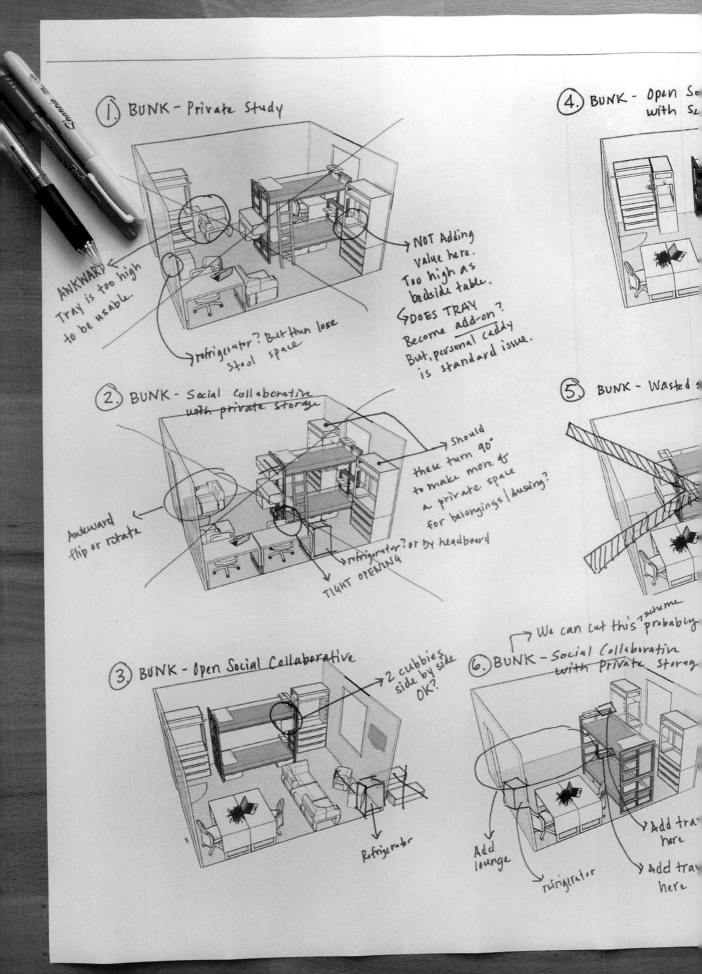

1. BUNK – Private Study

NOT Adding Value here. Too high as bedside table.
DOES TRAY Become add-on? But, personal caddy is standard issue.

AWKWARD → Tray is too high to be usable.

refrigerator? But then lose Stool space

2. BUNK – Social Collaborative with private Storage

Should these turn 90° to make more of a private space for belongings / dressing?

Awkward flip or rotate

refrigerator? or by headboard
TIGHT OPENING

3. BUNK – Open Social Collaborative

2 cubbies side by side OK?

Refrigerator

4. BUNK – Open S... with S...

5. BUNK – Wasted ...

We can cut this scheme probably

6. BUNK – Social Collaborative with Private Storage

Add lounge
refrigerator
Add tray here
Add tray here

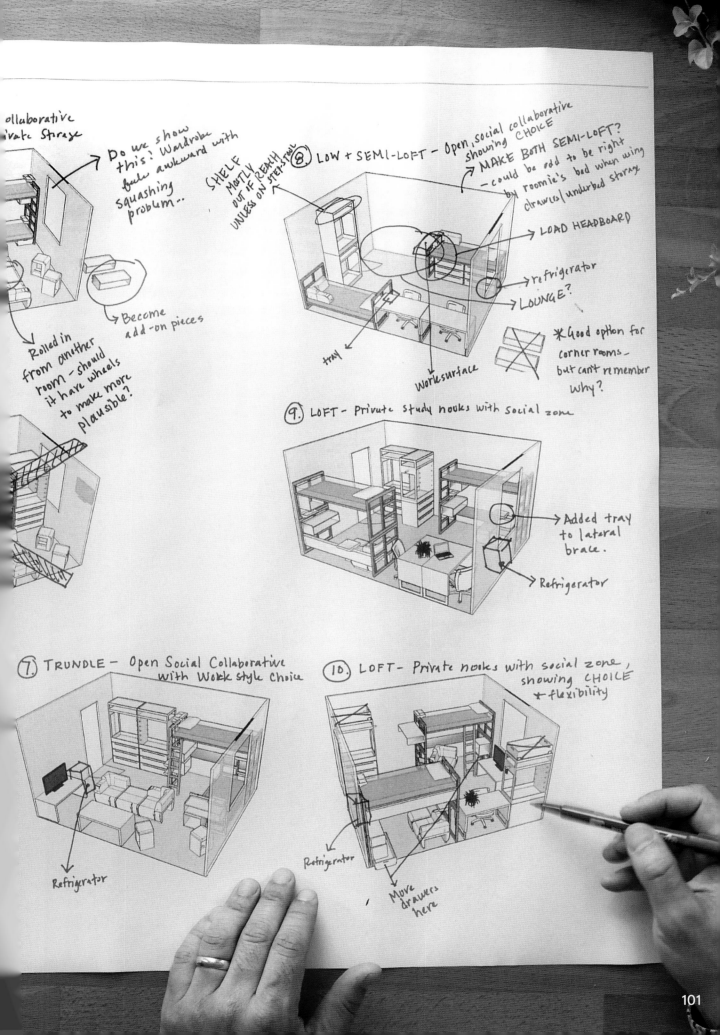

collaborative
private Storage

Do we show this? Wardrobe with feels awkward with squashing problem...

SHELF MOSTLY OUT IF REACH UNLESS ON STEP STOOL

Become add-on pieces

Rolled in from another room — should it have wheels to make more plausible?

⑧ LOW + SEMI-LOFT — Open, social collaborative showing CHOICE

MAKE BOTH SEMI-LOFT? — could be odd to be right by roomie's bed when wing crawler/underbed storage

LOAD HEADBOARD

refrigerator

LOUNGE?

* Good option for corner rooms — but can't remember why?

tray

Worksurface

⑨ LOFT — Private study nooks with social zone

Added tray to lateral brace.

Refrigerator

⑦ TRUNDLE — Open Social Collaborative with Work style Choice

Refrigerator

⑩ LOFT — Private nooks with social zone, showing CHOICE + flexibility

Refrigerator

Move drawers here

A High-Performance Place for Learning

Can rapid prototyping help us find new ways for design to support learning?

WHAT WE DID

We investigated opportunities for education environments to better match with today's learning models, specifically as those models shift toward personalization to support a diversity of learning styles. We worked with the Silicon Schools Fund, based in the San Francisco Bay Area, to partner with schools driving innovation in learning. After a preliminary review of existing research, we conducted site visits and interviews with key leaders at our partner schools to identify specific gaps where the design of the physical space was not meeting the learning needs and styles of the students.

In the next phase of our research, we prototyped furniture and fixture solutions designed to address identified needs related to a more personalized education model. Over the course of five weeks, we partnered with one school to develop multiple prototypes, test them with focus groups of students and teachers, and gather feedback to update and improve the designs for retesting. The findings helped us identify the design elements that best responded to the needs of today's students and facilitated the activities and behaviors necessary for high-performance learning.

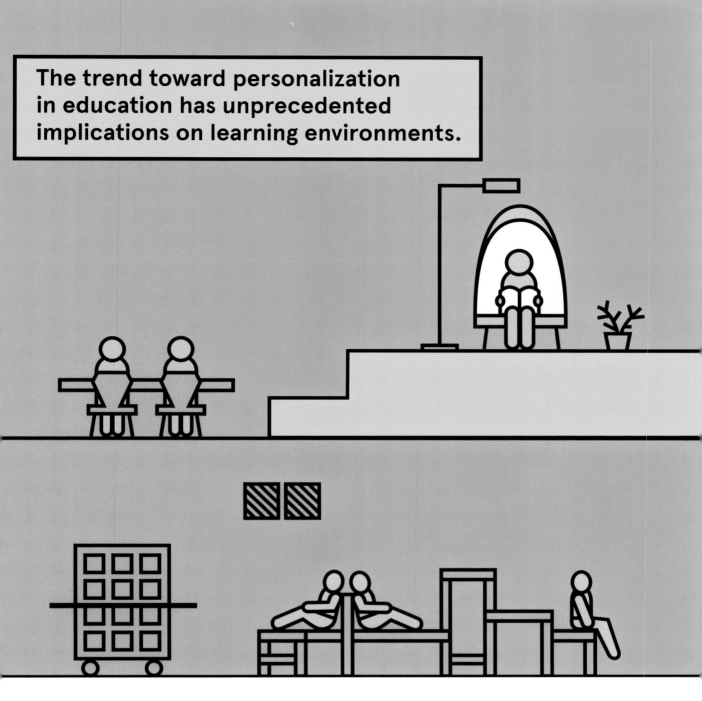

The trend toward personalization in education has unprecedented implications on learning environments.

THE CONTEXT

The manner in which we design, procure, and implement most learning environments today is a holdover of an industrial model. The focus remains, too often, on universal furniture provisions and self-contained classrooms designed on a square-foot-per-student allocation metric. This process does not reflect the diverse spectrum of activities and behaviors our schools need to support today.

The most progressive schools are moving **beyond a one-size-fits-all learning model** to become experts in **the business of learning personalization.** There is a significant opportunity for design to help learning environments keep pace with these unprecedented changes in education. Spaces that allow students to easily shift between different modes of learning, and that employ new strategies for zoning and allocating space, are key.

Experimentation with new design forms and solutions is necessary to meet this opportunity. Rapid prototyping processes in particular, which have shown success in other industries, are an opportunity to improve alignment between environment and pedagogy, with a focus on better supporting self-directed learners.

Many of today's learning environments are disconnected from the needs of students, educators, and schools. From our interviews with our partners, it became clear that schools are challenged to respond to the rapidly evolving learning landscape. All too often, even schools that attempt to design environments that enable student choice and flexibility are falling short of meeting student need.

We identified support for mode-shifting, focusing, and better definition of spatial zoning as primary needs. To gather insights quickly, we took a rapid prototyping approach. This enabled us to start small and iterate through multiple ideas. By employing this approach in active learning environments, and eliciting direct feedback, we quickly identified several approaches to meet the new demands of today's schools.

WHAT THIS MEANS

To allow mode-shifting

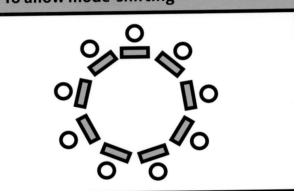

Design in the round
Designing for students to position themselves in a circular formation encourages interaction and allows them to quickly find a spot.

Make spaces inviting
Providing fun, comfortable spaces is very attractive to students and motivates them to move quickly into an activity.

Create standing settings
Places designed for standing facilitate quick changes between activities and optimize ergonomics.

Integrate fluid technology
Seamless technology helps students shift toward and between collaborative activities easily, particularly when sharing of digital information is required.

Full-scale prototyping is advantageous in the long run because it accelerates conversations among all parties... It can help you work out design challenges, recognize new opportunities, get acquainted with the physicality and feeling of a space, and get your community excited about the possibilities.

– *Make Space*, Scott Doorley & Scott Witthoft

WHAT'S NEXT

Our next step is to develop a framework for measuring the performance of educational spaces that goes beyond a square-foot-per-student metric and embraces the reality of new learning environments. We also continue to explore possibilities to develop our prototype solutions into new products for forward-thinking education environments.

To better support focus

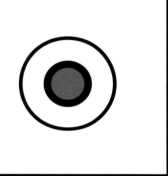

Find the sweet spot
In education, too much or too little enclosure lacks effectiveness. Aim for somewhere in-between.

Cover from the front, or from behind
To get into the zone, students need to shield themselves from distraction.

Provide a haven for more than one
Sheltered space has the power to enable two students to focus in the space at the same time.

To redefine spatial zones

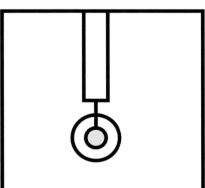

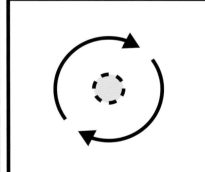

Rethink the wall
A central element can define a zone even more effectively than a perimeter boundary, such as a wall. When walls are helpful, lower height can provide a boundary while allowing for visual connection.

Consider usability
Elements that move can also be disruptive. Special attention needs to be paid to the user's interaction, as well as weight and noise from movement.

Facilitate mobility
Temporary elements are very effective for defining just the right zone when and where it is needed. These can signal a certain type of activity or behavior.

Graphic Learners

Can graphic design play an active role in improving elementary education?

We explored opportunities to leverage graphic design as an educational tool in elementary school environments. Our goal is to enrich the learning environment with educational content through simple, unconventional design solutions. We began this research by interviewing educators, not-for-profit leaders focused on using design to improve education, and designers with prior experience developing graphic programs for schools.

With Publicolor, a New York–based not-for-profit, we visited an East Harlem school to help illuminate the particular challenges of an environment faced by many students, particularly in lower-income communities. Based on this experience, we developed a series of design concepts for the use of graphic design to improve educational environments, which we then reviewed with educators in the Tri-State Area for initial reactions, feedback, and suggestions.

MOST SCHOOLS ARE NOT UTILIZING THE SCHOOL BUILDING AS PART OF THE EDUCATIONAL PROCESS. AS A RESULT, MANY LEARNING SPACES ARE CURRENTLY A MISSED OPPORTUNITY FOR AMBIENT LEARNING.

THE CONTEXT

In a competitive and fast-changing global economy, education has never been more important—and successful education starts young. Yet many of today's school environments are dark, harsh, and uninspiring for today's elementary school students. This represents a fundamental failing to start students off on the right foot, and a challenge that we believe great design can help solve.

Great schools, and the designers who help create them, use design to brighten space, promote school spirit, and inspire and engage students. But even many of the best schools are still missing an opportunity to leverage their buildings—and the walls, floors, windows within—directly in the educational process.

Only 55 percent of K–12 students are engaged in the learning process, according to a 2013 Gallup State of America's Schools report.

PERSPECTIVES

Publicolor, a NY-based non-profit, is one of many organizations leading the charge to improve education outcomes through the possibilities of design.

By involving students in the improvement of their own environments, they have seen significant success in improving student outcomes and engagement. Involving students in the application of our solutions could have similar results.

THE RESULTS

The design of education environments can serve not only aesthetic, inspirational needs but also practical ones. The integration of architecture and environmental graphic design communicates and reinforces core concepts and ideas related to students' ongoing studies. Importantly, this opportunity applies to all learning environments—low cost can yield high-impact results.

We believe creative, unexpected design intervention can assist current schools that are struggling to keep students engaged, and also act as a catalyst for a new type of school environment that sets a precedent for high-performance learning facilities. The success of not-for-profits such as Publicolor in using design to improve student outcomes serves as inspiration for our ideas.

WHAT
THIS MEANS

We identified a set of core educational areas or concepts with the greatest opportunity, then developed a series of design solutions to demonstrate the possibilities for each.

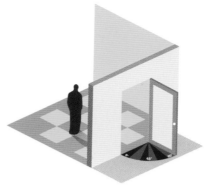

Show Measurement at the Student Scale

Use the physical environment to communicate measurement relative to other subjects or students' own experience.

Connect Language to Physical Objects

Install words onto objects themselves, using multiple languages to provide short lessons in translation.

Make History Personal

Display historical individuals or items in a way that invites interaction and students placing themselves into the tableau.

Let Structure Communicate Structure

Use school buildings to highlight architectural, engineering, and sustainability concepts, processes, and ideas.

Integrate Learning and Playing

Involve students in the creation and application of graphics, and make them interactive or changeable to keep the process going. Outdoor surfaces and playgrounds are an opportunity as well.

WHAT'S NEXT

Based on outreach to educators, we believe there is significant opportunity to implement these solutions in education environments.

We are developing a series of design solutions that can be implemented easily in existing and new facilities in partnership with our education designers. We are also exploring opportunities to create solutions that can be implemented, and easily changed, directly by students and/or teachers.

Cultural Transformation:

Museums

114 **What Is the Future of the Museum?**

Project Name: Museum Futures: Programming for the Next Generation
Research Team: Maddy Burke-Vigeland, Bevin Savage-Yamazaki, Nina Murrell,
Kristie Alexander, Gloriana Arias, Christine Barber, Iona Bruckner, Nick Bryan,
Louise Burnett, Nina Charnotskaia, Vanessa Churchill, Ashley Claussen, Jane Clay,
Hannah Dewhirst, Christine Durman, Lindsey Feola, Kimbro Frutiger, Traci Garner,
Aaron Gensler, Heidi Hampton, Allison Hausladen, Alexander Hohman, Ellen Hudson,
Richard Jacob, Robert Jernigan, Stephen Klimas, Namrata Krishna, David Lam,
James Lawrence, Sarah Lawrence, Diana Lee, Caroline LeFevre, Amanda MacDonald,
Carmen Martinez Fernandez-Barja, Melissa Mayer, Ines Mendez, Meghan Moran,
Maria Nesdale, Suzan Ozcelik, David Pakshong, Heather Pfister, Tim Pittman,
Maria Saenz, Hannah Sargent, Meng Sung, Amelia Tabeling, Joe Tarr, Jessica Tracey,
Brian Vitale, Ellyn Wulfe

What Is the Future of the Museum?

Perspectives on the evolution of the museum from people leading the charge

Museums are evolving to accommodate new active, individualistic, and tech-driven experiences. They must do so without sacrificing their core missions and audiences.

WHAT WE DID

We conducted a yearlong study of the evolving relationship between museums and their constituencies, with a focus on strategies to build and reinforce museums' relationships with their audiences and communities. We held roundtable discussions with influential museum leaders in Chicago, Houston, New York, London, Los Angeles, and San José, Costa Rica. These discussions explored innovations in audience engagement and operational models, and how these changes are rescripting the role of museums in their communities.

Following the roundtables, we conducted a survey of museum leaders to gather more detailed information on the topics surfaced during our discussions. The survey captures the input of 96 cultural leaders from across North America, Costa Rica, and London and represents a wide range of museum types, sizes, and governance models. We structured the survey as a tracking study to capture leaders' current perspectives on the museum experience, operations, architecture, and role in the community, both today and in the future.

THE CONTEXT

Museums today face both overt and subtle challenges. Institutional missions must be negotiated with shifting demographics, evolving visitor expectations, funding realignment, and ever-escalating technologies. Ideally, this leads to a richer and more memorable visitor experience, and encourages visitors to become museum advocates. But often conflicting goals and strategies can make this a challenge to achieve, from how (and how much) to embrace new technology as a part of the visitor experience, to who to consider as their core audience and how to best engage them.

Museums across the country, and the world, are meeting these challenges in myriad ways. Institutions are rethinking and reworking their spaces to promote deeper understanding of their collections and missions, greater interactivity, a fuller range of activities, and increased revenue stability. As they meet this challenge, a perspective on current approaches to engaging visitors and evolving facilities, as well as a picture of what's to come, can help guide museums as they meet an uncertain future.

The museum experience will become more interactive and self-directed.

As museum leaders look to the future, they see a shift to a greater level of visitor control and new methods of audience engagement. Today's emphasis on in-person, personal, museum-curated experiences will evolve to accommodate digital engagement (on- and off-site), self-directed entry experiences, and visitor curation. As museums seek to expand their reach, a greater focus on youth-oriented programming will also emerge.

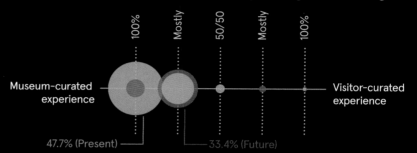

Museums were already community focused; they'll become even more so.

Expanded hours and nighttime operation were prioritized by roundtable participants and survey respondents in an effort to appeal to a larger segment of the population and accommodate working professionals. A move toward greater institutional partnerships for programming and promotion, paired with a shift toward community engagement, is also an opportunity for museums to expand their influence and relevance.

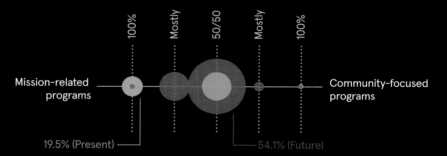

Museum design will follow suit, becoming more public, welcoming, and flexible.

While museums are often examples of iconic, civic architecture, the thinking is shifting. Tomorrow's museums will be more welcoming and embrace the public, the temporary, and the flexible in new ways. Leaders also see a shift toward a more equal balance between active and contemplative spaces. Accommodating the active and the public without sacrificing the traditional, quieter museum experience many visitors expect will be key to future museums' success.

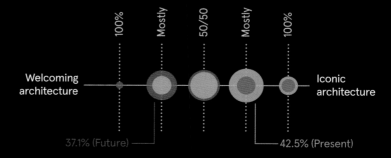

"Museums should be enjoyable, curious, allow us to see beauty, and fill us with wonder."

– Maria Balshaw, Director, Whitworth Art Gallery

WHAT THIS MEANS

Museums are uniquely positioned to blend education and recreation. Roundtable participants stressed the importance of taking risks in the creation of **new programs and experiences,** while avoiding "least-common-denominator" strategies. Engaging adults in more learning opportunities on-site while creating new strategies to meet younger constituents where they are is a key opportunity.

Architecture must play a **balancing act.** Digitized collections and self-directed experiences are on the rise, but museum leaders worry that over-emphasis on technology is displacing human interaction. The importance of welcoming, contemplative spaces must be balanced with the pull of iconic architecture and activity-focused programming.

Clear, mission-aligned success metrics are necessary. Participants noted an increasing expectation for quantifying value and success from philanthropic donors, while stressing the pitfalls of unproductive metrics. They see a shift toward more **mission-driven metrics** in the future, along with a greater balance between public and private funding.

To **attract and retain audiences,** museums must strengthen their presence in their communities. Lifestyle and retail activities compete for visitors' attention, but can also play a **synergistic role.** Museums must define their target audience(s) and tailor programming accordingly, including a comprehensive and often district-level approach to the visitor experience.

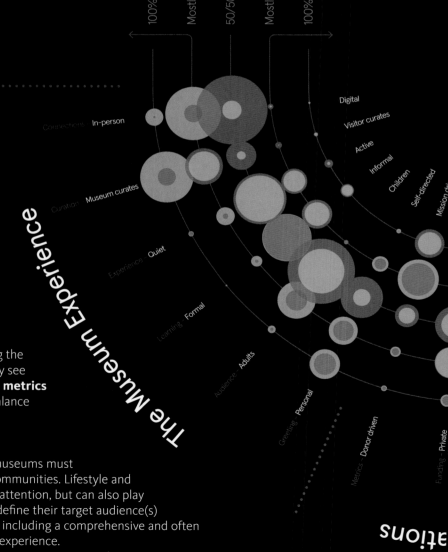

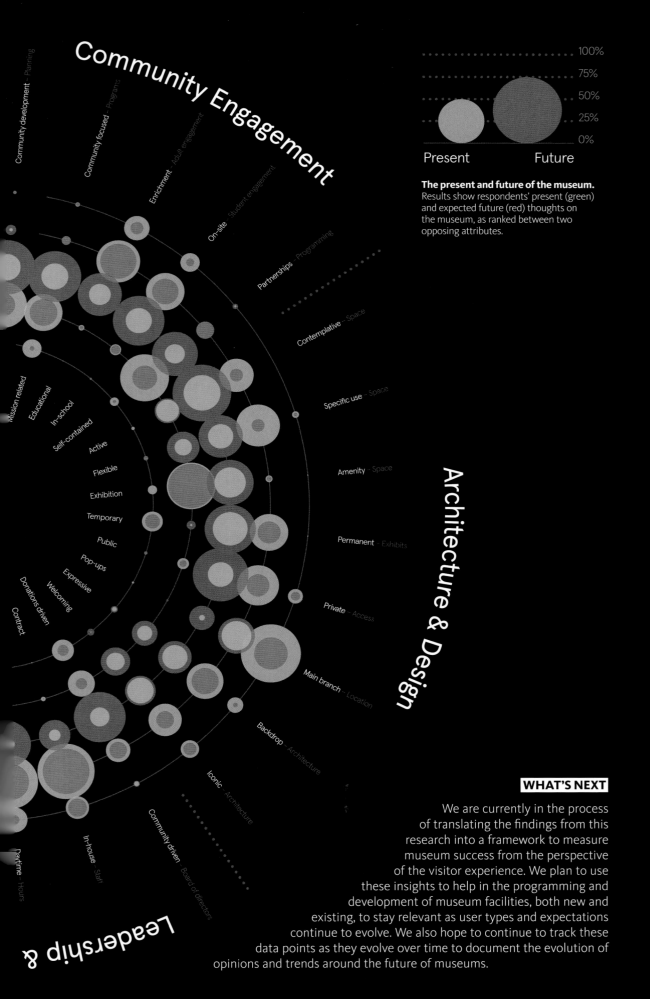

Community Engagement

Community development – Planning
Community focused – Programs
Enrichment – Adult engagement
On-site – Student engagement
Partnerships – Programming
Contemplative – Space
Specific use – Space
Amenity – Space
Permanent – Exhibits
Private – Access
Main branch – Location
Backdrop – Architecture
Iconic – Architecture
Community driven – Board of directors

Mission related
Educational
In-school
Self-contained
Active
Flexible
Exhibition
Temporary
Public
Pop-ups
Expressive
Welcoming
Donations driven
Contract
In-house – Staff
Daytime – Hours

Leadership &

Architecture & Design

100%
75%
50%
25%
0%

Present   Future

The present and future of the museum.
Results show respondents' present (green)
and expected future (red) thoughts on
the museum, as ranked between two
opposing attributes.

WHAT'S NEXT

WHAT'S NEXT

We are currently in the process
of translating the findings from this
research into a framework to measure
museum success from the perspective
of the visitor experience. We plan to use
these insights to help in the programming and
development of museum facilities, both new and
existing, to stay relevant as user types and expectations
continue to evolve. We also hope to continue to track these
data points as they evolve over time to document the evolution of
opinions and trends around the future of museums.

Cultural Transformation:
Health & Wellness

A Breath of Fresh Air

Can workplace and building design help filter polluted air?

For design to be an effective tool in the fight against air pollution, we need to look beyond filtration and focus on energy conservation, clean energy generation, and resilience in building design.

WHAT WE DID

We conducted a comprehensive review of existing research and information on the topic of air pollution in China, including current trends aimed at addressing this urgent issue. After collecting this information, we identified specific target areas and ways in which we felt design could address air pollution problems, both indoors and outdoors. We determined several locations in Asia with the greatest opportunity, then created experiments to test our designs. By tracking and comparing fine particulate matter (PM2.5) data for our experimental sites with other meteorological data from the region, we were able to determine trends from year to year. We also used surveys to gain insight into the effect of air pollution on people's daily lives and health.

THE CONTEXT

The World Health Organization has set the allowable AQI (Air Quality Index) level at 50; it is not unusual for Shanghai residents to experience levels over six times that amount. Many commuters wear particulate masks on their way to and from work, and even while working on days when AQI levels rise above 300. Pollution in China is an urgent problem that not only affects indoor air quality and occupant health, but also contributes to increased energy consumption to filter and circulate indoor air, reduced natural daylighting due to heavy smog, and decreased productivity and overall well-being among workers.

As our clients continue to seek LEED certification for new projects, addressing issues of daylighting, energy consumption, and ventilation is an ongoing challenge in such heavily polluted environments. Local economies and communities also suffer as people remain reluctant to breathe outside air, and become less willing to leave their homes and workplaces.

PM 2.5

PM2.5 levels signify the fine particulate matter content of air, specifically particles that are below 2.5 microns in diameter, small enough to lodge deeply into the lungs or be absorbed by your skin, hair, and ultimately bloodstream.

Concerns about air pollution are part of daily life in China.

In a survey we conducted with 150 residents, respondents stressed both the significant challenges air pollution adds to their daily lives, and expressed a feeling of helplessness about solving the problem—when asked if there was anything they could do to improve air quality, 4 of 5 respondents said no.

53%
of people discuss air pollution at least once a week.

72%
of people feel air pollution is the issue that affects their daily life the most.

74%
of people wear a mask at least once a week or more.

80%
of people don't believe the air is getting better.

81%
of people claim to suffer from respiratory illness related to poor indoor air quality.

Air pollution isn't just a respiratory issue; it has broad-reaching effects.

Contaminated air not only affects respiratory health but also contributes to decreased daylighting. Smog clouds concentrate and dissipate over hours, days, and seasons, and our designs need to not only provide clean indoor air, but also be able to respond to fluctuating levels of daylight. Interestingly, while it was originally believed that pollution in Shanghai was worse in winter months due to increased coal burning, through analyzing meteorological data, we determined that it was also due to a seasonal change in wind direction.

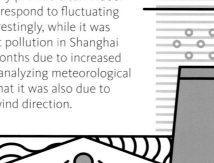

Traditional air filtration helps building air quality, but also compounds broader issues via increased energy consumption.

The importance of dramatic energy reduction and clean energy generation in building design may be one of the biggest takeaways from our research. Significant amounts of energy are consumed to filter air. Our own research shows a 7 percent increase in energy consumption in commercial office buildings (COBs) with the addition of air pollution filtration systems, even in those that achieve LEED Platinum certification. COB energy demand accounts for 60 percent of the total energy demand in metropolitan cities. If 7 percent is added to the existing 60 percent, it only creates a larger problem if that energy is 70 percent supplied by coal, as it is in China. Personal home filters are even worse, adding 1,280 grams of pollutant an hour at the energy source, while filtering only 62 grams in that same hour.

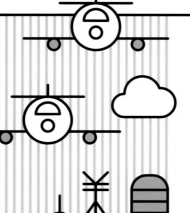

Much of the energy consumption and pollution in China are due to U.S.-owned and other foreign-owned industry.

In thinking about energy conservation, those living outside of China should also consider the impact of buying goods that are manufactured in China. A recent study conducted by Peking University and UC Irvine found that 24 percent of pollution on the U.S. West Coast can be linked to manufacturing U.S. products in China.

We can't rely on air pollution reduction; we need to design buildings to address this issue now.

Reducing air pollution is absolutely necessary, but it is not something we can take for granted. We must continue to design buildings to withstand high levels of pollution. In China, the carbon cap will not be put into effect until 2030, which is more than a decade away. Even after the carbon cap, pollution migration still remains a major threat as countries such as Iran, Pakistan, Bangladesh, and Mongolia continue to be big polluters in the region, with their pollution often drifting over to China.

We must continue to encourage the use of public transit and reduce pollution due to automobile traffic.

Currently, 77 percent of survey respondents commute by some means other than automobile, but car sales continue to increase. China has 128 car owners per 1,000 capita compared with 809 in the U.S., but the sulfur content in China's fuel is significantly higher. Through government planning bureaus, we must use design to shift the focus away from the luxury and convenience of automobiles, and encourage increased use of public transit.

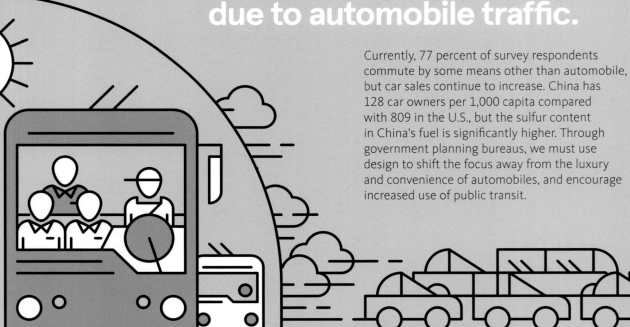

Public education must emphasize that air pollution is a problem not unique to China, and that it can be resolved.

Our research also uncovered a general lack of understanding about the topic of pollution—the sources of pollutants, what it means to talk about particulate matter, and how pollution has changed historically—not just in China, but in other major cities as well. By instead emphasizing cleanliness and the idea of "clean" design, we can simplify conversations to express the benefits of a pollution-free environment to our clients, colleagues, and communities.

PERSPECTIVES

In the 13th century, King Edward was the first person to try to ban the burning of coal in England. A consensus was not reached, and even today we are still arguing over coal as a source of energy.

WHAT'S NEXT

It remains a tremendous challenge to reduce indoor air pollution while also reducing energy consumption within a building. It is vital that we take the lead in designing buildings throughout Asia that address both issues simultaneously.

An Easier Hospital

Can better wayfinding improve the patient, visitor, and staff experience in healthcare settings?

Wayfinding is an important yet often underperforming aspect of many healthcare environments, potentially hindering the patient, visitor, and staff experience.

WHAT WE DID

We conducted a comprehensive audit of third-party research related to wayfinding in healthcare settings to identify potential areas that could benefit from improved wayfinding strategies. Based on our initial studies, we formulated several hypotheses on where strategic interventions could improve the patient, visitor, and staff experience through wayfinding. We then surveyed 25+ healthcare professionals to test and verify our hypotheses. The surveys and supporting research informed the development of our *The Value of Comprehensive Wayfinding in Healthcare* guidebook, a resource for healthcare system operators, planners, and architectural designers to create best-in-class hospital wayfinding systems.

THE CONTEXT

Healthcare settings are often large, complex environments that for many are visited infrequently, and often in times of physical or emotional stress. Many health systems have traditionally focused their resources on impacting the efficiency of medical care delivered. As a result, hospitals have not focused resources on the visitor, or staff, experience—which includes, but is not limited to, wayfinding. Too often this results in a discrepancy between the quality of care delivered and the overall quality of the experience, a situation that can negatively impact patient satisfaction levels, as well as the perceptions of visitors and community members. Faced with increased competition and an eye on improving patient outcomes and satisfaction levels, hospitals and medical systems are increasingly looking to improve the patient and visitor experience as a differentiator in the marketplace.

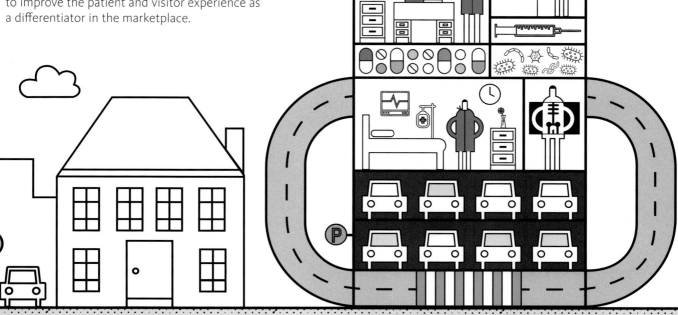

THE RESULTS

Wayfinding is a key aspect of the healthcare experience.

Ninety-five percent of those surveyed identified wayfinding as being "extremely important" to the patient and visitor experience. When well executed, wayfinding has been shown to reduce patient and visitor stress, reinforce institutional branding, and improve operational efficiency. Currently, many healthcare facilities are missing the mark: of the healthcare professionals we surveyed, 65 percent rated the wayfinding at their facilities to be worse than the medical care provided. As a result, patients and visitors are more likely to have negative experiences. Facility operations and workflows for staff are also negatively impacted by poor wayfinding.

Basic interventions—signage, naming conventions, pathways, and entrances—should be the first priority for improving wayfinding.

Building identification signage, directional signage, pathway definition, entrance definition, and landmark definition are currently not given enough priority in hospital design. As a result, they are often ineffective and confusing. Once the basics are working, there are opportunities to improve the experience by providing a more integrated and comprehensive wayfinding system. Human factors like staff training and knowledge, as well as digital factors like apps and digital directories, can work with the built environment and signage to aid different populations in wayfinding—and enhance their overall experience.

An integrated approach to wayfinding that includes human, physical, and digital interfaces provides the most opportunity to enhance experience and improve satisfaction levels.

The most effective wayfinding systems are multidimensional and address many aspects of the user journey from beginning to end. They are also human-centered, empowering a diversity of user types to find their own way and build mental maps that make the journey easier.

"Hospitals are realizing they have a design problem as patients and visitors struggle to navigate the maze of the modern medical complex. Confusing layouts and signage add to patients' anxiety at a time when many are feeling ill and are coming to the hospital to undergo tests and procedures."

– "A Cure for Hospital Design," Laura Landro, *The Wall Street Journal*

WHAT THIS MEANS

A reprioritization to focus on designing, implementing, and maintaining effective wayfinding systems can reduce patient stress and anxiety, improve facility operations and workflows, and have profoundly positive impacts on the confidence and well-being of patients and visitors.

Make destination points easily identifiable.
The use of medical terminology in signage can overwhelm patients. For example, a parent taking their child for treatment of an inner-ear infection may not understand what the Otolaryngology Department is, but will understand "Ear, Nose, and Throat."

Identify important locations with distinctive design cues. This could be a unique entryway, piece of furniture, or storefront. It should be clearly visible and easily described—for instance, by having a recognizable color, shape, or object.

Clearly mark pathways and reinforce navigational cues. Visual cues include creative naming signage, directional signage, graphics, landmarks, and view corridors. They must occur frequently along a path to provide reassurance to people as they navigate, making reorientation easy and seamless.

Multiple forms of communication (visual, verbal, and digital, for example) should be integrated into an optimal wayfinding strategy. Interactive kiosks or visitor help desks can supplement pathways and signage by providing directional printouts, or they can be sent to a patient's or visitor's smartphone.

WHAT'S NEXT

We continue to use our publication, *The Value of Comprehensive Wayfinding in Healthcare,* as our primer on how to understand and design wayfinding systems for healthcare environments. The guide provides a recommended methodology for beginning a new wayfinding project or refreshing an existing system. It can also help healthcare organizations begin to think about their wayfinding earlier in the design process of a new building or renovation project. Ultimately, this guide will enable critical conversations about what is important to a successful wayfinding experience and also provide a basic tool list and an approach for creating those experiences.

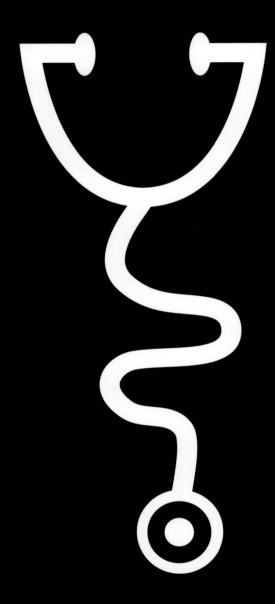

How Good Design Can Improve Public Health

Blog, originally published on GenslerOn.com

By the year 2050, a staggering 70 percent of the planet's population will live in urban areas. That rate of change holds significant ramifications, not the least of which is that Non-Communicable Diseases (NCDs) are the leading cause of death globally and will be proportionately represented in growing cities. In recent times (as well as historically), a strong relationship exists between the design of the built urban environment and public well-being. Improved sanitation requirements, building regulations, and the development of hospitals and healthcare systems significantly reduced epidemics of cholera, tuberculosis, and other contagious health threats that plagued cities in 19th and early 20th centuries.

During the 21st century, however, these threats to public health have been replaced by a different epidemic: a significant rise in the percentage of adults living with chronic health conditions such as obesity and diabetes. Studies indicate these instances of NCDs are related to lifestyle choices such as inactivity and unhealthy eating habits, resulting in diseases that are both debilitating and expensive.

There are other obvious diseases associated with urban health. Problems affecting emotional well-being are associated with living in the city—people living in cities have a 21 percent increased risk of anxiety disorders and a 39 percent increased risk of mood disorders. Similarly, the impacts of poor health in urban workplaces are enormous. Employers bear the costs which stem from lost productivity and absenteeism. This alone provides a compelling argument for addressing the well-being of employees through scalable solutions aimed at reversing unhealthy lifestyles.

As planners, designers, and architects, we can bring about a meaningful improvement in the general well-being of our society by designing physical environments that promote healthier lifestyles. Design professionals can address health and wellness for urban dwellers both at work, and outside of work. These two realms are converging to support the larger goal of total well-being.

As a result, design is evolving to address well-being at multiple scales, ranging from city-wide transformations at a macro scale to integrating well-being design into the work environment at the micro scale. The idea that design can positively influence a person's well-being is starting to transcend every project typology. A codified set of ideals and drivers embedded in design strategies and priorities are being incorporated into newly adopted health elements of general plans in cities throughout the United States. These health elements consider the emotional and physical well-being of urban dwellers as a function of the man-made environment. They incorporate various design responses—active design, social connectivity, and transit for instance—that make a significant difference on our holistic well-being.

At the urban scale, increasing activity by improving walkability and offering alternative modes of transportation are fundamental strategies for combating the growing global epidemic of obesity, heart disease, and diabetes. The direct correlation between workplace productivity, well-being, and the city will only evolve as more of the planet's population moves to the urban cores. Well-being is not a state; it's a lifestyle. Our cities, buildings, and workplaces, at all scales, must evolve to support healthy lifestyles.

– By Claudia Carol, AIA, Senior Associate, Gensler

The Hospital Left Behind

What do we do with underutilized or closed hospital infrastructure?

WHAT WE DID

We identified strategies for adaptive reuse and redevelopment opportunities for underutilized medical facilities, with a goal to benefit owners and users, as well as the communities the hospitals serve.

Our methods included interviews with hospital executives and other healthcare professionals, as well as architectural project teams; a review of historical events that directly impacted hospital facility growth and decline; and the identification of industry benchmarks to better understand key components for successful facility transitions.

We also gathered secondary research and case studies identifying the economic parameters that drive real estate decisions to repurpose or demolish buildings; and analyzed metrics from independent industry organizations such as the American Heart Association, The Advisory Board, DHG Healthcare, PwC, Kaufman Hall, among others. Using this information, we held roundtable discussions, design charettes, and think tanks with service providers, industry analysts, and design professionals to explore effective strategies that would later inform a speculative design project to illustrate our findings.

THE CONTEXT

The healthcare market is undergoing a major transformation in how and where it delivers services. This is impacting service providers' real estate strategies in profound ways. Just as patient care is shifting from a reactive, episodic service model to one of continuous wellness, healthcare facilities must adapt to this new continuum of care.

As a result, the U.S. is rife with shuttered or under-utilized hospitals. These facilities vary in size, shape, design, context, and age, and have come to symbolize the state of the healthcare real estate market. Together these are the hospitals left behind, and the phenomenon only promises to grow. The question of what to do with underutilized or closed hospital buildings is of vital importance, not only to the buildings' owners and operators, but to the patients and communities they were built to serve.

THE RESULTS

When facing the challenge of adapting legacy healthcare infrastructure for new purposes, it's critical that stakeholders have a solid understanding of **what works—and what doesn't.** More often than not, the real opportunities for hospital reuse reside slightly "off stage" and away from the glow of critical praise and preservation dialogue. The vast numbers of the hospital buildings left behind **are not considered historic or iconic.**

To understand when, and in what way, a building is worth reusing, we developed a process to identify the highest and best use for a given building. By exploring demographic and trend data specific to a building's location, in context of the costs and opportunities for converting the building to different uses—whether **workplace, residential, hotel, or other healthcare uses** —the process helps clarify the options for redevelopment, and ultimately aids in making the final and best decision.

PERSPECTIVES

"When you think about a public hospital, obviously there is a central mission, and it is critical to maintain that mission. On the other hand, if everything you do is a negative cash flow, you're not going to be able to keep your doors open."

– HOSPITAL ADMINISTRATOR

In many cases, decidedly un-iconic buildings can be the best candidates for re-engagement. Using what we learned during our research, our team then speculated on the possibilities for one such building. We used the opportunity to test our ability to apply what we've learned by identifying the highest and best use for the property, and then assess ways we could **"hack" the building** to improve its value and benefit the community as a whole.

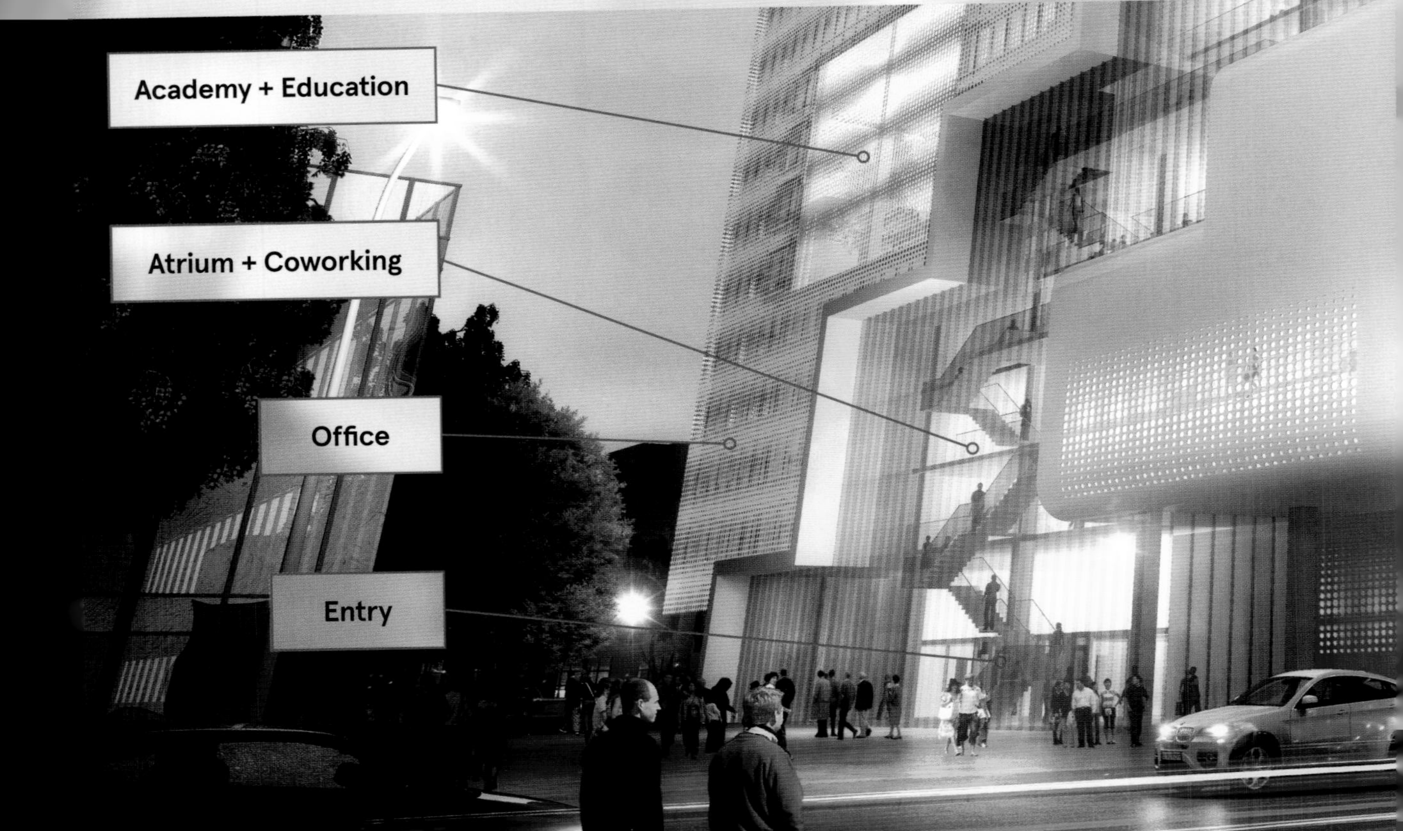

Academy + Education

Atrium + Coworking

Office

Entry

Residential

Hotel

Event Space
+ Garden

Healthcare
Incubator

Restaurant
+ Events

Public Lawn

Community Retail

The architectural options for hospital reuse are initially quite straightforward: you can either **renovate, repurpose, or raze** the building. However, the underlying factors that inform which path a client chooses are as nuanced and varied as the buildings themselves.

We ultimately identified **eight critical factors** our clients must consider when undertaking a hospital reuse project:

1 - CURATE YOUR TEAM. You're not just picking a team of architects, planners, and facilities managers; you need the right people at the table to help calculate capital and operational expenditures, as well as analyze market need and opportunity.

2 - START THE RIGHT CONVERSATION. Make the conversation strategic and informed, and have the right people in the room. The client side of the equation must include the C-suite, not just the facilities manager.

3- KNOW YOUR COMMUNITY. This means understanding demographics, but also the nuances and personality of a community. Sustained and meaningful community engagement is tantamount to success.

4 - INFRASTRUCTURE ALWAYS RULES. Respect the bones of your building, and understand how it can—or cannot—be adapted to work for you. The opportunities, or limitations, of infrastructure may be the key factor in deciding whether a building can be saved.

5 - UNDERSTAND YOUR OPTIONS. Learn how residential, hospitality, learning, workplace, and clinic programs work with legacy infrastructure. Paired with the needs of the local community, this will help you identify the best usage options.

6 - THINK SCULPTURE, NOT SURGERY. Don't be afraid to make a big, inspirational move that goes beyond the pragmatic. The intervention should be a provocation, not an homage to the past.

7 - SOMETIMES THE SMARTEST OPTION IS NOT TO BUILD. Sometimes you don't need more space, just better use of space. Look for ways to make processes more efficient—embarking on a new project should be the last resort.

8 - KNOW YOURSELF. At the end of the day, it's critical to understand your own risk profile. If it's the right decision, as one source put it, "don't be afraid of the wrecking ball."

We continue to share our findings within the industry, and help clients with underutilized facilities explore the best opportunities for their revival.

Engagement & Experience

Brands of all types—from hotels to sports teams—are connecting with consumers in increasingly sophisticated ways, aligning with and expressing personal values in search of like-minded customers, and creating unique experiences that differentiate and delight.

Engagement & Experience:
Brand Strategy

Emotional Consumerism in India

What drives brand loyalty and consumer decision making in India?

WHAT WE DID

We designed and conducted an online, panel-based survey of 1,000 adult consumers from India to understand the impact of emotional connection on their relationships with brands. This survey builds on prior research we conducted with U.S. consumers, which identified the importance that shared values play in fostering brand loyalty. Respondents first named their favorite brands, then chose the one that is most important to them. They were then asked a number of additional questions about their relationship with that brand in detail, as well as about their own values, priorities, and purchasing behaviors. We used this data to understand the level of emotional connection respondents have to a brand, and analyzed this in relationship to their broader responses and demographic profile.

THE CONTEXT

The Indian retail industry continues to evolve rapidly, particularly with a steady influx of international brands into the market. For those that make the right value proposition and connection to Indian consumers, the potential benefits are huge—but understanding how is a challenge. As India's retail sector becomes more organized—currently, organized retail is less than one-tenth of the market share of overall retail in the country—the concept and behaviors of shopping will undergo a dramatic transition.

To stay ahead of the curve, brands must understand how, and why, consumers forge emotional connections with their favorite brands. For local brands, the opportunity will be to remain relevant among growing competition; for brands new to the market, the opportunity is to establish lifelong relationships for the first time.

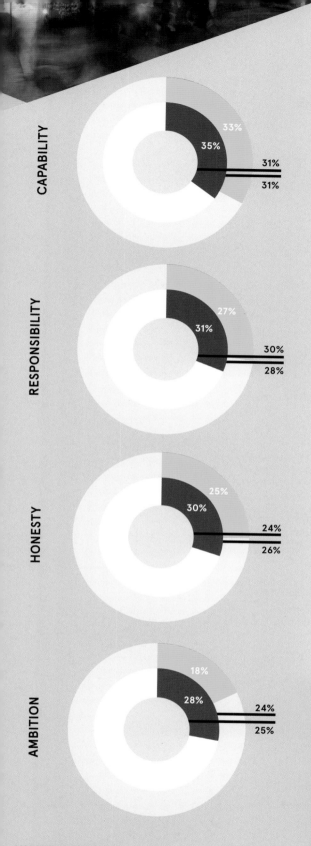

CAPABILITY
33%
35%
31%
31%

RESPONSIBILITY
27%
31%
30%
28%

HONESTY
25%
30%
24%
26%

AMBITION
18%
28%
24%
25%

VALUES ALIGNMENT

● **PERSONAL VALUES**

○ **BRAND VALUES**

— **U.S. DATA COMPARISON**

Data represents the percent of respondents ranking each value important, both personally and to their favorite brand.

THE RESULTS

Emotions are what differentiate brands from commodities. In India this is especially important—four out of five consumers consider themselves brand savvy, with strong opinions about brands and the values they stand for. Our survey shows that brands in the technology sector are the most effective at making these emotional connections—33 percent of respondents noted their favorite brand was in this sector. Automotive, financial, and clothing brands also fare well, while food, retail, and sports brands rank the lowest. Compared with our United States data, the prevalence of "favorite" financial brands, and the comparative lack of connection with food and beverage brands, is notable; financial brands ranked lowest in the United States, and food and beverage ranked near the top.

Quality is key to brand loyalty—and that's universal. In both India and the United States, our survey results underscore that quality is the most important component of loyalty. Today's Indian consumers are more materialistic than previous generations, and many are stretching their budgets to acquire their favorite brands as they enter the growing middle class. This stretch makes delivering on quality even more paramount, as consumers are willing to spend but can't frequently replace products that come at a premium. If the quality isn't there, loyalty will be lost quickly.

Innovation outranks familiarity for Indian consumers. After their expectations for quality are met, alongside other pragmatic factors like trust and effectiveness, consumers rank innovation as a key brand attribute contributing to loyalty—a notable difference from their U.S. peers, who prioritize familiarity. This may be a result of the steady influx of new brands to the Indian market, resulting in a consumer focus on what's new instead of what's known.

81% of Indian consumers consider themselves brand savvy.

75% of consumers in India interact with their favorite brand by making purchases in-store.

48% of consumers in India report visiting the store to see what's new.

WHAT THIS MEANS

Connect with consumers' daily lives. For consumers to feel a connection to a brand's set of values—defined in our survey as what the brand stands for, or the stated beliefs that are core to its purpose or position—it's important for brands to proactively communicate and demonstrate consistently the values they stand for. In India this is especially important, as values alignment is often a more significant contributor to brand engagement than it is in the U.S.

Make your value proposition personal. People don't always buy for logical reasons. They buy for emotional reasons, and this emotional spark occurs most often when a consumer is able to connect with a brand at a personal level. The strong alignment between personal and brand values from our respondents illustrates the point—capability, responsibility, honesty, and ambition rank as consumers' top personal values, as well as the top values they perceive in their favorite brands.

Leverage in-person interaction. With the growing presence of online retail in India, just as in other global markets, the opportunity to touch, feel, and experience a brand in person is often minimal—but when it happens, the payoff can be significant. In-store connections with consumers can go a long way to strengthening brand relationships—75 percent of consumers in India interact with their favorite brand by making purchases in-store, and 48 percent report visiting the store to see what's new. While product availability is often the reason our respondents report store visits, their experience is ultimately driven by staff friendliness and helpfulness.

ATTRIBUTES CONTRIBUTING TO BRAND LOYALTY

Innovation

Price

Familiarity

Effectiveness

Trust in the Brand

Quality

● INDIA   ● UNITED STATES

"**India is like a kaleidoscope.** Every time you turn it, you get a different perspective— enticing, different, and "real." The basic requirement for understanding Consumer India is to recognize that there are no simple algorithms to segment it. It is the methodological nuances that allow one to get at the heart of this opportunity."

— *Winning in the Indian Market*, Foreword by C. K. Prahalad

WHAT'S NEXT

We plan to build on the findings of this project, and parallel surveys undertaken in the U.S. and China, by conducting a global comparative analysis to understand similarities and differences among consumers in each country. The findings of this analysis will deliver additional insights to inform our design work for local and multinational brands.

Consumer Multiplicity in China

How does brand behavior, and loyalty, vary among Chinese demographic groups?

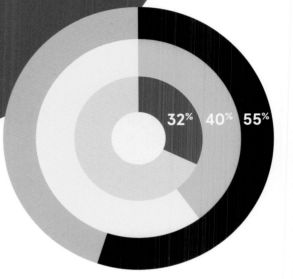

32% 40% 55%

BRAND AFFINITY IN CHINA BY CITY TIER

The more metropolitan the city, the more likely its consumers are to report a strong emotional connection to their favorite brands.

- ● TIER 1 (LARGE CITIES)
- ● TIER 2 (MEDIUM CITIES)
- ● TIER 3 (SMALL CITIES)

WHAT WE DID

We conducted an online, panel-based survey of 1,000 adult Chinese consumers to identify patterns in consumer behavior among various demographic groups in China. We analyzed the data according to location, gender, and brand type to better understand how consumer values correspond with brand values for specific demographic groups. To inform our location analysis, we categorized China's major population centers into first-, second-, and third-tier cities according to criteria such as economic development, GDP, transportation systems, urban infrastructure, and historical and cultural significance. Across demographic categories, we then measured the frequency and intensity with which consumers connect to and engage with brands, and the brands particular consumer groups identify with most.

THE CONTEXT

As China continues to undergo rapid economic development, its consumer class is increasing in both scale and sophistication. The number of products and services available to Chinese consumers continues to grow, and they are concurrently becoming more and more discerning in their purchasing decisions. The behaviors and brand affinities of various consumer groups also show distinct characteristics, offering opportunities for brands to better target consumer groups.

93% of respondents said that they are **very likely to recommend their favorite brands to friends or family.**

50% of respondents said they **are willing to wait in a long line or travel a long distance** to purchase branded products.

85% of consumers acknowledge the financial value of branded goods and services, and **are willing to pay more for the real, authentic products.**

45% **say that friendliness of staff impacts level of satisfaction greatly.** Helpfulness (21%), product availability (41%), and speed and efficiency (41%) influence satisfaction as well.

THE RESULTS

Connection drives consumer behavior. The top three components that contribute to brand significance for respondents in our sample are a genuine connection with the consumer, alignment with personal values and style, and the ability to make the consumer feel good. Staff friendliness and helpfulness are also key factors in determining positive brand experiences, indicating that even in the digital age of online shopping, customer service is still essential. Additionally, 93 percent of respondents said they are likely to recommend their preferred brands to family or friends, proving word of mouth is still one of the most effective ways for brands to spread their message.

Men consider themselves as brand savvy as women.
In fact, among Chinese consumers between the ages of 18 and 34, men actually report themselves as being slightly more brand savvy than women. The diversity and availability of products targeted at men don't currently reflect this—products that build greater connection with men have an opportunity to compete in a less crowded but equally valuable consumer space.

International brands struggle outside first-tier cities.
Consumers in first-tier cities are highly engaged with their favorite brands, and feel these brands express their personal values. Their favorite brands are often international or global entities, reflecting a consistency among global consumers in major cities. Consumers in second- and third-tier cities are different—they are more loyal to local brands, and overall see less connection with brand values; their decisions focus more on economic value than brand identity.

Retail banking is a particular opportunity area.
The majority of the trends and relationships identified in our data apply across various industries with only slight variation. The retail banking industry appears to have particular opportunity for improvement—consumers indicate that they often remain loyal to banking brands simply because they don't have better options from which to choose.

WHAT THIS MEANS

Expansion beyond first-tier cities requires a different approach. International brands have been successful connecting to savvy consumers in major, global cities in Asia—beyond these, they still face challenges engaging local consumers. To expand more deeply into the Asian market, they must tailor their values to meet the needs of consumers who have a more local mindset, and understand that competition is more price-driven in these markets than in others.

Grow local brands by aligning values. Local brands have the opposite challenge from that faced by their international competitors: scaling values and personal connection with consumers to maintain their foothold in second- and third-tier cities, while gaining traction in first-tier cities where competition and alignment with international brands is already strong.

Don't forget the men. Men in Asia report being as brand savvy as women, if not more so. Brands should explore the possibilities of additional goods and services intended specifically for men. The food and beverage industry, in particular, showed a high prevalence of male consumers expressing connection to brands.

ATTRIBUTES CONTRIBUTING TO BRAND LOYALTY

Trust in the Brand

Innovation

Familiarity

● CHINA   ● UNITED STATES

PERSPECTIVES

WHAT'S NEXT

We plan to segment the data to address five industries of interest: fashion retail, retail banking, food and beverage, technology, and automotive. Three of the five industries show similar patterns to the U.S. The two anomalies are food and beverage and retail banking. We want to better understand why this is true.

We will build on the findings of this project, and parallel surveys undertaken in the U.S. and India, by conducting a global comparative analysis to understand similarities and differences among consumers in each country. The findings of this analysis will deliver additional insights to inform our global retail strategy and design work.

"Despite China's growing significance on the world stage and an explosion of new Chinese material and lifestyle opportunities, local culture remains intact and, to those with cultural curiosity, knowable. In order to establish a productive relationship with the Chinese people, we—business people, politicians, students and tourists—must reorient ourselves to engage with a profoundly different worldview."

– *What Chinese Want: Culture, Communism, and China's Modern Consumer*, Tom Doctoroff

Brand Engagement: People and Passion

Blog, originally published on GenslerOn.com

Brands are people; people are brands. This statement may resemble clichéd jargon, but it's true. Here's why: Consumers actively choose brands based on personal values and aspirations, which is not so different from the way we choose our friends, significant others, or spouses. This kind of alignment of personal priorities sparks real emotion and connection. And companies don't create brands, people do. Companies create new services, products, names, logos; but it's customers—people—who give them life and longevity by making them a part of their own lives. This kind of engagement is emotional, not transactional. It's all about people and passion.

Strategies to achieve that level of customer-brand engagement can be developed by any company, large or small, using social media, local events, partnerships with other relevant brands, grassroots community efforts, etc. The point is to open the door for customers to connect with your brand in ways that are authentic to you, and relevant to them. Our brand engagement survey points to an opportunity to define and articulate your values —what the company or brand believes in—and then to demonstrate through words and actions that what your customers believe in matters to you, too.

Of course, established brands have terrific opportunities to spark emotional connections with customers, too. What's unique about brands with long legacies behind them is the opportunity to create elements of surprise, which can spark very emotional reactions with customers old and new. Do something no one expects, with no expectation of reward. Maybe it's showing a longtime customer that you remember their name or favorite product, or you remember something important about their life—small details that let them know they're important to you. Or maybe it's forging a new partnership between your brand and another like-minded brand, creating new and different, even unexpected, experiences that keep customers coming back for more.

It's all about understanding who your client is and what matters to them, and then connecting with them on a personal level. In today's high-tech world, social media follows or likes, online comments, or mobile app interactions are often the way we connect—even with

our closest friends and family members—and these connections are often a big part of a brand's engagement strategies. Social media and mobile technology are simply additional tools in the relationship-building toolbox. The key is to include customers in the equation to provide a sense of ownership in your brand.

The good news is that the use of social media and other tech-fueled tools is a successful way to open the door to two-way conversations with today's consumers, and that's the first step in giving customers a sense of ownership in your brand. The social media phenomenon of the 21st century continues to expand with Facebook's 1.1 billion global users leading the pack. Meanwhile a new breed of socially driven retail platforms is emerging. In examples like the Hunt, users either help each other find items or help to validate other users' choices, and this kind of online camaraderie leads to advocacy, which leads to sales. Brands have the opportunity to use these platforms to create communities, or join existing ones. Bloggers, long recognized as highly effective influencers, should similarly be considered as virtual stockists—access to an online distribution network that a brand is unlikely to reach on its own.

Last but not least, social media offers a unique window into customers' personalities and passions. Paying attention to even casual, semi-anonymous messages on Twitter can offer insights into when, where, and why a customer is using your brand in more qualitative ways that traditional forms of research can't offer. It also allows you to respond personally, and show that you're listening, and that you care.

Connecting with customers on an individual, personal basis is often the missing piece in the engagement puzzle—only a few leading brands have mastered these human connections, even in the virtual world. Fortunately there are more and more tools that brands can quickly employ to join and start conversations. A focus on people and the relationships between them is the best way to add emotion to the mix and drive lifelong loyalty.

– By Jill Nickels, Senior Associate, Gensler

Brands Go Global

Why do some brands thrive in new markets while others fall flat?

WHAT WE DID

We brought together retail experts from São Paulo, Bangalore, and Shanghai to gather and interpret secondary market research in each of these cities. These local insights, paired with our global knowledge of retail trends and successful brand expansion strategies, helped to identify global growth opportunities and strategies for retailers. Our investigation focused on the automotive, banking, apparel, technology, hypermarket, and luxury retail sectors, but allowed us to document findings that could apply to all industry sectors.

Teams in each city gathered market research; investigated local consumer trends, retail prototypes, preferences, and business practices; documented common partnership models; and conducted photo surveys and interviews. Each team then presented their findings in a live, online webinar, as well as during a face-to-face client event attended by retail and retail-center clients. We also documented our work in a series of *GenslerOn* blog posts.

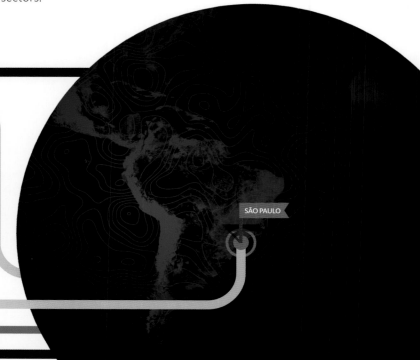

São Paulo is Brazil's cultural capital, with rich and colorful traditions. Global brand experiences that **engage all of the senses** and reflect Brazil's vibrant, lively culture can really resonate with local consumers.

SÃO PAULO

AN UNDERSTANDING OF **LOCAL CONTEXT** AND AN **OPENNESS TO EXPERIMENTATION** ARE NECESSARY FOR BRANDS LOOKING TO EXPAND AND SUCCEED GLOBALLY.

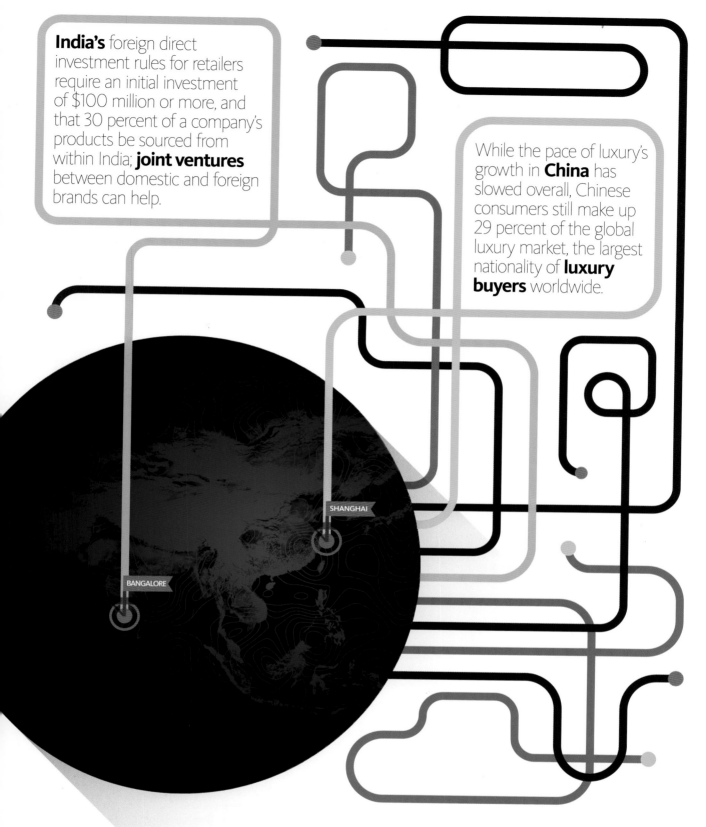

India's foreign direct investment rules for retailers require an initial investment of $100 million or more, and that 30 percent of a company's products be sourced from within India; **joint ventures** between domestic and foreign brands can help.

While the pace of luxury's growth in **China** has slowed overall, Chinese consumers still make up 29 percent of the global luxury market, the largest nationality of **luxury buyers** worldwide.

BANGALORE

SHANGHAI

THE CONTEXT

We are currently in the midst of a massive global brand migration. The shopping experiences once exclusive to London, Paris, New York, and Tokyo are now emerging in numerous cities around the world. The fuel of this growth lies in an expanding global middle class nearing one billion people, with the most dramatic growth concentrated in Asia, Latin America, and Eastern Europe; in Asia alone, the middle class grew by 600 percent from 2000 to 2014.

The increased buying power and desire for a global class of products and experiences present significant opportunities for existing and established brands looking to expand into new markets—but growth does not come easy. As retail brands go global, they face unique opportunities and challenges in each market they enter.

BE LOCAL AND CONTEXTUAL,
BUT DON'T FORGET YOUR ROOTS.

Our research underscores three basic guidelines for successful entry into any new market:

KNOW YOUR AUDIENCE.

Formulaic store designs and merchandise strategies from a brand's native home don't always fly in increasingly savvy global urban markets. Understand your core customer—their preferences, behaviors, and cultural customs—and have a strategy to address those local tastes. Research-based design solutions are a must, and ensure an informed approach tailored to the products and experiences local consumers crave.

FIND THE RIGHT PARTNERS.

Successful brand expansions don't happen alone. Acknowledge that success requires solid relationships that can guide you through complex business or political structures and bring local market know-how. Strategic partnerships and consultants with "boots on the ground" can help deliver the appreciation of the region's shopping habits and dynamics required.

EMBRACE PERSONALITY AND EXPERIMENTATION.

In an experience-based economy, consumers seek out the new and different, and brick-and-mortar retail stores increasingly resemble innovation labs. Brands have to be bold and address consumers in a way that meets their unique needs, habits, and desires. This means accepting an interpretive approach, having an open dialogue with core customers, and being willing to express a global brand through a local lens.

You can't be successful in new markets if you're not successful back at home, but that doesn't mean delivering the same thing in every city. In the three global cities that we studied, we found unique characteristics that underscore specific opportunities in each market:

IN SÃO PAULO:

Consider luxury on all levels. The young population of Brazil's cultural capital seeks a lifestyle of wealth and wellness. Retailers should focus on delivering luxury, top-notch service, and unique social experiences with design at the core. Local business partners also prove particularly crucial to successful navigation of São Paulo's financial and legal structure. Many global brands partner with mall operators to enter the city's retail landscape, joining spaces that are especially popular with women for the convenience, comfort, and security they provide.

IN SHANGHAI:

Experience and global cachet reign. Shanghai's roots as a world-class financial hub are firmly planted thanks to more than 25 years of rapid growth. Sophisticated residents gravitate toward global brands, and seek unique and compelling experiences. Shoppers are also well equipped and tech savvy. Online shopping is skyrocketing, and stores that integrate the online world with the in-store experience and offer opportunities to learn about new brands or products in immersive environments are well poised for success.

IN BANGALORE:

Embrace the diversity of a growing consumer base. India's rapid urbanization and changing government regulations open doors for global retailers to invest in Bangalore's growth, and deliver new products and experiences. The social fabric of India is tightly woven and shopping is often a family activity, centered on a special event. A deep understanding of this market's diversity—from young, tech-savvy urbanites to aspirational rural consumers—is critical to success.

PERSPECTIVES

"Today's global retailers get it. They have become **more strategic in their expansion** and in avoiding the operational pitfalls of entries into developing markets ... The leaders are also identifying the unique challenges of each market ..."

– A. T. KEARNEY'S GLOBAL RETAIL DEVELOPMENT INDEX

Consumer trends and hot markets continue to evolve and expand as new cities and countries enter the global retail stage and attract interest and investment. Continuing to document the unique perspectives and needs of each of these markets is imperative as brands seek to stay relevant in order to deliver both globally and locally.

Engagement & Experience:
Customer Experience

Experience Reigns

How does design transform the user experience, and can we measure and track its business impact?

WHAT WE DID

We conducted a series of client roundtables across five cities—Los Angeles, New York, San Francisco, Shanghai, and Washington, DC—to explore the meaning of experiential design (ExD) through the perspective of our clients and to examine how we might better measure and track its business impact. Client participants included senior executives representing a wide range of lifestyle enterprises that focus on experience, such as retail, real estate, hospitality, entertainment, transportation, and technology companies.

The first two roundtables, in New York and Los Angeles, hosted expert panel discussions with thought leaders at the edges of experiential design: two futurists, a robot designer, a trend analyst, and a food and sensory experience artist participated. Other roundtables used gamification, facilitated conversations, and one-on-one interviews to gather insights. These were intentionally open conversations meant to spark ideas, reflect the spirit of the cities they were held in, and cast a wide net across multiple industries to capture any and all ideas around what makes a great experience.

At the completion of the roundtables, we analyzed the conversations and grouped the key themes into six broad categories.

"

Design things for people's eyes, if your eyes
see something interesting, your feet will follow.
Make sure there are interesting elements,
no blind walls.

LA :: **WING T. CHAO,** *Master Planner,*
Developer, Architect

You don't always need something crazily new—
just get rid of the frustrations and time-wasters.

NY :: **CARLA DIANA,** *Product Designer, Artist,*
Creative Consultant

We are eliminating most computer-based training.
How can we expect somebody to be trained
through a computer and then learn to engage,
when engagement is our number-one issue?

SF :: **MARY BURNS,** *Director of Merchandise*
Operations & Experience Planning & Integration,
Walt Disney World and Disneyland

Experiences that are new and emotional—novel
or tap into the unknown—leave lasting memories
that can be recalled even decades later.

SHG :: **DANIEL WEI,** *Senior Vice President,*
Mia Group

[People] . . . are looking for something that puts
them out of their day-to-day world . . . I think they're
looking to be able to hold onto something . . .
and be present in the moment.

DC :: **KIRSTEN COBB,** *Director of Entertainment*
& Events, Nickelodeon

"

Companies increasingly seek to create great experiences for their customers. But though the word is used frequently, "experience" has a variety of meanings to those who employ it. Service models, immersive environments, digital interaction, products, events, and brand activations all fall under the umbrella. The best experiences combine all of these elements to create a holistic, long-term engagement with the user.

As consumers increasingly choose to have experiences rather than owning things, **designers will need to pay as much attention to creating emotional space as they do physical space.** One point that's universally agreed upon: consumers are smarter and savvier, and their expectations are higher than ever. A one-dimensional, one-note experience falls flat and fails to impress. In response, companies are beginning to focus on new ways to measure the return on their investment as they leverage experience as a means to deliver improved brand loyalty and business performance.

The continued pace of technological innovation cannot be ignored. As future generations spend more time in the digital world, they may not even think of virtual experiences as being different from "real" ones, potentially rendering the strategies and vocabulary we use to understand experience, space, and behavior obsolete. And as data mining becomes more sophisticated, technology will enable increasingly customized and personalized experiences.

People are living, working, and socializing in all kinds of environments, at all hours of the day. As a result, **we have come to expect experiences that combine and facilitate multiple types of interactions, delivered in spaces that serve several purposes and cater to a wide range of needs.**

Engage all five senses.

Activating emotions through the senses is central to creating great experiences. Understanding how sensory stimuli—sight, sound, smell, touch, and taste—affect emotions and behaviors is a powerful aspect of design experience. Stimulating and exciting the human senses on a variety of levels throughout an experience serves to deepen emotional connections and create lasting memories.

THE RESULTS

We analyzed and synthesized the results across our five roundtable discussions, and developed strategies based on the themes our clients identified as important aspects of design experience:

Tap into emotion.

The ability to capture hearts and minds is key to eliciting powerful emotions. Experiences that allow individuals to connect in new and meaningful ways can inspire us to feel, behave, and think differently. Design can evoke emotions by signaling permission to experience something positive and new, or provide guardrails and guidance that can be springboards to adventure, freedom, and exhilaration. Many of the most effective and innovative experiences are successful precisely because they tap into the most basic human emotions.

Be consistent from real to virtual.

Emerging technologies, such as robotics and artificial intelligence, sensors and the Internet of things, are increasingly blurring the lines between the virtual and the real world—with virtual experiences serving as extensions, articulations, or even replacements for physical space. The ultimate goal is to create engaging, seamless interactions that feel the same across digital and human domains. The creation of a strong narrative that will merge the two worlds is critical to building meaningful relationships and rich experiences that work on both sides of the line.

Anticipate needs and solve problems.

The best experiences are those that anticipate user needs, solve problems, are intuitive to use and understand, and deliver the right solutions at the right time. Whether responding to people's increasingly busy lives or releasing them from the pressures of time and place, the best-designed experiences give people the freedom to choose their manner and level of interaction with a brand, product, or service.

Sometimes this means taking away negative aspects from an existing experience, rather than adding anything new. Solving problems simply, elegantly, and intuitively can be a game-changing design innovation that transforms the way people perform everyday tasks. This is especially true in "burden categories" such as healthcare and transportation.

Create something unique and new— but also familiar.

The most memorable experiences are often those that feel completely novel, or offer unique or unexpected qualities that surprise and delight. They change our perspective and invite us to look at the world in new ways. Ironically, many of these novel experiences are effective precisely because, in all their novelty, they still feel somehow familiar. Introducing a known quantity, then flipping it on its head, is a powerful technique for creating a meaningful experience.

Consider every element.

Compelling design doesn't stand on its own. Customer experience now involves a greater number of touchpoints across multiple channels, where the experience is only as satisfying as the weakest link in the chain. The most immersive experiences are those in which every element along the user's journey has been carefully considered, from the enticement to an experience, through the entry, engagement, exit, and extension. It's important to identify the interactions that matter most, so that every point of contact delivers the highest consumer value.

WHAT THIS MEANS

Measuring experience requires a common lexicon. Experience means different things to different people. In order to measure outcomes, we need to develop a common language around experiential elements to ensure that we are talking about experience in the same way. Consistency and a common language are the keys to measurement.

Measuring experience is measuring people. Experience designers treat people as a medium in the experience. Therefore, understanding human behavior is a core element of the discipline. In order to measure experience, we must first understand people. That means expanding our research toolkit to include psychographic analysis as well as demographic analysis, and adding ethnography to survey data. The goal is to understand not just what kinds of choices people make, but why.

Measuring experience will be different for each industry. Because experience is so broad and encompasses so many elements, there is not a single solution that fits every experience. In order to measure, we will need to develop different metrics and rubrics for each industry.

WHAT'S NEXT

Our next phase of research will be to conduct a nationwide survey among 2,000 consumers to identify the attitudes and values of those individuals who are design-oriented or have conscious awareness of design's impact. We will conduct parallel ethnographic research among consumers across five cities, ranging from big to small, to better understand the design elements that help create great experiences from the consumer perspective. This variety of research methods will help us uncover how consumers think about design, how they talk about and identify aspects of experiences, and identify consumer "archetypes" that map to different experiences.

APRIL 13
2016
SHANGHAI,
CHINA

D

ROUNDTABLE
SHANGHAI

INTRODUC

MO
AMO
ME MO
ME MO
EXPE
EXPE

+ ROLE
PLAYER

AGENDA

WINE + BITES

TIM
XIAOMEI

NEW/ WHT EXD

WHAT'S YOUR

GINN   HAN

SHOES OFF

SOCKS

"NEW SOCKS"
AWKWARD BUT HAPPY
W/ NEW SOCKS,
NO MORE SOCKS
VERY SERVICE
ORIENTED.

T/ PAUL PAIRET

TELLING/ ARIEL
MARGALITH

OGRAPHICS/
HAN ZANTINGH

ACKNOWLEDGE
MAKING MENT

ESS

STEPS

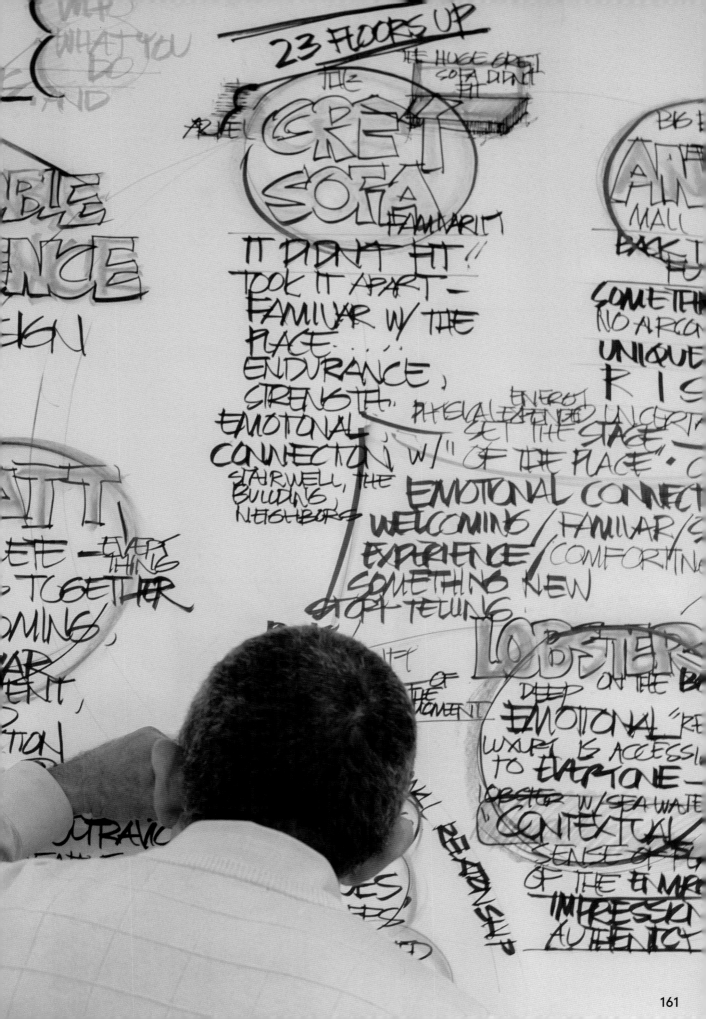

Experiential ROI

Can we measure the investment return on customer experience?

Increasingly sophisticated consumers are forcing an alignment of business and store design goals, with customer experience rising to the forefront as the key differentiator for retailers.

WHAT WE DID

We conducted an investigation into the connection between store design, customer experience, and retailer success. Our goal was to develop a framework and metrics that go beyond traditional store design elements to consider the customer experience more fully, and to draw direct connections between environmental design and business outcomes.

To begin, we reviewed existing research on store design and consumer behavior in the retail setting, and conducted interviews with industry experts, designers, and innovators. We then explored existing theoretical frameworks specific to customer experience and store design. This knowledge helped us develop deeper insights into how consumers perceive value in the retail context, as well as a theoretical construct for understanding and designing for optimal customer experience.

THE CONTEXT

Retail is an industry that is heavily dependent on metrics. Design—though appreciated viscerally and indirectly in business outcomes—lacks robust business-focused metrics as well as a framework to better assess its value. **While quantifying the value of design is notoriously difficult, the importance of design to retail success has never been greater.** In an increasingly competitive market of online, offline, and multichannel operators, it is a strategic imperative to design a store experience that is compelling and differentiating.

The need to maximize experience dovetails with an ongoing evolution of how, and where, retailers connect with their customers. The 1980s saw the emergence of a customer-focused mindset in marketing and store design—and a parallel focus on market segmentation and measuring customer satisfaction. Store design at this time became more expressive of brands, but the customer relationship was primarily single-channel. In the 1990s, the Internet gave rise to e-commerce, disrupting the industry and calling into question the need for physical locations.

At the turn of the century, traditional retailers were scrambling to stay relevant. Though e-commerce didn't replace physical retail, as some expected, it did create a fundamental shift in how consumers perceive value. **In recent years, it has become clear that customers are going to stores less for purely utilitarian needs, and more for hedonic or experiential needs such as social connection or entertainment.** As a result, the basis of competition is shifting from products and services to broader customer experiences.

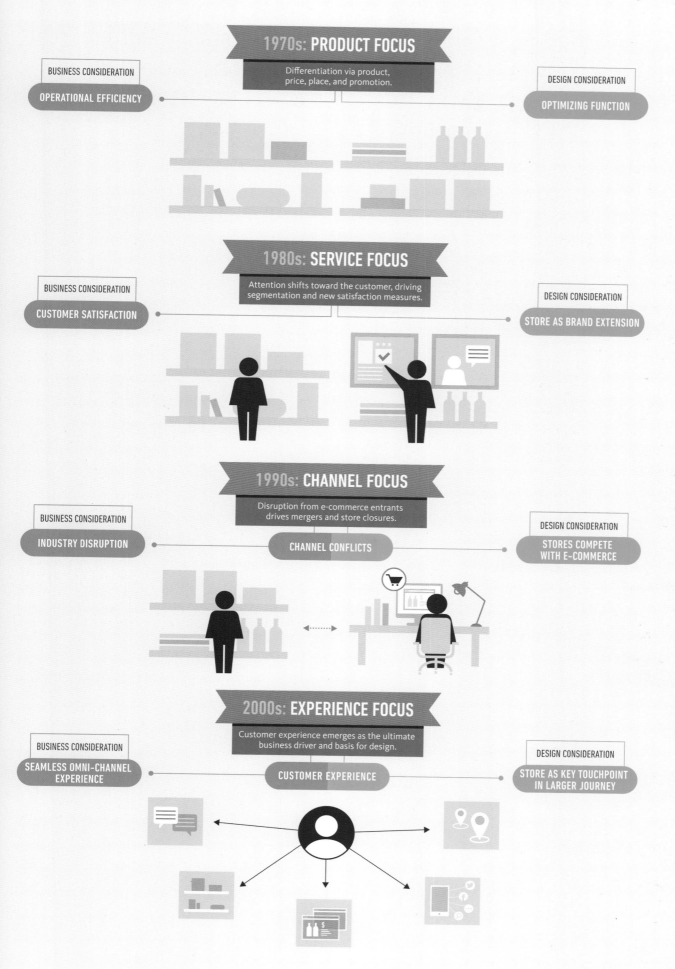

1970s: PRODUCT FOCUS

Differentiation via product, price, place, and promotion.

BUSINESS CONSIDERATION
OPERATIONAL EFFICIENCY

DESIGN CONSIDERATION
OPTIMIZING FUNCTION

1980s: SERVICE FOCUS

Attention shifts toward the customer, driving segmentation and new satisfaction measures.

BUSINESS CONSIDERATION
CUSTOMER SATISFACTION

DESIGN CONSIDERATION
STORE AS BRAND EXTENSION

1990s: CHANNEL FOCUS

Disruption from e-commerce entrants drives mergers and store closures.

BUSINESS CONSIDERATION
INDUSTRY DISRUPTION

CHANNEL CONFLICTS

DESIGN CONSIDERATION
STORES COMPETE WITH E-COMMERCE

2000s: EXPERIENCE FOCUS

Customer experience emerges as the ultimate business driver and basis for design.

BUSINESS CONSIDERATION
SEAMLESS OMNI-CHANNEL EXPERIENCE

CUSTOMER EXPERIENCE

DESIGN CONSIDERATION
STORE AS KEY TOUCHPOINT IN LARGER JOURNEY

The value equation for brick-and-mortar retail is shifting from a transactional to an experiential model. Stores designed to optimize the customer experience build long-term loyalty and rise above the competition.

PERSPECTIVES

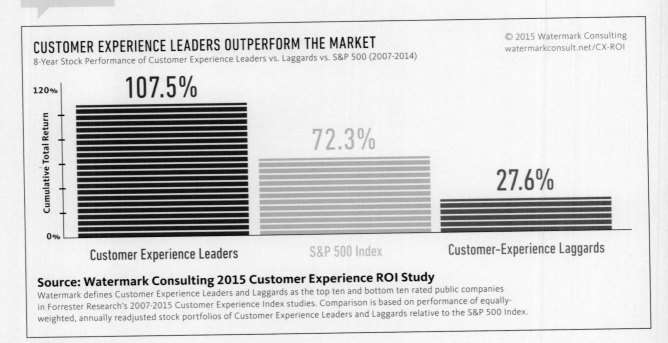

CUSTOMER EXPERIENCE LEADERS OUTPERFORM THE MARKET
8-Year Stock Performance of Customer Experience Leaders vs. Laggards vs. S&P 500 (2007-2014)

© 2015 Watermark Consulting
watermarkconsult.net/CX-ROI

120%

107.5%

72.3%

27.6%

0%

Cumulative Total Return

Customer Experience Leaders   S&P 500 Index   Customer-Experience Laggards

Source: Watermark Consulting 2015 Customer Experience ROI Study
Watermark defines Customer Experience Leaders and Laggards as the top ten and bottom ten rated public companies in Forrester Research's 2007-2015 Customer Experience Index studies. Comparison is based on performance of equally-weighted, annually readjusted stock portfolios of Customer Experience Leaders and Laggards relative to the S&P 500 Index.

THE RESULTS

Customer experience has already proven demonstrable value on an empirical and anecdotal basis. A positive customer experience shows a stronger correlation to loyalty than customer satisfaction, which is typically based on a single transaction or point in time. Findings shown above from Watermark Consulting (www.watermarkconsult.net), a U.S.-based customer experience advisory firm, note dramatic differences in the eight-year stock performance for customer experience leaders. Another by McKinsey notes improvements in revenue growth, customer satisfaction, and employee engagement (along with a decrease in cost to serve customers) for companies that designed for an end-to-end customer experience.

It is no longer sufficient to simply have well-priced and well-displayed products in a well-located, well-designed store. Retailers must design for the entire customer experience—and that does not necessarily begin nor terminate at the store. In this increasingly omni-channel world, traditional metrics such as sales per square foot are also becoming less meaningful. However, despite the mounting evidence and growing business case for customer experience, few companies actually do it well.

Part of this challenge is the lack of visibility to the customer journey across the retail organization. The tools to measure correlations and design performance within the retail space are also lacking. To address this gap, we propose our Framework for Designing Customer Experience, which focuses on the customer journey and integrates multiple perspectives, including those of the company, customer, and frontline staff.

WHAT'S NEXT

The next chapter for this research is the convergence of business analytics and design thinking to create experiences that engage customers on a cognitive, emotional, social, and psychological level for superlative returns. This will require the development of new performance metrics and benchmarks in regard to store and customer experience design, as well as an evolved approach to the process of retail design and strategy. To begin this process, we are conducting in-depth research and applying expanded metrics to evaluate the impact of design on customer experience, and, ultimately, key performance indicators on the project level.

FOCUS ON EXPERIENCE, NOT JUST SATISFACTION.
Designing holistically for the customer experience drives stronger brand loyalty and profit growth.

LEVERAGE CUSTOMER AND BUSINESS DATA TO UNDERSTAND EXTERNAL AND INTERNAL ISSUES.
Organizational and customer insights must be an integral part of the design process.

DON'T NEGLECT THE PRE-DESIGN AND POST-DESIGN PHASES OF A PROJECT.
Designing for customer experience requires upfront alignment—and ongoing assessment—of strategic goals, market intelligence, and design performance metrics.

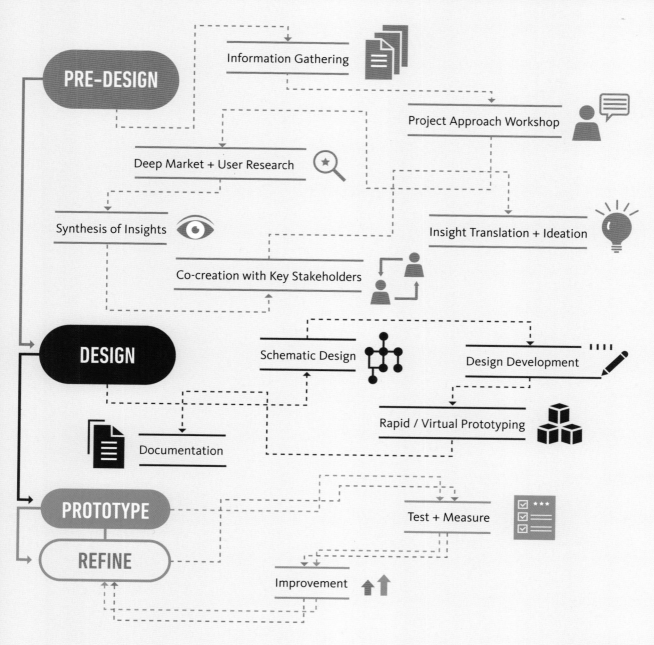

Engagement & Experience:
Sports

168   **#Winning the Fan Engagement Game**

Project Name: Factors of Engagement with Sports Brands
Research Team: Kate Kirkpatrick, Evan Hathaway, Tom Milavec

#Winning the Fan Engagement Game

Is winning the only factor that significantly affects sports brand engagement?

> *Being a #winning team is about much more than wins and losses—having a great fan experience makes the difference.*

THE CONTEXT

Of all the brands in Gensler's 2013 U.S. Brand Engagement Survey, sports brands had the highest engagement rankings—more than cars, technology, clothing, or food. This earlier research also showed not just sports as the brand vanguard, but the NFL's preeminence within it: just 18 percent of self-identified NFL fans said they would ever consider seeking out a replacement team. The popularity of fantasy football has increased overall fan engagement—studies show fantasy football makes people more likely to watch NFL games on television and attend them—while social channels like Twitter and Instagram give fans a sense of personal access to players' lives.

In spite of these positives, the NFL is facing a number of thorny issues, including decreased game-day presence, troubling findings regarding player safety, and periodic public outcry over players' off-field behavior. To maintain and grow their enviable competitive position and expand revenue, NFL franchises must capitalize on factors other than winning to heighten fan engagement. For winning franchises, there's an opportunity to build on the increased loyalty and money that good performance generates; for losing franchises, there's an opportunity to boost revenue streams and in turn, they hope, revive winning ways.

WHAT WE DID

Building on sports brand data from Gensler's 2013 U.S. Brand Engagement Survey, we conducted a targeted investigation into how sports fans relate to their teams, and what makes them more (or less) of a fan. Because the National Football League (NFL) dominates the American sports market and permeates its culture like no other professional sports league, we decided to focus our exploration on the NFL. Our methods included an online survey of adult U.S. football fans, analyzed against other data sources on fan equity and NFL stadium performance.

Our survey asked fans what factors might make them more or less of a fan, from building a new stadium to more community involvement, and also asked them to tell us how long they would tolerate chronic losing and still remain a fan. We analyzed this data against Emory University's 2014 Fan Equity rankings, a statistical model developed by two college professors that quantitatively measures the economic impact of a loyal and active fan base, which we saw as a proxy for fan engagement. We also looked at a composite index of NFL stadium rankings and the 32 NFL franchises' win-loss records since 2000. This data helped us understand what factors besides winning allow NFL franchises to maintain or increase brand engagement.

FACTORS IN FAN ENGAGEMENT OTHER THAN WINNING

Respondents ranked each factor on a 1-to-10 scale. A score of 10 would make them "way more of a fan," and a score of 1 would make them "way less of a fan."

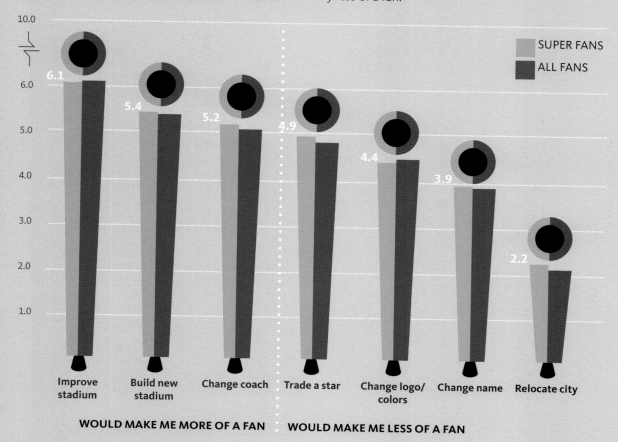

| | SUPER FANS |
| | ALL FANS |

10.0 — 6.1 — 6.0 — 5.4 — 5.2 — 5.0 — 4.9 — 4.4 — 4.0 — 3.9 — 3.0 — 2.2 — 2.0 — 1.0

Improve stadium · Build new stadium · Change coach · Trade a star · Change logo/colors · Change name · Relocate city

WOULD MAKE ME MORE OF A FAN   **WOULD MAKE ME LESS OF A FAN**

THE RESULTS

The stadium experience drives fan engagement.

A good or great game-day environment can be the difference between highly engaged fans and lackluster ones. Survey respondents, whether casual or super fans, identified improving their favorite franchise's current stadium and building a new stadium as the two factors most likely to make them more of a fan.

Our side-by-side analysis of Emory University's rankings, win-loss records from 2000–2015, and a composite index of NFL stadium rankings shows that teams with highly ranked stadiums have higher fan equity than teams with poorly ranked stadiums, and that teams with better-ranked stadiums also enjoy better winning percentages, suggesting a positive cycle of stadium experience, results, and equity/engagement.

We love you the way you are.

Great sports brands invoke a sense of tradition and closely align with their home city's civic identity. Gensler's 2013 U.S. Brand Engagement Survey revealed that sports brand fans value tradition and stability far more than innovation and change. Franchises that underestimate the power of these preferences risk alienating fans.

Relocating a team to another city, changing its name, and changing the logo and/or the team's colors were the three factors survey respondents said were most likely to make them less of a fan. Moving away from the current site, even for a better facility, was also a detractor. This is further proof that the stability of a team's brand is paramount to maintaining fan engagement.

Higher equity/engagement correlates with a lower tolerance for losing.

Despite their preference for legacy and stability, highly engaged fans expect results and are less likely to be patient in the face of chronic losing. When asked how long they would tolerate losing, fans of teams high on Emory University's rankings expressed less of a willingness to be patient than fans of teams with lower equity scores. Two exceptions to this finding were the Dallas Cowboys and New York Jets, with mediocre 15-year records and highly acclaimed stadiums.

Know the difference between winning and #winning.

While nothing boosts fan engagement like good on-field results, any sports franchise, from a perennial championship contender to a long-term bottom-feeder, can become a #winner if it envelops its brand in an aura of quality and tradition and stays connected to the fans. Unlike average consumers, whose tastes and loyalties are fickle, sports fans want to remain loyal through good times and bad. An engaged fan base of a #winning franchise even enjoys a shared sense of commiseration during losing seasons, while lower-engagement fan bases are simply turned off by poor on-field performance. To keep fans engaged, sports franchises must give their fans something to be proud of each season, whether it's a great stadium, a resonant brand, or a team that involves itself with the local community.

Use the stadium to energize your fan base.

#Winning franchises tend to have great stadiums. Great stadiums function as important pieces of civic architecture, connect franchises and their brands to the communities around them, and give viewers at home something to be proud of. They fuel a sense of being a #winning organization and have a significant capacity to boost overall fan engagement. That energy and pride remain long after the final whistle sounds, and so franchises cannot underestimate the importance of presenting invigorating game-day experiences. Whether they can translate #winning into winning the Super Bowl? That remains to be seen.

Engage fans outside the stadium walls.

While a great game-day experience goes a long way toward boosting overall fan engagement, franchises must also viscerally connect with the fans who watch from home. Gensler's 2013 U.S. Brand Engagement Survey revealed that a majority of fans prefer online engagement with their favorite team to in-person engagement (likely related to our survey respondents' saying lower ticket prices would make them bigger fans). Our more recent NFL-focused survey reinforced that importance of engaging with fans outside the stadium walls: respondents identified increased community involvement as one of the factors that would make them more of a fan.

WHAT'S NEXT

We plan to build on the findings of this research project by facilitating discussions with Gensler sports clients and industry experts to refine our understanding of the ways franchises can position themselves as #winning to sustain fan engagement through win-lose cycles.

Through additional research, we will seek to conclusively determine how stadium design influences actual on-field athlete and team performance. These inquiries and the results they surface will continue to shape our approach to sports brand strategy and stadium facility design.

"What separates loyal fans from everyone else isn't the number of years they have rooted for a team or the number of games they have watched. Rather, it's the simple fact that they consider the team they support **their** team. In what could be considered a sort of pseudo-family, teams and loyal fans share success as well as failure."

– "The Value of the Loyal Fan," Joseph Yi, *Sports Networker*

50

12

Engagement & Experience:
Hospitality

Beyond Boutique

How can boutique hotels cater to the desires of today's travelers?

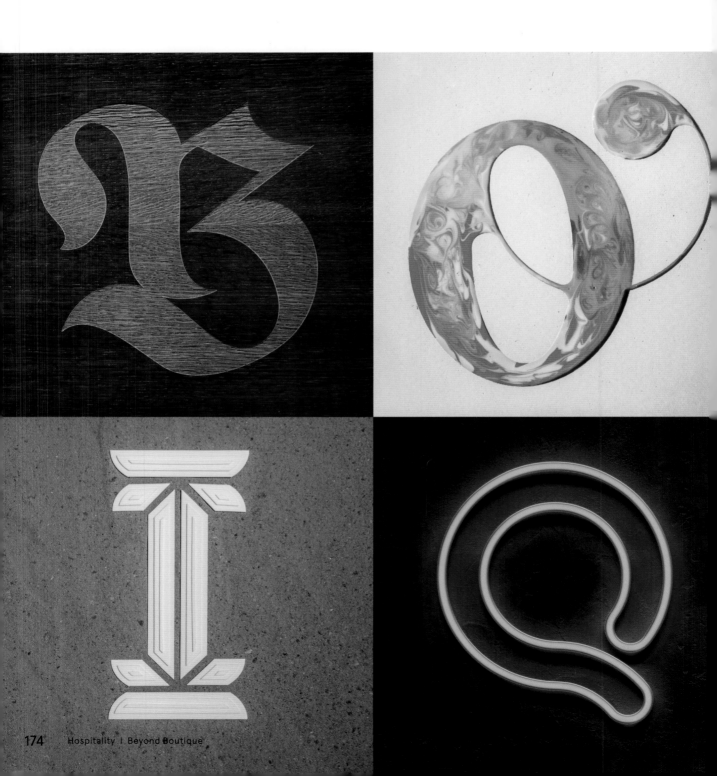

WHAT WE DID

We started by identifying current trends and perspectives on boutique hotels, including documenting the various definitions different brands/groups use to define "boutique." To understand the growth and evolution of boutique hotels, we created a timeline of key developments and properties alongside case studies of selected hotels in Los Angeles. We then investigated up-and-coming trends to identify both the current criteria that define a successful boutique hotel, and those that will be essential to the design of future boutique hotels.

THE CONTEXT

While some consider size the most important factor in determining whether a hotel is a boutique hotel or not, many believe it has more to do with the approach or attitude of the hoteliers in creating the look-and-feel of the property. Unlike many corporate hotel chains, which have consistent branding among many locations, boutique hotels are typically privately owned and strive for a one-of-a-kind experience. Nonetheless, while most boutique hotels began as independent endeavors, many larger corporate brands have caught on to the allure of these properties and now have boutique-oriented sub-brands, or in rare cases, smaller boutique hotels within larger hotels.

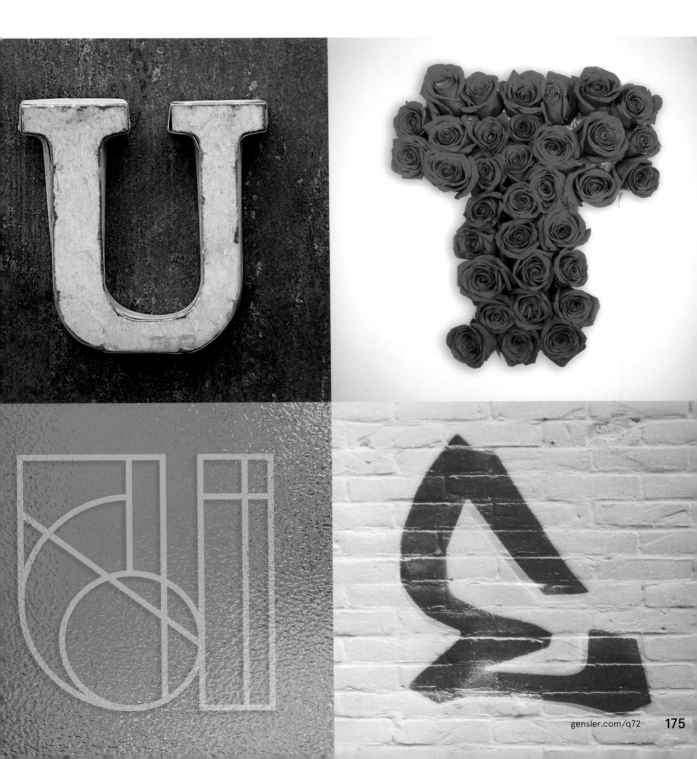

Travelers who select boutique hotels are not just seeking a more intimate stay outside the standard luxury hotel offering. **They are also looking to experience their destination through their lodging.** This is achieved by hotels that become an integral part of the neighborhood in which they exist, and do everything they can to reflect and be a part of their local community. Our review of trends and case stories identified a series of strategies and characteristics common to many successful boutique hotel properties that achieve this hyper-local sense of place.

One way that boutique hotels often become neighborhood fixtures is through repurposing of old iconic buildings. Whether within an old theater, factory, or apartment building, a hotel that operates inside a historic landmark creates a unique sense of place and authenticity. These hotels also often strive for a residential look-and-feel, with design schemes and decor varying among rooms. In line with the growing popularity of Airbnb, these hotels make guests feel as if they have their very own apartment in the neighborhood, not just a hotel room.

The inclusion of social and community spaces in the building is also a key strategy, with the ultimate goal of creating a place where locals, not just travelers, want to be. Many hotels work with artists, designers, and chefs to integrate custom features into their design and experience—whether an art piece or a menu inspired by regional cuisine. And to entice the locals to visit, these hotels focus on creating a sense of community with vibrant social experiences, serving as ideal hangout spots for their neighborhoods, and mixing visitors and regulars for a feeling that's more neighborhood coffee shop than hotel lobby.

HOTELS WITH A CAUSE

Through regionally inspired art and architecture, local cuisine, and community-based education and entertainment programs, these properties will draw like-minded guests to share in the experience of giving back to local ecologies and residents.

EXPERIENCE-BASED LODGING

In exchange for smaller rooms, these properties will cater to younger, more active travelers with larger, well-designed common areas and events within the hotel to encourage interaction and socializing among guests.

UNIQUE SERVICES

Many boutique hotels may be too small to deliver the services of a traditional four- or five-star property. Instead, they can compete with unexpected services, often delivered via staff who wear multiple hats to keep costs down.

BEYOND ECLECTIC

Boutique hotels have achieved success by forgoing generic travel experiences in favor of contemporary, eclectic design elements. Maintaining a unique nature in a market increasingly filled with properties billing a one-of-a-kind experience will be the key challenge for the boutiques of the future.

As boutique hotels continue to develop and promote their individual personalities and offerings, the next step may be exploring ways to match travelers to the hotel that fits their interests or style best. Many hotels have already created apps in which guests can check in and out, and create profiles indicating their background, interests, and reason for travel. Groups of boutique hotels could leverage this at a larger scale, joining together to create a network in which travelers select their destination, lifestyle, and desired activities to easily find the hotel that is right for them.

PERSPECTIVES

"Growth in boutique hotels, defined as upscale, smaller properties focused on design, technology, local culture and standing out from the cookie-cutter hotel crowd, has exploded in the last decade. According to research firm IBISWorld, the boutique hotel industry, which comprises about 5 percent of the market, has grown 6.1 percent per year since 2009, and it expects that growth to accelerate through 2019."

– "Major Hotel Brands Compete for Space in The Boutique Hotel Trend," Ismat Sarah Mangla, *International Business Times*

Engagement & Experience:
Living

182 **Design for Active Aging**

Project Name: Foundations of Design for Active Aging
Research Team: Rob Jernigan, Charrisse Johnston, Ben McAlister, Helen Lin

Design for Active Aging

Can design better support today's active aging population?

WHAT WE DID

We investigated and documented trends for Baby Boomers and the market for aging seniors, focusing on demographic shifts and the unique physical, mental, and social needs of this population. We read and summarized research findings from 170 documents produced by government organizations, professional associations, academia, corporations, and the popular press. We also interviewed industry experts and attended panel discussions and conferences on aging in place. Our goal was to identify current innovations and industry trends in senior-living housing types, and to document design opportunities to create successful "active aging" communities.

THE CONTEXT

Today's 50- and 60-year-olds don't see themselves as "old" and don't view aging as a time of physical decline. They're eschewing living and community situations that make them feel otherwise and expect to continue living life to the fullest. As their numbers grow, they have the demographic heft and buying power to back that up— Baby Boomers today outspend other generations by an estimated $400 billion each year on consumer goods and services, accounting for 50 percent of total U.S. consumer spending.

These actively aging Boomers are looking for housing options to support their lifestyles and allow them to live a long, purposeful life. And their lifestyles are anything but traditionally "senior"—today's seniors are better educated than any of their predecessors, and are a well-connected, tech-enabled population. As consumers, they are as savvy as these characteristics would suggest. As a result, **we recognize that the U.S. active aging population is a group with discerning tastes and a hunger for good design.**

TODAY'S AGING POPULATION IS ANYTHING BUT TRADITIONALLY SENIOR

U.S. POPULATION 2015–2050

- 15% — 2015 UNDER 18
- 23% — 2015 OVER 65
- 21% — 2050 UNDER 18
- 21% — 2050 OVER 65

⸜ UNDER 18
● OVER 65

2015   2050

U.S. Census Bureau, December 2012

PERCENTAGE OF PEOPLE WHO FEEL "OLD" BY AGE GROUP

- 10% — –50
- 14% — 50–59
- 31% — 60–69
- 47% — 70–79
- 77% — 80+

"80 is the new 60," *UBS Investor Watch*, October 2013

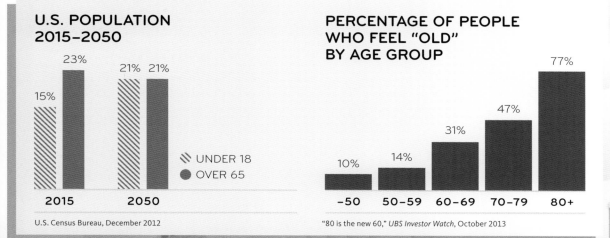

We identified four major themes that define our design approach for an actively aging population:

Together, these factors underpin psychological, social, and physical health. By intervening to support an aging population across these factors, we can increase quality of life and "active" life expectancy. Design interventions across scales—from thoughtful urban planning, to buildings integrated with transportation and social service systems, to personal products and technology with a wellness focus—can help address these trends.

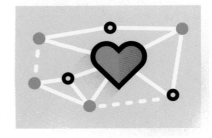

CONNECTIVITY

The ability to maintain relationships with neighbors, coworkers, family, friends, and community members—both in-person and online.

CHOICE

Living in a location that fits one's particular preferences, participating in activities that one chooses, and making one's own decisions about healthcare.

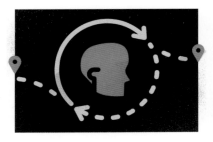

INDEPENDENCE

Relying on others as little as possible for personal care and getting around, including use of public transportation, ride-sharing, and walking.

WELLNESS

Not only staving off disease but also managing long-term illness to lead a productive and fulfilling life.

SENIOR HOUSING ON COLLEGE CAMPUSES

Campuses can deliver the cultural and lifestyle amenities an aging population desires, and an aging population can bring welcome diversity (and income sources) to college towns.

Creating vibrant places that meet the needs of an active aging population requires bringing new approaches and disciplines to the table. We are working with multidisciplinary teams across Gensler's offices and practices to share expertise and insights, and continue to develop these ideas to create a holistic approach to design for active aging.

"There is less difference in aesthetic taste between young people and Boomers than there is between Boomers and their elders."

– An executive at a global consumer products company

WHAT THIS MEANS

BRANDED RESIDENTIAL PROPERTIES

If and when a move is required, this population is seeking a different type of aging community. Stress urban living with "active aging" amenities.

AGING-IN-PLACE TECHNOLOGY

Use architecture, design, and "smart" technology to allow people to stay in their homes as long as possible—at the high levels of aesthetic and performance quality they've come to expect.

RETAIL HEALTHCARE

Reposition medical services to focus on healthy lifestyles and an experience that feels more like retail than healthcare. Consider underused retail environments, from malls to supermarkets, for potential locations.

AGE-FRIENDLY CITIES

Urban environments designed to foster multigenerational living meet both aging-in-place preferences and the urban lifestyle this segment prefers.

Organizational Strategy

The who, what, and how of work are in a constant state of flux, driven by the pressures of global competition, emerging technologies, and the ongoing need to inspire and motivate employees to maximize performance. As a result, organizations are focused on the value proposition of workplace design more than ever before.

Organizational Strategy:

The Workplace
Surveys

U.S. Workplace Survey 2016

How does the physical workplace help employees innovate?

WHAT WE DID

Gensler's U.S. Workplace Survey 2016 is the most recent installment in our 10-year Workplace Survey research effort. We surveyed a panel-based sample of over 4,000 U.S. office workers in 11 industries to understand where, and how, work is happening today, and the role design plays in employee performance and innovation. Our goal was to provide critical insight into how the workplace impacts overall employee experience, and to identify ways to leverage workplace design and strategy to unleash the power of the whole organization.

We conducted the survey using Gensler's proprietary Workplace Performance Index™ (WPI) online survey tool, which is built upon a core set of validated questions gauging workplace effectiveness and functionality that we have used and refined over the past 10 years. Respondents represented all generations and roles in the workplace, companies of various sizes, and were geographically spread across the U.S.

THE CONTEXT

The nature of work and the places in which work happens are both facing significant—and potentially volatile—paradigm shifts. Unemployment has fallen since our last survey in 2013, but despite overall job growth, workforce participation is at the lowest levels since 1978. Over two-thirds of the workforce is disengaged from their work, and workplace stress is on the rise, afflicting 8 out of 10 workers. Companies are struggling to attract and retain good talent, just as emerging technologies and coworking trends empower more workers to step out of the corporate structure and become freelance consultants—40 percent of the U.S. workforce is estimated to be independently employed by 2020.

For the majority of the U.S. workforce, disengagement and stress are compounded by the physical work environment, which continues to challenge productivity and innovation. Smaller desks and less privacy are the norms for many at work today, at a time when continued urban migration is forcing many into smaller living situations as well. Other workplace trends are also compounding the issue—in particular, a rise in virtual or technology-enabled collaboration requires new ways of working that many organizations still struggle to support.

GREAT WORKPLACE DESIGN DRIVES CREATIVITY AND INNOVATION

THE RESULTS

As workplace designers and strategists, we know intuitively the impact of workplace design on innovation. **Our 2016 data uncovers a statistical link between the quality and functional makeup of the workplace, and the level of innovation employees ascribe to their companies.** Respondents with a higher WPI score (Gensler's aggregate measure of workplace effectiveness and functionality) also report higher innovation index scores (an average of six validated questions focused on innovation, leadership, and creativity).

Our analysis also helps to fit workplace into the broader picture of what truly matters to employee performance. At-work relationships, particularly with one's manager; the level of meaning or purpose an employee sees in their organization's work; and whether the workplace reflects that their company prioritizes collaboration are statistical predictors of organizational innovation. This need to prioritize collaboration must be addressed alongside the critical need to support focused work for today's knowledge workers. Innovators report that they are **five times more likely to have workplaces that prioritize both individual and group work.**

By comparing employees with the highest innovation index scores—those in the top quartile or 25 percent—to those in the bottom quartile, we were also able to identify a broader suite of behaviors and spatial attributes that make the biggest difference for the most innovative employees in our sample.

Innovators have better designed workspaces of all types. Every office space we measure—from individual desks, to meeting rooms, common areas, and bathrooms—is rated significantly higher on design look and feel by the innovators in our sample. And not only is the design better, innovators are also leveraging the whole office to greater effect. **Innovators spend less time at their desks,** instead collaborating and socializing from conference rooms, open meeting areas, and café spaces. They also spend more time working away from the office, averaging 74 percent of an average week in the office compared to 86 percent for respondents with the lowest innovation scores.

Innovators have more choice in when and where to work. This speaks to both a management issue—they are more autonomous at work, better able to work in the places and ways that suit them best—and the variety of their spaces. **Innovators have greater access to amenities** in or near their office locations, and report using amenities twice as often. All of this adds up to more engaged employees, with a stronger connection to the organization: **innovators report more meaning and purpose in their work,** have stronger relationships with their managers, and are more satisfied with their jobs.

EMPLOYEES WITH A WPI SCORE OF 50 OR LESS HAVE AN AVERAGE INNOVATION RATING OF 2.6

EMPLOYEES WITH A WPI SCORE OF 90 OR MORE HAVE AN AVERAGE INNOVATION RATING OF 4.4

INNOVATIVE INDEX

WORKPLACE PERFORMANCE INDEX (WPI)

Innovators have **2x** more access to amenities.

How can design help employees innovate?
By identifying the key differentiators for employees with high innovation index scores, we developed a set of action items every organization should take to optimize the workplace and improve performance and innovation:

Invest in the Individual

Employees at innovative companies have better designed and more functional workspaces, no matter how open—and if those functional aspects are managed, an open office can be as effective as a private one.

Diversify Group Work Spaces

Innovators have access to, and use, a greater variety of workspaces in and out of the office, particularly for non-focus activities. They are also less likely to report having to work in the same space, and less likely to socialize at their desks.

WHEN WE CONTROL FOR THE FACTORS THAT ARE MOST IMPORTANT TO INDIVIDUAL WORKPLACE PERFORMANCE, ANY SPACE TYPE CAN BE HIGHLY EFFECTIVE.

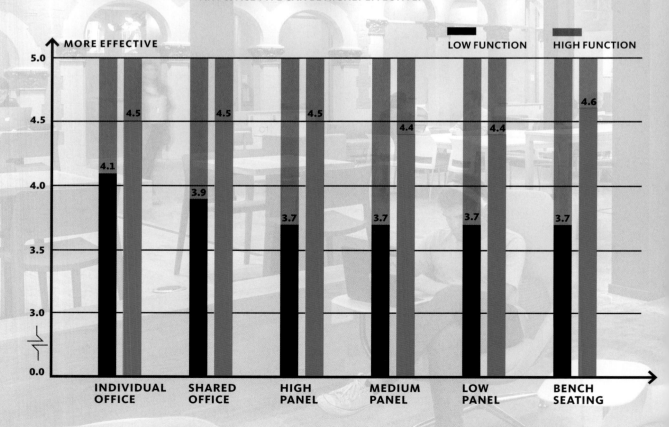

LOW FUNCTION   HIGH FUNCTION

MORE EFFECTIVE

	LOW FUNCTION	HIGH FUNCTION
INDIVIDUAL OFFICE	4.1	4.5
SHARED OFFICE	3.9	4.5
HIGH PANEL	3.7	4.5
MEDIUM PANEL	3.7	4.4
LOW PANEL	3.7	4.4
BENCH SEATING	3.7	4.6

5.0
4.5
4.0
3.5
3.0
0.0

> **"Mounting evidence suggests that the habits encouraged by mobile technology—namely, talking in public to someone who is not there —are tailor-made for hijacking the cognitive functions of bystanders."**
>
> – "Cellphones as a Modern Irritant," Douglas Quenqua, *The New York Times*

Empower the Whole Community

The ability to work wherever is best for the task at hand shouldn't be a perk just for leadership. Invest in strategies to increase autonomy, and connect every employee to the purpose behind their work and the broader organizational community.

WHAT'S NEXT

These ideas apply across organizations in every industry and geography, but the best solutions are project- and company-specific. Organizations must gauge their current state and opportunity across these factors to identify areas with the greatest need for improvement, and target workplace investment for maximum impact.

FROM 2013 TO 2016, CHOICE FELL AT EVERY LEVEL OF THE ORGANIZATION. SENIOR LEADERSHIP CONTINUES TO REPORT GREATER CHOICE THAN PROFESSIONAL OR ADMINISTRATIVE STAFF.

% WITH CHOICE (2016)

% WITH CHOICE (2013)

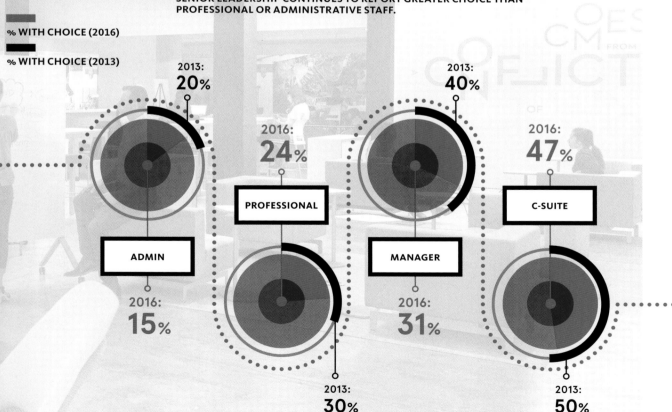

ADMIN
2013: 20%
2016: 15%

PROFESSIONAL
2013: 30%
2016: 24%

MANAGER
2013: 40%
2016: 31%

C-SUITE
2013: 50%
2016: 47%

U.K. Workplace Survey 2016

Can we make U.K. office environments work better for everyone?

WHAT WE DID

We surveyed a panel-based sample of over 1,200 U.K. office workers in 11 industries to gauge current state of the U.K. workplace and uncover opportunities to improve employee performance and experience. Our goal was to uncover detailed insights into the connection between workplace design and organisational innovation, and identify key strategies to improve U.K. office environments. Similar to surveys launched in the U.S. and Asia, we gathered responses using Gensler's proprietary Workplace Performance Index™ (WPI) online survey tool. Respondents represented all the generations and seniority levels in the workplace, companies of various sizes, and were geographically spread across the U.K.

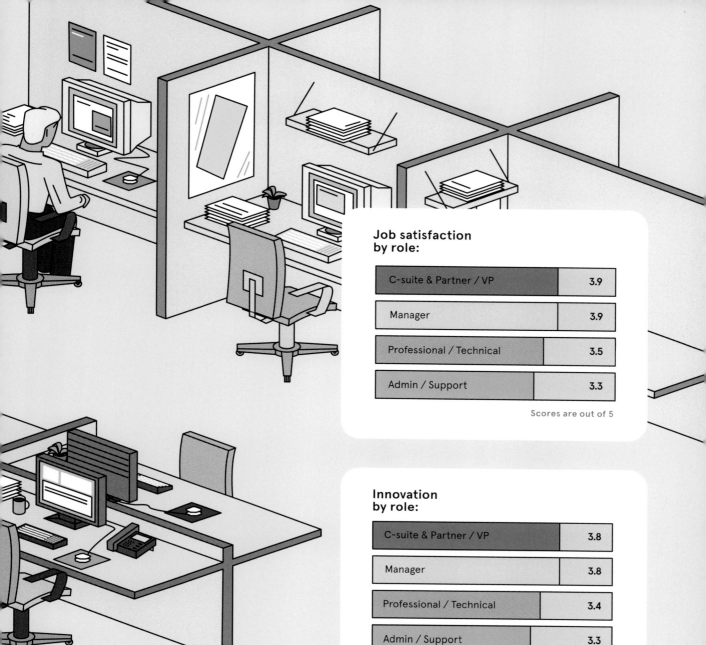

Job satisfaction by role:

C-suite & Partner / VP	3.9
Manager	3.9
Professional / Technical	3.5
Admin / Support	3.3

Scores are out of 5

Innovation by role:

C-suite & Partner / VP	3.8
Manager	3.8
Professional / Technical	3.4
Admin / Support	3.3

Scores are out of 5

PERSPECTIVES

Despite being in a period of economic recovery, the latest figures from the Office of National Statistics show that U.K. GDP per worker is lower than all other G7 nations, with the exception of Japan.

THE CONTEXT

Just after Gensler's last U.K. Workplace Survey in 2008, the U.K. entered a period of economic decline that saw U.K. GDP drop by a staggering 2.6 percent in the first quarter of 2009. The recession has had a significant impact on the workplace, as companies have been forced to reduce their costs while maintaining or even improving productivity levels. Many have become smarter in their use of space and have developed new, more efficient ways of working, while others have not. As U.K. productivity continues to lag behind other nations, it is critical that the physical work environment performs at maximum effectiveness to support how work happens today, and to meet changing needs in the future.

THE RESULTS

The U.K. workplace significantly favours those in management positions. It may come as no surprise that employees in leadership positions have higher-performing workspaces, but the gulf between the haves and the have-nots in the U.K. workplace is dramatic and it poses a significant challenge for organisations looking to innovate. The starkest representation of the difference is in the allocation of private offices—89 percent of those in senior leadership have private offices, compared to 23 percent at lower levels of the organisation— and the impact shows across all performance and experience metrics.

WPI scores by role:

Role	Score
C-suite & Partner / VP	76
Manager	72
Professional / Technical	63
Admin / Support	62

Scores are out of 100

Effectiveness ratings by work setting:

Work Setting	Rating
Private Office	4.2
Shared Office	4.0
Room with 3 or More	3.5
Workstation with High Panels	3.7
Workstation with Medium Panels	3.8
Workstation with Low Panels	3.5
Desk or Bench without Panels	3.6

Scores are out of 5

Choice versus no choice:

70%

30%

% **Do not have choice** in when and where to work

% **Have choice** in when and where to work

Over 8 million U.K. employees work in open plan environments and many of these environments are not optimally designed. The U.K. has an established open plan culture, and the majority of workers are in open plan environments particularly at lower levels of the organisation. However, the basic open plan environment often fails to support work activities as well as those providing a variety of enclosed environments, with job satisfaction, performance, and at-work relationships suffering as a result. Key to this problem is a lack of alternative spaces for work. Our data shows that open plan environments can be just as effective, if not more effective, as more enclosed ones, but on the condition that employees have a range of spaces in which to work more effectively and use them optimally.

Legacy workplace behaviour and lack of choice are a drag on performance. Having not only variety, but also the freedom to work wherever and whenever it's most effective, are key performance drivers for U.K. workers and workers across the world. Employees who rate their organisations highly on innovation measures also report having greater choice, and use a wider range of workspaces to get their work done. Working this way requires not only the right spaces, but also the right behaviours—change management can help the transition to open environments and activity-based work settings achieve greater success.

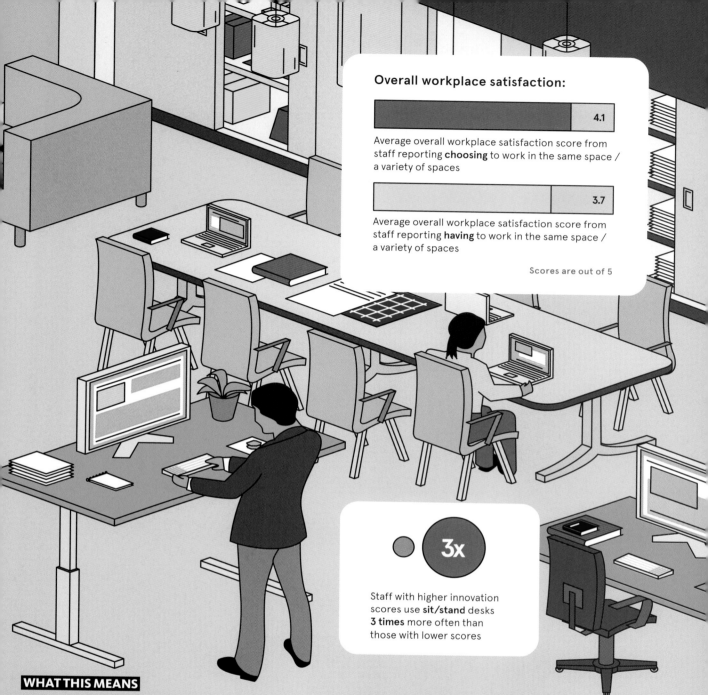

Overall workplace satisfaction:

	4.1

Average overall workplace satisfaction score from staff reporting **choosing** to work in the same space / a variety of spaces

	3.7

Average overall workplace satisfaction score from staff reporting **having** to work in the same space / a variety of spaces

Scores are out of 5

3x

Staff with higher innovation scores use **sit/stand** desks **3 times** more often than those with lower scores

WHAT THIS MEANS

We need to take a more considered approach to the open plan. Effective workplaces must support both individual and group work, and open plan environments without access to a range of alternative settings and enclosed spaces are challenged to do both. If adopting an open strategy, the right—and separate—spaces for individual and collaborative work are key. And for some organisations, becoming more open may not be the best option. The enclosed office is not necessarily the enemy, but one size very much does not fit all.

Expand workplace variety and choice. British workers are still using their desks for most work activities and this appears to be to the detriment of performance. Give employees a greater variety of spaces, and the choice to work when and where suits their current tasks and work styles best, and their satisfaction and performance will improve.

Match space to job needs, not role. Employees who report that the spaces in their offices are assigned by job requirements, rather than hierarchy, are much more likely to also report an optimal workplace experience. Given the current challenges of workplace performance across all levels in the U.K. workplace, strategies that match space to need rather than seniority are an opportunity to engage and improve at all levels of the company.

WHAT'S NEXT

We continue to analyse data gathered via this survey and other, individual WPI surveys to uncover industry and client-specific insights into how best to leverage workplace design to maximise organisational performance and innovation.

Asia Workplace Survey 2016

Can the Asian workplace embrace experimentation and balance to create a distinct identity?

As Asian companies focus on competitiveness in a global market, they must explore a new, more balanced workplace identity to help them differentiate.

WHAT WE DID

We surveyed a panel-based sample of over 2,000 Asia office workers in 11 industries focused in six major metropolitan areas—Bangalore, Beijing, Hong Kong, Shanghai, Singapore, and Tokyo—to understand the Asian workplace from the perspective of the worker.

The data collected represents respondents across nine key industries, and a wide distribution of ages and organizational roles. Survey questions explored not only the current state of the workplace—how, and where, employees are working, and how effective those spaces are—but also organizational dynamics, including relationships with teams and managers, and the impact of hierarchy on employee performance and experience. Similar to surveys conducted in the U.S. and U.K., we gathered data using Gensler's proprietary Workplace Performance Index™ (WPI) survey tool.

THE CONTEXT

Today, Asian countries and companies are laser-focused on global competitiveness, and looking for new ways to aspire to excellence, self-sufficiency, and new product and service development to rival the West. Yet today's Asian workplaces still tend to adopt a common, Western narrative, resulting in mostly open plan workspaces combining workstations, offices, and conference rooms. This hand-me-down model of workplace design, a paradigm exported from the U.S. as countries quickly modernized and sought Western-style workplaces in an increasingly global business climate, may now be holding Asian companies and employees back. As organizations continue to focus on talent attraction and business innovation, the **Asian workplace is increasingly in need of a new, differentiated, and home-grown approach to workplace design.**

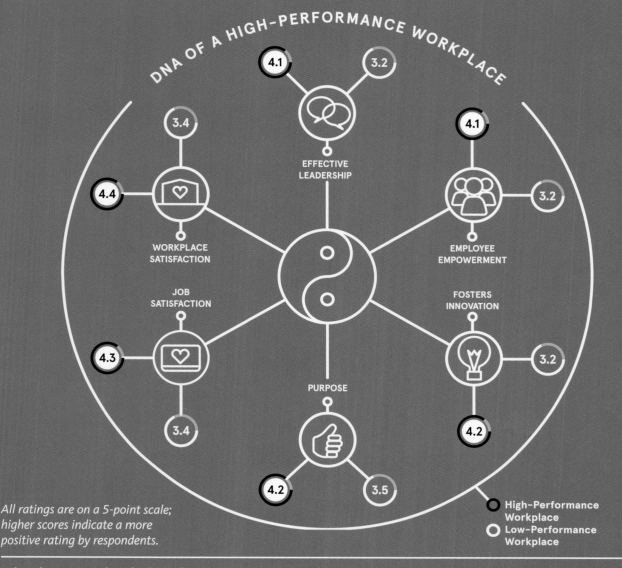

EFFECTIVE
LEADERSHIP
4.1   3.2

EMPLOYEE
EMPOWERMENT
4.1   3.2

FOSTERS
INNOVATION
4.2   3.2

WORKPLACE
SATISFACTION
4.4   3.4

JOB
SATISFACTION
4.3   3.4

PURPOSE
4.2   3.5

○ High–Performance
Workplace
○ Low–Performance
Workplace

*All ratings are on a 5-point scale;
higher scores indicate a more
positive rating by respondents.*

What do we mean by a high-performance workplace?
A high-performance or "balanced" workplace is one that effectively prioritizes both individual and collaborative work.
Employees who rate their workplace highly for both also score better across key performance indicators, as shown above.

THE RESULTS

To help companies be more innovative, have happier employees, and create coherent teams, **the Asian workplace needs to find a better balance of spaces for focused and collaborative work in line with work style and job requirements.** On this, the Asian workplace is similar to those across the world—Gensler's 10 years of workplace survey investigations in the U.S. and U.K. have proven the importance of a workplace environment that effectively supports the myriad activities of today's knowledge workers, and in particular, the need to balance individual and group efforts.

This desire for balance fits with cultural themes that unify Asia—from slokas in Sanskrit, to Buddha's middle path, to the Chinese philosophy of ying and yang, the need for balance is deeply connected to culture and spirituality. For the respondents to our Asia Workplace Survey, the impact of achieving this balance in the workplace is also clear—**respondents in balanced workplaces are more satisfied with their jobs, see their companies as more creative and innovative, have better relationships with their managers, and enjoy greater work-life balance.**

Equally clear, however, is a desire among our respondents to seek new ways of working that push beyond the boundaries of the traditional, Western workplace design and experience. Unlike the U.S. and U.K., in which a collaborative work environment proved to be a key statistical driver of organizational innovation alongside managerial relationships and meaning in one's work, in Asia the key driver after meaning and relationships is **feeling empowered to experiment with new ways of working.** Flexibility in day-to-day job scope, and a lack of hierarchy in how workspaces are assigned, also prove important factors to Asian office workers today.

Manager relationships, feedback, and freedom to work the way one works best are all more highly rated for employees in high-performance/balanced environments.

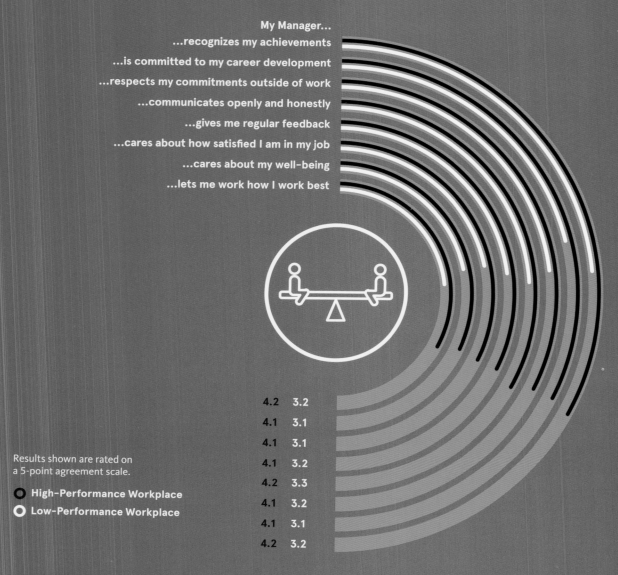

My Manager...
...recognizes my achievements
...is committed to my career development
...respects my commitments outside of work
...communicates openly and honestly
...gives me regular feedback
...cares about how satisfied I am in my job
...cares about my well-being
...lets me work how I work best

High-Performance	Low-Performance
4.2	3.2
4.1	3.1
4.1	3.1
4.1	3.2
4.2	3.3
4.1	3.2
4.1	3.1
4.2	3.2

Results shown are rated on a 5-point agreement scale.

○ High-Performance Workplace
◯ Low-Performance Workplace

WHAT THIS MEANS

Balance builds relationships. Employees in balanced workplaces see their managers in a more positive light, are able to communicate more openly and honestly, better receive feedback, and reported higher work-life balance and job satisfaction. The quality of relationships is also a key factor in creating a culture of creativity and innovation at work.

Mobility enhances performance. Employees in balanced workplaces spend an average of 20 percent less time in their primary workplace or office location, consistent across countries and industries. By having the capability and infrastructure to work outside of the office, they may also be able to shorten travel time in Asia's larger urban centers, increasing their productive working time. Organizations should encourage employees to work from alternative settings, experimenting with not just the how but also the where of their work,

while at the same time being sensitive to local culture and expectations.

Prioritize autonomy and choice. Employees who can choose their own work settings are 1.5 times more likely to work in a balanced environment, and also report higher scores across performance indicators. Choice in when and where to work, paired with a variety of spaces in which to work, is also a key aspect of empowered mobility and experimentation.

Experimentation helps innovation. The central theme of flexibility and the ability to experiment with new ways of working permeated the results of our Asia Workplace Survey. Empowering experimentation, and encouraging employees to take risks in search of new and better ways to work, is of paramount importance.

Balanced workplaces encourage employees to spend more time working away from the office.

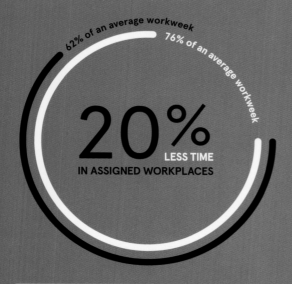

62% of an average workweek

76% of an average workweek

20%
LESS TIME
IN ASSIGNED WORKPLACES

Employees in balanced workplaces have more choice in when and where to work.

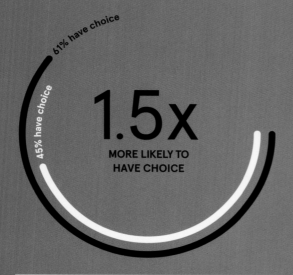

61% have choice

45% have choice

1.5x
MORE LIKELY TO
HAVE CHOICE

Experimentation with new ways of working is better supported in balanced workplaces.

"East Asia has the lowest proportion of engaged employees in the world, at 6 percent, which is less than half of the global mean of 13 percent. The regional finding is driven predominantly by results from China, where 6 percent of employees are engaged in their jobs—one of the lowest figures worldwide."

– *State of the Global Workplace*, Gallup

WHAT'S NEXT

To give the Asian workforce, and workplace, its due, the imperative is clear—move beyond workplace models adopted from the West, and find the right balance of workspaces, activities, styles, and cultures to poise Asian companies for competitiveness in the future.

Organizational Strategy:

Office
Evolution

The Indian Workplace

How has India's history influenced the development and current state of its workplace?

WHAT WE DID

We researched the evolution of work and the workplace throughout India's history, beginning in the pre-colonial era and ending in the present. Focused, comprehensive information that specifically addresses the sociocultural and economic factors that have defined and influenced the Indian workplace are not easily available. In response, we designed this study to begin mapping the changing Indian workplace. We relied on published third-party research, interviews, questionnaires with service sector industry leaders, workplace observations, and focus groups. Our research focused on shifts in demography, workforce, trade and commerce, politics, urban infrastructure, and technology.

PRE-COLONIAL   1520–1770 *a time of prosperity*

Pre-colonial India thrived under the rule of the Mughal (Islamic) and Maratha (Hindu) Empires. During this time, Europeans began to arrive and expand trade routes, influencing local politics, religion, and economic forces. The economy was strong, exporting spices, sugar, textiles, and opium to Europe by sea, which resulted in the formation of coastal cities. For these city dwellers, **work and commerce were heavily male-dominated, hierarchical, and rooted in the service sector,** relying on low-tech resources and often housed in small, poorly lit spaces. Employer-employee relations were more akin to the "master and servant" relationship, which informed the nature of the workplace. As customary in India, these workers used low seating and low tables to conduct business and manage transactions. Throughout the 1700s, European traders continued to arrive in increasing numbers, resulting in political and economic stability that lasted for decades.

COLONIAL   1773–1946 *life under foreign rule*

At the turn of the 18th century, Portuguese, French, Dutch, and British settlers had long-established businesses and trade routes connecting India to Europe. The British East India Company eventually gained market and political dominance after defeating the ruling Maratha Empire in a series of wars that ended in the early 19th century. This shift of power effectively transformed (and consequently devastated) India's economy, moving the country from a manufacturer of goods and services, to an exporter of raw materials destined for factories in Europe. During this time, a massive railway system was developed to connect rural villages to India's growing cities. **The introduction of electricity and the telephone in the early 20th century added small comfort and efficiencies to India's service sector workers, but availability was extremely limited.**

THE CONTEXT

The current form of the Indian workplace, specifically in its growing service sector, is largely the result of a Western typology that was introduced into India in the 1990s with little regard for the local context. While this form has evolved over time, its evolution has been driven primarily by business and real estate shifts and less by demands or desires specific to the Indian cultural context.

There is a growing realization that a maturing, global Indian workforce needs a workplace that speaks to their ethos and mores. The challenge remains for designers to discover what this "Indianness" is and reflect it sensitively, appropriately, and creatively. A lack of focused, comprehensive information that specifically addresses sociocultural and economic factors in India is a key challenge to achieving a more culturally appropriate approach to workplace design.

PRE-LIBERALIZATION   1947–1990 *political and economic reform*

The mid-20th century brought economic and political independence to India through an effort of nationwide civil disobedience led by Mahatma Gandhi, the Indian National Congress, and other political organizations. The new government—modeled after Russian socialism—heavily regulated industry, putting tremendous emphasis on public sector funding of large infrastructure projects,

leaving the private sector to focus on consumer goods. Women began to slowly enter the workforce during this period, but remained the minority. The introduction of air conditioning expanded basic office comforts, but **workplaces remained basic, dense, and highly pragmatic.**

POST-LIBERALIZATION   1991–PRESENT *an emerging, reformed global economy*

Liberalization and globalization have driven rapid change in this period, and the workplace has become increasingly diverse (though still male-dominated) and also increasingly urban-based. From the 2000s, **to accommodate the boom in IT-enabled services, workplace typologies have been transplanted from the West as multinationals set up business process outsourcing (BPO) operations.** This new business powered India's resurgence at a global scale and

simultaneously drove significant societal shifts. Unfortunately, the buildings that have been developed largely ignore local cultural mores and any meaningful references to the context. Though in certain cases, retrofitting modifications have made the spaces more user-friendly, these interventions were often poorly thought-out and executed, displaying a typical shoddiness more reflective of operational efficiency than good design.

Workplace design has a significant effect on employee performance and engagement. There is a growing realization, presently, that a maturing, global Indian workforce needs a workplace that speaks to their ethos and mores. As designers, we must respect this "Indianness" and reflect it sensitively and appropriately.

What works elsewhere in the world may not work with the same degree of effectiveness in India.

The challenge in India is for both architects and corporations to recognize its rich cultural history, vast landscape, and how its evolution of work impacts the modern workforce. To understand how to improve workplace design in India, business owners, architects, and designers need to be informed by a deep understanding of workplace evolution, through time, as well as the forces that affected that evolution.

To begin developing a conception of and design strategy for the Indian workplace, we identified

10 KEY FACTORS

to address as we look to the future

 1

Hierarchy

Indian culture remains hierarchical and the workplace must respect this separation. Management expects a level of distinction (separate elevators, for example) and a higher quality of service and design.

 2

Religion

Sensitive accommodation of religious and cultural differences is paramount. Prayer rooms accommodating a variety of faiths should be accommodated in the workplace.

 3

Demographics

Unlike many nations in the West, India's demographics skew young: 60 percent are under 35, and by 2020 the average Indian will be only 29 years old.

 4

Gender

Currently only 15 percent of the urban workforce is women. Though women are the minority, cultural needs require significant attention to separation between genders such as modesty panels at workstations, mother's rooms, and security for women in the workplace.

 5

Food

A large portion of the Indian population is vegetarian, and separation of vegetarian and non-vegetarian food is extremely important. Significant importance is placed on meals, which often consist of multiple items, and dedicated (non-toilet) handwashing statements are necessary.

WHAT THIS MEANS

With the gradual shift to knowledge-based work, keeping employees engaged and motivated is the imperative Indian businesses and workplaces must face today. Employee engagement and satisfaction are affected by a variety of factors—and a workplace that speaks to one's culture is essential. Employees view their workspaces as a symbol of whether or not they are valued by their employers. Workplaces must respond to India's uniqueness and reflect solutions that come from within, celebrating cultural differences and identity.

Work Styles

The Indian workforce has adopted technology quickly and is highly dependent on telephone and virtual communication, particularly as teams become more global. Growing focus on employee retention necessitates investment in learning and training activities.

Hospitality

Food service is extremely important for both internal and external meetings. Infrastructure must be provided for food preparation, and accommodations for added staff focused on food service and cleanup.

Location

Lack of available real estate has driven many offices to be located far from infrastructure, requiring independent power, water, and often sewage systems. Continued urbanization will require new approaches.

Sustainability

Corporate attention to sustainability is increasing. Larger floor plates create issues for daylight penetration, and heavy (often round-the-clock) space utilization requires extra attention to durability and housekeeping.

Transportation

Infrastructure and location challenges make for very long commutes. Arrival and departure amenities are required to enhance employee experience; many companies have dedicated bus fleets.

WHAT'S NEXT

India is a vast country with extreme variations. A one-size-fits-all workplace does not do justice to the multicultural, multilingual, and multigenerational workforce. What would work in the south of the country might not necessarily work in the north. To extend our research, we hope to conduct an in-depth study to develop more location-specific findings to improve the Indian workplace.

Legal Innovation Lab

How will lawyers work in the future?

FUTURE PROOF:
**ADAPTABLE &
RECONFIGURABLE
DESIGN**

Law firms are ready for change, and are seeking progressive, tech-enabled workplace strategies that improve efficiency while enhancing their ability to attract, retain, and support talent.

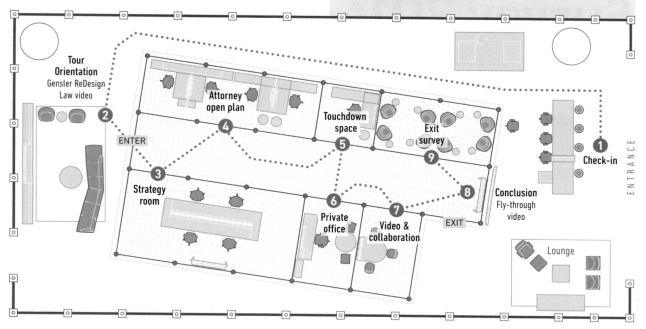

Innovation Lab We led 600+ conference attendees on a guided tour highlighting progressive workplace strategies tailored to attorney needs and work processes.

Tour Orientation Gensler ReDesign Law video ②

ENTER

③ **Strategy room**

④ **Attorney open plan**

Touchdown space ⑤

⑥ **Private office**

⑦ **Video & collaboration**

EXIT ⑧

Exit survey ⑨

ENTRANCE

① **Check-in**

Conclusion Fly-through video

Lounge

WHAT WE DID

We designed and built a "legal innovation lab" in partnership with the Association of Legal Administrators (ALA) and leading technology, software, and furniture manufacturers.* The lab was comprised of a series of vignettes used to share and test ideas for the future legal workplace. We developed the strategies and design solutions showcased in this exhibit based on the findings of our prior research into the legal workplace, including a roundtable of legal leaders and an analysis of our workplace performance data for lawyers and legal staff. At the end of the exhibit, we gave all attendees an exit survey, and analyzed the results of over 250 survey responses on the current state of the legal workplace as well as their firms' openness to change.

THE CONTEXT

The practice of law is undergoing a fundamental transformation. Our previous research and experience highlight numerous shifts, from a market in which lawyers' clients are increasingly cost-conscious and value-focused, to a growing focus on teamwork and quality-of-life concerns. The design of the future law office must address these rapidly changing influences and align with a fundamental reengineering of how legal work is, and will be, done.

We anticipate the law office of the future to be smaller, more flexible, more collaborative, more client-focused, and more technology-enabled—employing workplace qualities many associate with business or management consulting firms today. Yet we also know that lawyers will continue to have workplace needs specific to their profession and tasks. An exploration of progressive workplace strategies through the lens of legal work today is necessary to create future work environments that continue to support legal work while adapting to new realities of the profession and market.

Exit survey results

Q: How receptive are the firm's partners to change?
PERCENT RESPONDING "RECEPTIVE," BY FIRM SIZE (EMPLOYEES)

AVERAGE

82% 50 OR LESS

70% 51–500

84% 501 OR MORE

78%

*Bernhardt Design, Steelcase, Microsoft, Thomson Reuters, Herman Miller, Knoll, Hitplay, Creative Wood, POI Business Interiors, Interface.

THE RESULTS

Change is a fact of life for law firms today, and leadership is fully aware—**three in four survey respondents noted their firm's partners are receptive to change.** This need for change centers around two central premises: the need to improve real estate efficiency to stay lean and cost-competitive, and the need to evolve to attract talent and accommodate new ways of working.

Space efficiency and reduction trends we've observed in the marketplace are confirmed by our respondents. The majority of firms have off-site archives, and one in three (36 percent) have off-site data centers. Off-site administrative functions currently exist only for 17 percent of respondents, with the most among larger firms.

Despite these initiatives, the majority of respondents reported that their firm continues to lease more space than is necessary. Larger firms are more likely to have excess space on their books. Recently designed firms are less likely to have excess space, confirming the focus on space reduction in recent years—though even among those whose offices have been redesigned recently, one in three reported their firm still has more space than is necessary.

Respondents noted the **adoption of new technology, managing an increasingly multigenerational workforce, and the war for top talent** as key trends impacting the legal industry, confirmed through discussions with attendees and a companion panel held at the ALA Toronto conference. Approaching these trends proactively is of vital importance for a firm's long-term survival. Panelists also felt they were lacking a consistent set of best practices by which to adopt these trends successfully, particularly given a future that is largely unknown.

KEY: FIRM SIZE (EMPLOYEES)
- 50 OR LESS
- 51–500
- 501 OR MORE

KEY: RECENCY OF DESIGN
- WITHIN THE LAST 3 YEARS
- 3–5 YEARS AGO
- 6 OR MORE YEARS AGO

Q: Does your firm/company have off-site facilites?
PERCENT RESPONDING "YES," BY FIRM SIZE AND BY RECENCY OF DESIGN

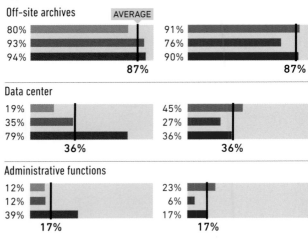

Off-site archives
80%	91%
93%	76%
94%	90%
87%	**87%**

Data center
19%	45%
35%	27%
79%	36%
36%	**36%**

Administrative functions
12%	23%
12%	6%
39%	17%
17%	**17%**

Q: Which of the following trends are affecting your business the most?
TRENDS RANKED FROM MOST TO LEAST, BY FIRM SIZE (EMPLOYEES)

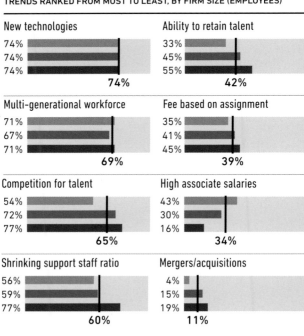

New technologies
| 74% |
| 74% |
| 74% |
| **74%** |

Ability to retain talent
| 33% |
| 45% |
| 55% |
| **42%** |

Multi-generational workforce
| 71% |
| 67% |
| 71% |
| **69%** |

Fee based on assignment
| 35% |
| 41% |
| 45% |
| **39%** |

Competition for talent
| 54% |
| 72% |
| 77% |
| **65%** |

High associate salaries
| 43% |
| 30% |
| 16% |
| **34%** |

Shrinking support staff ratio
| 56% |
| 59% |
| 77% |
| **60%** |

Mergers/acquisitions
| 4% |
| 15% |
| 19% |
| **11%** |

Q: Does your firm lease more space than actually needed?
PERCENT RESPONDING "YES," BY FIRM SIZE AND BY RECENCY OF DESIGN

47%	36%
59%	49%
76%	71%
57%	**57%**

Tech-enabled mobility is gaining wide acceptance.

When respondents were asked about the likelihood of their firms implementing the progressive work and workplace strategies highlighted in our exhibit, technology and out-of-office mobility topped the list, followed by in-office mobility and reduced paper. Importantly, all of these strategies are reliant on effective mobile work and tools as well as organizational policies that encourage flexibility and anywhere-working. Currently these strategies appear focused on attorneys—mobility for non-legal staff ranks lower in likelihood.

Adoption of open environments is tentative.

While firms appear focused on increasing choice and mobility, the parallel adoption of more open plan environments that often comes alongside these shifts is slower to be embraced. While early adopters exist, mostly in the U.K., U.S. firms have been more likely to seek efficiency via interior and/or smaller attorney offices, and multi-use spaces.

Talent and workforce shifts are top-of-mind.

Generational and talent issues ranked among the top trends impacting the legal business. This focus on talent, alongside the recognized importance of technology, may explain legal firms' interest in mobility and technology, and their tentative approach to adopting more open or shared workplace environments.

Flexibility is the first line of defense against uncertainty.

With an uncertain future ahead, our respondents noted the importance of keeping the workplace flexible to accommodate change. Three out of four respondents ranked the ability to reconfigure their workplace easily and quickly as important, and the importance appears to be even more paramount for larger firms. These strategies are all the more important as firms seek to carry less inventory, opting to manage staff fluctuations by reconfiguring furniture and density levels instead of allowing space to stay empty while waiting for future occupants.

Q: How important is it to reconfigure your workplace easily and quickly?

PERCENT RESPONDING "IMPORTANT TO VERY IMPORTANT," BY FIRM SIZE (EMPLOYEES)

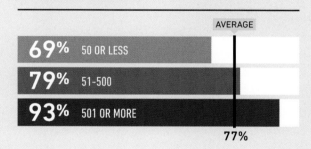

AVERAGE

69%	50 OR LESS
79%	51-500
93%	501 OR MORE

77%

Respondents noted significant openness to change, underscoring that dramatic shifts will continue in the legal workplace. Our findings suggest that as law firms increasingly embrace alternative workplace strategies, their focus will be on those that help them maximize space efficiency while also improving the workplace experience. Building in flexibility from the start is a key example, and allows today's work environments to adapt to and support future needs while ensuring firms get the most out of their real estate investments.

Q: How likely is it that your firm will implement some of the ideas seen at the exhibit?

UNLIKELY | SOMEWHAT LIKELY | VERY LIKELY

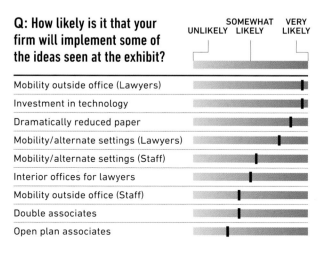

Mobility outside office (Lawyers)
Investment in technology
Dramatically reduced paper
Mobility/alternate settings (Lawyers)
Mobility/alternate settings (Staff)
Interior offices for lawyers
Mobility outside office (Staff)
Double associates
Open plan associates

City / Building / Desk

What might the future of work look like and how could this reshape our cities?

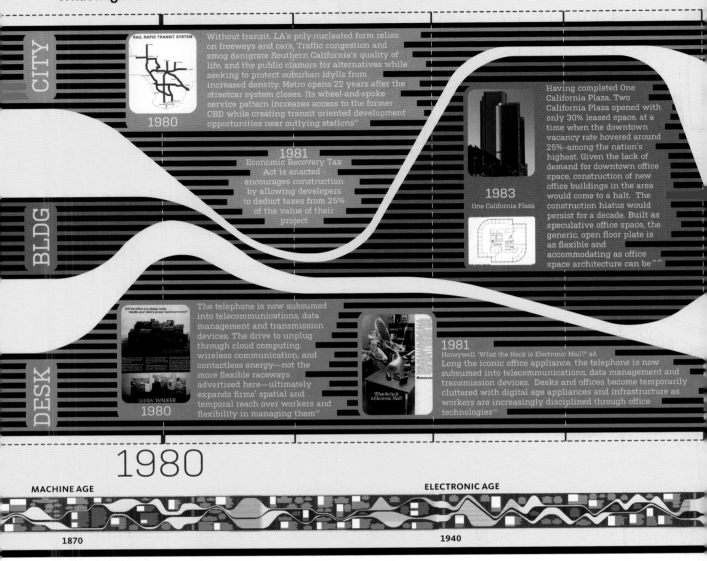

CITY

RAIL RAPID TRANSIT SYSTEM

Without transit, LA's poly-nucleated form relies on freeways and cars. Traffic congestion and smog denigrate Southern California's quality of life, and the public clamors for alternatives while seeking to protect suburban idylls from increased density. Metro opens 22 years after the streetcar system closes. Its wheel-and-spoke service pattern increases access to the former CBD while creating transit oriented development opportunities near outlying stations[s]

1980

1981
Economic Recovery Tax Act is enacted · encourages construction by allowing developers to deduct taxes from 25% of the value of their project

Having completed One California Plaza, Two California Plaza opened with only 30% leased space, at a time when the downtown vacancy rate hovered around 25%-among the nation's highest. Given the lack of demand for downtown office space, construction of new office buildings in the area would come to a halt. The construction hiatus would persist for a decade. Built as speculative office space, the generic, open floor plate is as flexible and accommodating as office space architecture can be[s, e]

1983
One California Plaza

BLDG

DESK

Will the office you design today handle your client's power needs tomorrow?

The telephone is now subsumed into telecommunications, data management and transmission devices. The drive to unplug through cloud computing, wireless communication, and contactless energy—not the more flexible raceways advertised here—ultimately expands firms' spatial and temporal reach over workers and flexibility in managing them[s]

SHAW WALKER

1980

1981
Honeywell. 'What the Heck is Electronic Mail?' ad
Long the iconic office appliance, the telephone is now subsumed into telecommunications, data management and transmission devices. Desks and offices become temporarily cluttered with digital age appliances and infrastructure as workers are increasingly disciplined through office technologies[s]

What the heck is Electronic Mail?

Honeywell

1980

MACHINE AGE

ELECTRONIC AGE

1870

1940

WHAT WE DID

We conducted a three-year research project with the University of California, Los Angeles (UCLA) think-tank cityLAB to investigate the future of office work, and its impact on the urban environment, using Los Angeles as a case study. At the onset of our research, we asked: Is the generic office building still relevant? Does Rem Koolhaas's 1993 "Typical Plan" still apply to today's world of work? If not, what is the future of this building type? And, because these buildings take up so much of the real estate in our cities, what would the urban impact be if their DNA were to change?

To investigate these questions, our multiyear project explored the nature of "work" and the spaces it inhabits through three sequential processes: Research, Formulation, and Design.

We researched the history and trajectory of office buildings and forms of 21st-century work to both challenge well-established narratives about urban centers and propose new ways to think about time, location, and the organization of work. Our research included published third-party studies, roundtable discussions with urban planning and workplace experts, and the development of models that proposed new strategies for office design as it relates to urban planning.

The outcomes highlight emerging ecologies and economies of work in Los Angeles with the power to transform how we address challenges presented by the central business district, urban land use, office buildings, desk configurations, and the spaces of everyday life on a broader scale.

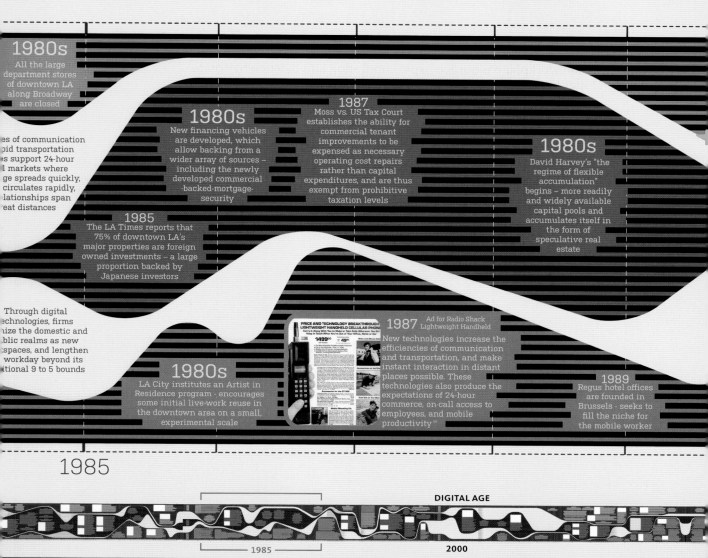

1980s
All the large department stores of downtown LA along Broadway are closed

...es of communication ...pid transportation ...s support 24-hour ...l markets where ...ge spreads quickly, ...lationships span ...eat distances

1980s
New financing vehicles are developed, which allow backing from a wider array of sources – including the newly developed commercial -backed-mortgage- security

1987
Moss vs. US Tax Court establishes the ability for commercial tenant improvements to be expensed as necessary operating cost repairs rather than capital expenditures, and are thus exempt from prohibitive taxation levels

1980s
David Harvey's "the regime of flexible accumulation" begins – more readily and widely available capital pools and accumulates itself in the form of speculative real estate

1985
The LA Times reports that 75% of downtown LA's major properties are foreign owned investments – a large proportion backed by Japanese investors

Through digital ...echnologies, firms ...ize the domestic and ...blic realms as new ...spaces, and lengthen ...workday beyond its ...itional 9 to 5 bounds

1980s
LA City institutes an Artist in Residence program - encourages some initial live-work reuse in the downtown area on a small, experimental scale

PRICE AND TECHNOLOGY BREAKTHROUGH LIGHTWEIGHT HANDHELD CELLULAR PHONE

1987 Ad for Radio Shack Lightweight Handheld
New technologies increase the efficiencies of communication and transportation, and make instant interaction in distant places possible. These technologies also produce the expectations of 24-hour commerce, on-call access to employees, and mobile productivity ™

1989
Regus hotel offices are founded in Brussels - seeks to fill the niche for the mobile worker

1985

DIGITAL AGE

1985   2000

THE CONTEXT

The notion of work has been historically structured around three distinct scales: the desk, the building, and the city. At the desk scale, work life has undergone a process of perpetual change due to innovations in technology, efficiency, and communication that continually challenge the way we consider and define a work "environment." At the scale of buildings and cities, new patterns of work are allowing—or in many cases, forcing—workers' lives to be entirely restructured. However, with instantaneous forms of communication and rapid flows of information, the physical dimensions that have historically bound each worker—the cubicle, building floor plate, or city district, for example—have become increasingly difficult to characterize.

The old binary oppositions of home and office, public and private, downtown and suburb, interior architecture and building design, now fail to describe the current world of work. The distinctions of the desk, the building, and the city—as they pertain to work—are inadequate. Los Angeles proves an excellent case study here, as the oldest post-war American city, and as such the model for many American cities. Like most American cities, Los Angeles' urban core was historically a place for industry, commerce, and work. When urban sprawl pushed the city boundaries outward and established many suburbs in the mid-20th century, Downtown Los Angeles retreated, losing much of its population, businesses, and vibrancy. Today, Downtown Los Angeles is experiencing a renaissance as a district that is rooted in work. How it continues to support businesses, workers, and visitors will be key to its resilience.

THE RESULTS: YEAR ONE

Our first year of research explored the history of Downtown Los Angeles within a broader genealogy of city planning, office building design, and technology. The re-emergence of Downtown Los Angeles challenges the definition of urban centers elsewhere; it serves as one potential location for work in the city among many. Technology has allowed modern knowledge workers to be more mobile, allowing the office and its typical interior to encroach on the airport, café, public park, plaza, automobile, and most notably, the home.

Our findings from year one charted the evolution of work activity in Los Angeles by rethinking the concept of a central business district in scalar, material terms: "city," "building," and "desk." They are outlined in the first publication in our series, *The Future of Office Work, Vol. 1: How We Got Here.*

THE RESULTS: YEAR TWO

Our second year of research focused on the conceptual and physical gaps within office design. How might traditional places for work be re-formulated? How might new professional alliances be forged to improve how we work, whether between urban planning and industrial design, or mobile technology and architecture? We investigated these questions via a series of roundtable discussions and panel presentations, during which leading academics and professionals proposed sites in Los Angeles that are most ripe for rethinking.

We organized the content from these discussions into a four-part publication, *-Less: Re-wiring Work*, the second volume of *The Future of Office Work* series. In this volume, we explore moving design and professional boundaries beyond the confines of the desk, building, and city to ultimately render work and the contemporary worker location-less.

WHAT THIS MEANS

Given Los Angeles' decentralized nature, it serves as an excellent case study for work that permeates beyond the downtown setting. The history of Downtown Los Angeles is a narrative of perpetual revisionism. It has been able to morph in ways more consistent with 21st-century forms of work, and as such is a lesson for other cities with similar struggles. As we chart this evolution, the existing scales of work are becoming less distinct, overlapping and intermingling instead.

WHAT THIS MEANS

Technology and the mobile worker are dissolving the traditional definitions of the workplace. The modern knowledge worker requires both mobility and some version of a home base, presenting challenges to consider for architectural and urban design applications. This dynamic workforce challenges the way we think about office design and office culture. Via this phase of work, we seek to raise the question: What would "location-less" work mean for the design and material form of a 21st-century downtown?

THE RESULTS: YEAR THREE

The conclusion of our three-year research collaboration offered paradigmatic future scenarios that re-conceptualize and critique the existing structures, locations, and boundaries of work within Los Angeles. We engaged industry and academic leaders from a multitude of fields, from real estate to mobility design, along with a group of graduate urban planning and architecture students at UCLA. Through a series of cityLAB and Gensler-led workshops, they collectively developed, designed, and tested new ideas. We then curated the three-year compilation of work—including books, pamphlets, posters, and videos—into a weeklong exhibition at the Architecture + Design Museum in Downtown Los Angeles. This event drew together LA city planners, architects, developers, and academics, and spurred new conversations about the potential futures of Los Angeles.

WHAT THIS MEANS

The city must reposition itself to accommodate and perpetuate the emerging ecologies of the workplace. The physical workplace holds a significant stake in the real estate market; it is imperative not only to be aware of the increasingly rapid change in the specific ways work is done, but also to harness the opportunity for change in the city as a whole—whether that is something as simple as adding electrical outlets by public benches, or as complex as rethinking transportation infrastructure.

WHAT'S NEXT

The collaboration with UCLA's cityLAB allowed the gap between academia and practice to dissolve by tapping into minds in design and related industries, and by providing a tangible context for academic theory. The process synthesized history and critical analysis with the realities of practice, such as building and city codes, legislation, and finance, adding another dimension of inquiry outside the boundaries of pragmatism, while simultaneously providing a foundation for more informed speculation. We continue to work with the City of Los Angeles to blur the boundaries between academia and practice, between space and the city.

"In this situation, public space ceases to exist. It appears as a 'sea' of possible meetings or—articulated by confessions, sermons, advertisements, reading voices—a continuum of 'interiors.' The world appears as one interior, as a fluid of information."

– "The Continuous Interior," Winy Maas,
FARMAX: Excursions on Density

Organizational Strategy:

The Employee Experience

For the Love of Purpose

What can we learn from not-for-profit employees about why purpose matters most?

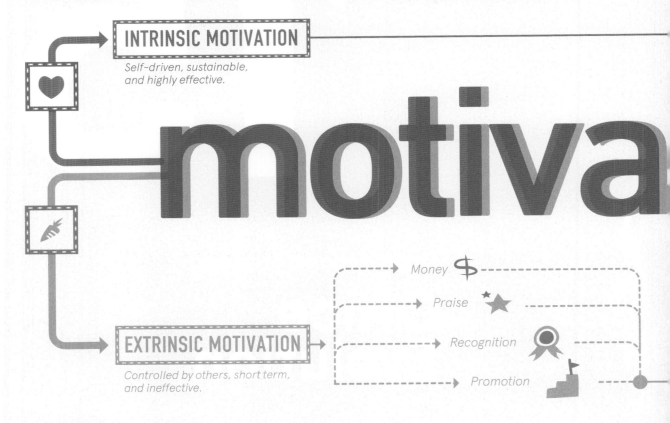

INTRINSIC MOTIVATION
Self-driven, sustainable, and highly effective.

motiva

EXTRINSIC MOTIVATION
Controlled by others, short term, and ineffective.

Money $
Praise ★
Recognition
Promotion

WHAT WE DID

We researched trends and drivers shaping the not-for-profit workforce to better understand their engagement, purpose, and motivation differentiators. We used this information to explore the "why" of not-for-profit work, and specifically the impact of intrinsic motivation and

meaning on employee performance and experience. These entwined forces not only help to explain the paradoxes of the not-for-profit employee, but reveal significant challenges—and opportunities—facing all organizations today.

THE CONTEXT

Less than one-third of the U.S. workforce is engaged in their work, a troubling statistic that has remained stagnant for almost two decades. As a response to this and other statistics on workforce dynamics, there is a growing assumption that work is "broken," and that it has become so due to the centuries-old belief that money is the main reason people work. However, the not-for-profit sector offers a subset of workers who stand in direct contradiction to the myth of a coin-operated workforce: intelligent, talented people who have chosen the path less-paid. On average, not-for-profit employees are more educated than the general workforce, yet they face a significant income gap, earning 10 to 30 percent less than for-profit employees in comparable mid-level positions and up to 75 percent less at higher levels.

A deeper understanding of why they make that sacrifice may not only provide us valuable insights into how the workplace environment can be designed to better support them, but also points to broader ways that design can contribute to a brighter era of work itself. While our research led to some encouraging findings, it also exposed a serious problem for not-for-profits:

WHILE ENGAGEMENT IS BETTER AMONG EMPLOYEES IN THE NOT-FOR-PROFIT SECTOR, TURNOVER IS STILL HIGH.

In fact, talent retention is cited in most industry surveys as one of the biggest challenges facing not-for-profit organizations. Our research presents an exciting opportunity for not-for-profits to engage their employees, reduce turnover, and achieve overall higher performance.

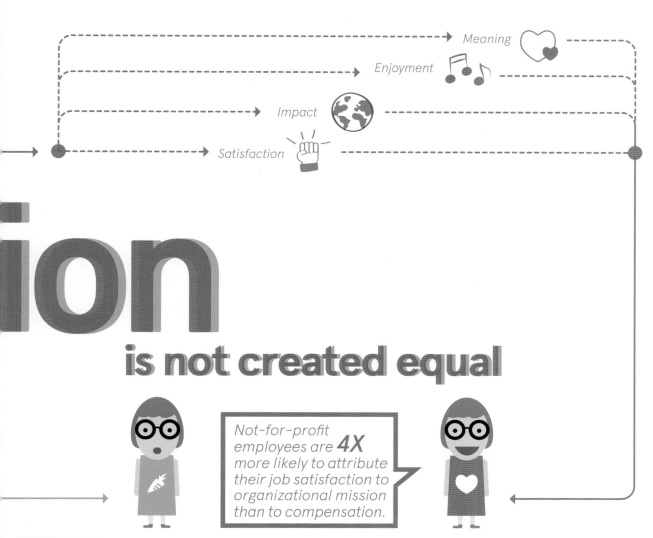

ion is not created equal

> Not-for-profit employees are **4X** more likely to attribute their job satisfaction to organizational mission than to compensation.

THE RESULTS

Why do not-for-profit employees choose their path? The results may seem obvious—they're largely driven to the sector by the opportunity to contribute to something meaningful. However, in digging deeper, this obvious conclusion became something much more profound: **Meaning comes from within, and is a key component of motivation and performance.** Intrinsic motivation, or self-determined action, is an innate human characteristic tied to curiosity, persistence, direction, a desire to learn, and an inner drive to take on challenges.

On the other end of the motivational spectrum is extrinsic motivation, action carried out to earn a reward or avoid punishment. In the realm of work, extrinsic rewards include raises, bonuses, promotions, and praise, but also deadlines, pressure, rules, and bureaucracy.

Studies have proven extrinsic motivation to be highly ineffective in driving performance, and is often an impediment to it. Nonetheless, extrinsic rewards remain at the core of most corporate engagement initiatives and performance strategies.

Employers have enormous power to facilitate intrinsic motivation; they can align work to individual strengths, reinforce connection to the mission of the organization, and de-emphasize extrinsic rewards and regulations.

To do so, employers must reimagine themselves not as enforcers of productivity, but enablers of meaning.

Workplace environments are a key lens through which employees "read" the culture of their organization, whether intentional or not. A well-designed workplace can be a powerful tool to foster intrinsic motivation, and reduce turnover as a result. Even better, the other organizational benefits made possible by an increase in intrinsic motivation include a more engaged, healthier, collaborative, self-directed, resilient, enthusiastic, and loyal workforce.

Most importantly, in a sector taking on some of the most daunting challenges facing society today, intrinsic motivation is a key driver of innovation. Incremental innovation may occur through extrinsic motivation, but true, game-changing transformational innovation—the kind that organizations across all sectors need today—only comes from a fire within individuals (a flame that can be fed or extinguished).

SUPPORT WHY PEOPLE WORK, NOT JUST HOW.

Gensler's Workplace Surveys have shown the potential for workplace design to have a positive impact on employee performance and engagement. We believe the next step goes beyond the functional to incorporate purpose more directly—expanding the definition of "high performance" to include environments that not only support how people work, but also why.

MAKE ENGAGEMENT A KEY METRIC, AND TRACK IT.

The workplace presents organizations with an unmatched opportunity to amplify engagement and emotionally connect with workers. In every design decision there is an opportunity to increase employee engagement: from site selection, building orientation, and spatial configuration, to the color of the paint on the wall.

MEANING IS A FEELING, NOT A MESSAGE.

Resolving the entrenched disengagement of the U.S. workforce will not take place through space-planning alone—the solution must be transformational. We must create environments where, more than just communicating mission, people experience mission and organizational meaning directly.

PURPOSE SHOULDN'T JUST BE FOR NOT-FOR-PROFITS.

Employees in not-for-profit organizations have a leg up—they've chosen a career path directly connected to motivation and purpose. Nonetheless, there are lessons to be learned for any organization and workplace. Grappling with design's power to drive purpose can be a key goal of any workplace.

HIGHER PURPOSE, HIGHER INNOVATION

Not-for-profit companies lead the workplace sector in purpose ratings (4.0), placing the industry closer to the rating of the highly innovative companies (4.3), according to Gensler's U.S. Workplace Survey 2016.

Employee ratings of personal and organizational purpose on a 5-point scale.

5.0

3.7 — Industry Average
4.0 — Not-for-Profit
4.3 — Innovative Companies

Through our research, we have learned the extraordinary power of meaning and intrinsic motivation in driving higher performance. Our results will inform processes to understand the opportunities for meaning within every project, and identify design principles that help deliver on that potential, culminating in an entirely new approach for not-for-profit projects, as well as a new vocabulary to talk about design. With mission and purpose at the core of all our not-for-profit work, the opportunity to marry space and meaning is unparalleled, and the lessons learned have the potential to drive positive change at a time when the world of work sorely needs it.

Employers must reimagine themselves not as enforcers of **productivity**, but enablers of **purpose**.

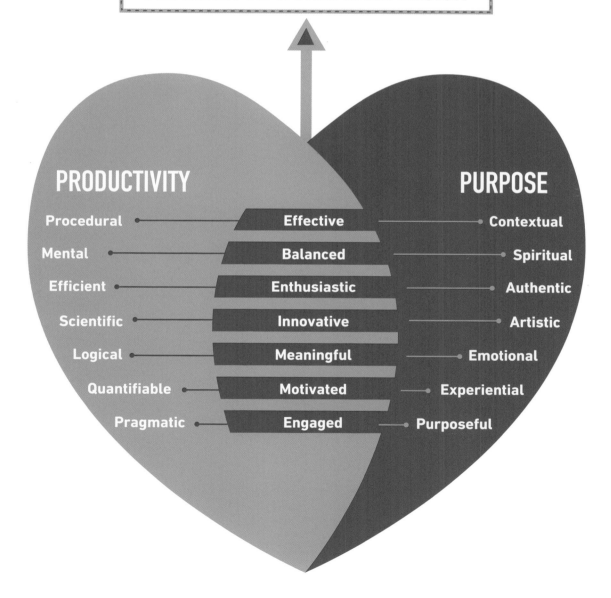

MEANINGFUL WORKPLACE DESIGN

PRODUCTIVITY

Procedural
Mental
Efficient
Scientific
Logical
Quantifiable
Pragmatic

Effective
Balanced
Enthusiastic
Innovative
Meaningful
Motivated
Engaged

PURPOSE

Contextual
Spiritual
Authentic
Artistic
Emotional
Experiential
Purposeful

Trading on Stress

Can better trading floor environments mitigate stress?

WHAT WE DID

We conducted secondary research to identify opportunities for design to improve the health and well-being of traders, addressing issues of stress and poor decision making often associated with today's trading environments. Our goal was to explore the neurological and biological considerations relevant to the financial workplace, alongside progressive ergonomic, technological, and design strategies relevant to creating healthier and more effective trading environments.

STRESSFUL TRADING ENVIRONMENTS CAN CONTRIBUTE TO:

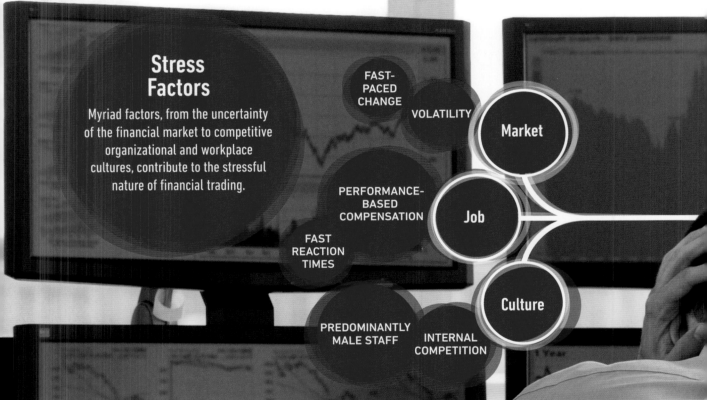

Stress Factors

Myriad factors, from the uncertainty of the financial market to competitive organizational and workplace cultures, contribute to the stressful nature of financial trading.

FAST-PACED CHANGE

VOLATILITY

Market

PERFORMANCE-BASED COMPENSATION

Job

FAST REACTION TIMES

Culture

PREDOMINANTLY MALE STAFF

INTERNAL COMPETITION

THE CONTEXT

Financial trading ranks among the most high-pressure and stressful knowledge worker occupations. With success or failure hinging on the traders' ability to instantaneously process, analyze, and react to multiple and increasingly fast-paced streams of information, debilitating stress and high burnout rates have become all but endemic for traders, a startling state for a profession where most workers are only in their 20s or 30s.

A typical trader's workday begins long before market opening with research and preparation, and extends long after closing, recapping the day's efforts and planning for the next. While the market is open, turnaround times for trades are often measured in seconds or even milliseconds, with traders performing a delicate balancing act between risk-taking and risk avoidance. One wrong decision or even an incorrect keystroke can spell disaster.

POOR DECISION MAKING, EXACERBATED MARKET VOLATILITY, AND COMPROMISED EMPLOYEE WELL-BEING.

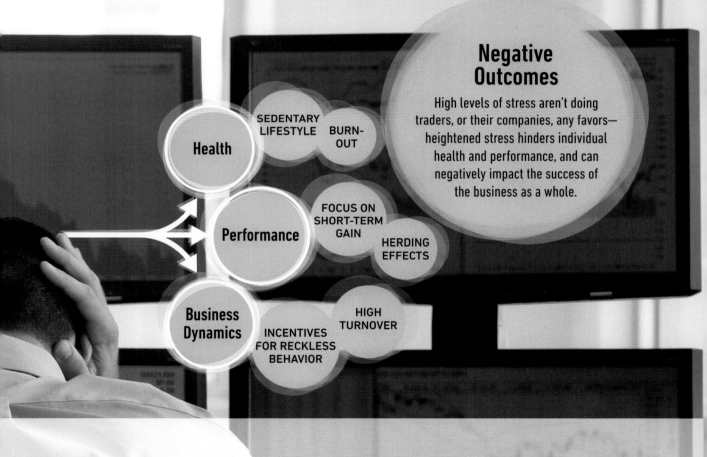

Health

SEDENTARY LIFESTYLE   BURN-OUT

Performance

FOCUS ON SHORT-TERM GAIN

HERDING EFFECTS

Business Dynamics

INCENTIVES FOR RECKLESS BEHAVIOR

HIGH TURNOVER

Negative Outcomes

High levels of stress aren't doing traders, or their companies, any favors—heightened stress hinders individual health and performance, and can negatively impact the success of the business as a whole.

But change is on the horizon. The financial crisis still looms large over Wall Street, causing firms to question industry and company norms. With clients seeking change, this research project is a critical step in helping our trading firm clients redefine both their workplace and, in turn, their work culture.

By understanding the current physical characteristics of trading floors and the potential to map behavior and space, financial firms can redesign these environments to mitigate stress, shape positive behavior, and break the risk cycle. The potential rewards are profound. It is not just the health and well-being of traders at stake, but in many ways the health of financial markets themselves.

THE RESULTS

While the technology and increasingly high-pressure processes of trading have changed drastically in the digital age, the trading floor itself has seen little workplace design innovation. **In contrast to the dramatic changes in other corporate workplaces, trading floors remain defined by dense, unvarying linear layouts more akin to a factory or production floor.** These layouts ignore the potential benefits of more progressive workplace strategies characterized by openness and collaborative spaces, support of focus, and variety of work settings.

To begin the research, we identified broad areas in which the physical trading floor environment might help improve the employee experience. From that initial list, three topics revealed themselves as having the strongest potential for positive impact: control, sensory stimuli, and behavioral ergonomics. Additional factors to consider include acoustics, amenities, density, indoor air quality, lighting, lines of sight, mobility, and temperature/humidity.

WHAT THIS MEANS

CONTROL OF THE PHYSICAL ENVIRONMENT MAY MITIGATE RISK-SEEKING BEHAVIOR.

Traders are prime candidates for "control illusions" in their daily practices. They are prone to seek and overestimate their control of the market—the greater this feeling of control, the worse their performance. We are exploring the possibility that familiarity and certainty within the immediate work environment may reduce the need to control the uncontrollable.

CURATE SENSORY STIMULI TO MINIMIZE STRESS, RATHER THAN AMPLIFY IT.

The quality of light and sound cause physical reactions that affect performance and cognitive state. Prolonged exposure to fluorescent lighting in the absence of natural light is associated with dampened moods, a particular problem for traders working long hours. Views and sightlines also impact experience, especially when providing connections to nature.

CONSIDER POSTURE CAREFULLY.

Proper posture has been shown to improve cognitive function, emotional disposition, and decision making. Open or expansive postures may even improve confidence and minimize errors. This improved confidence does come with a caveat—open postures are also associated with increased levels of risk and dishonesty.

❝ Our sense of sight and sound are heightened under stress. Sensory stimuli spark a chain of both physical and mental reactions in the body. ❞

— Dr. John Coates, Senior Research Fellow,
Neuroscience and Finance,
University of Cambridge

WHAT'S NEXT

Our next step is to conduct fieldwork examining the daily activity of the trader, to better understand the presence of stress-inducing factors on a typical trading floor. As a part of this phase, we will be creating an infield toolkit to analyze both cultural and physical characteristics of the work environment—from employee posture and routines to light and sound qualities. It is our expectation that these innovations will yield qualitative data that can be evaluated to develop a new standard of best practices for the design of future trading floor environments.

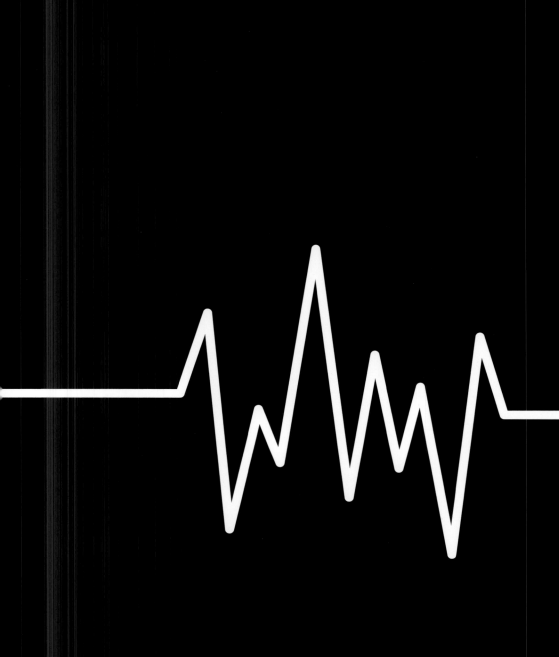

Stress, Performance, and Workplace Design

Blog, excerpt, originally published on GenslerOn.com

Gensler's Financial Services Firms practice area is investigating the connection between stress, performance, and workplace design—and they've focused on a notorious hotbed of stress: the trading floor. The team recently published the first stage of their research, Trading Stress for Wellness. We spoke with research team members Rocco Giannetti, Kimberly Kelly, and Braxton Satterfield to learn more about the project.

· · · · · ·

Interviewer: You note that stress isn't just a well-being issue for traders, it's an issue for their performance with potential impacts on the market as a whole—can you elaborate?

RG: Following the financial crisis of 2008–2009, there were a lot of theories around risk-taking and rewards in financial markets. Stress and risk-taking are directly correlated, and connecting trader stress, environmental factors, and market performance seemed like an obvious and very timely research study.

BS: By better understanding the role of stress on the trading floor, we can potentially provide design solutions that improve well-being for traders. Less stress should improve trader performance and, in turn, market performance.

KK: Market performance is a key element of this research study. Unlike other occupations, trading can use the market as a measurable stress variable. This allows us to compare what's happening in the environment with what's happening in the market.

Interviewer: Based on your research, what's the one design intervention each of you think has the greatest potential to reduce stress and improve performance on trading floors?

KK: Shaping posture is a huge opportunity to impact stress through design. Our secondary research suggests that posture not only is a reflection of stress level, but can also impact stress level, which in turn impacts the way we think and evaluate risk. For me, this is a new way of looking at ergonomics.

RG: I would challenge the whole notion of proximity and visual communication. Traders have traditionally been seated closely together to enable cross-communication and leadership oversight. By leveraging technology, we can likely facilitate the same level of cross-communication and oversight while giving traders more room to breathe.

BS: One of the greatest opportunities is rethinking the design and layout of the trading desk itself, and prioritizing elements like privacy and natural views over high density, basically a flip of the current approach which puts head count first. Our focus is on the trading industry, but the research findings could have implications for better workplace design across all industries.

Live + Work + Play in Tokyo

What is the next generation of Tokyo's "third places"?

WHAT WE DID

We documented the situation of today's Tokyo workforce and real estate, including government plans, key industries, demographics, and both current and future development sites. We then identified our potential users' behavior patterns, and attempted to envision a "day in the life" of a worker in Tokyo, supported via online surveys and in-depth interviews of 20 people who live and work in the city. We used this information to identify the needs and priorities of the Tokyo workforce. Our team then proposed conceptual design solutions to address these needs, focused on spaces people occupy when they are not at home and not at work, commonly referred to as "third places."

"Jitan,"

the Japanese word for the shortening of time, is the core concept behind our investigation and design solutions.

THE CONTEXT

Tokyo is expected to see a massive amount of redevelopment over the next decade, resulting in upwards of 28 million square feet of new office space. As the city undergoes a change of such magnitude, the way its residents live and work will be similarly transformed, creating new opportunities for developers and the built environment to respond to new needs while increasing the market value of their existing or upcoming properties. Mixed-use development and public spaces such as plazas, parks, retail centers, and cafés are common strategies considered to meet these needs; we believe solutions that go beyond these standards can deliver even greater value. Our research seeks to identify these opportunities, and develop nontraditional and unexpected design solutions to meet the needs of Tokyo's diverse working population.

THE RESULTS

Tokyo workers are facing a shortage of time driven by long work days and long commutes. The long hours spent getting to and from home, often far from the city center given Tokyo's massive population and geographic reach, are exacerbating this challenge, and preventing many workers from achieving a sense of well-being. Overall, Tokyo workers' lifestyles are dominated by work; it is often challenging for them to find time for non-work-related activities. Even when at the office, the challenges of dense urban environments are top of mind for workers—employees face problems of noise and lack of meeting rooms when at the office, and lack of public internet and appropriate workplaces when away from it.

As a result, Tokyo workers are currently struggling to balance life, work, and play. Work is taking the brunt of their time and effort, and even it could be better supported. We see opportunities for a next generation of the third place to help better achieve balance and enrich quality of life by promoting more effective use of time and space. "Jitan," the Japanese word for the shortening of time, is the core concept behind our investigation and design solutions.

We hope to promote more effective use of time, a high quality of life, and a sense of well-being through the offering of specific programs, services, and experiences—and placing these amenities in the locations where they will deliver the most value.

We developed three concepts to demonstrate opportunities to improve the well-being and experience of the diverse Tokyo workforce. While each addresses life, work, and play together, the balance between the three aspects varies by scenario, potential users, and specific needs of each proposed location.

time gained to devote to non-work activities

DISTRIBUTED URBAN HOSPITALITY

Sometimes work needs to happen away from the office; for many Tokyo workers, this remains a struggle. Located in central Tokyo, these spaces would provide supplementary meeting and collaboration spaces with a high level of personalized business hospitality services and experiences. Distributed among existing office buildings and hotels, this concept creates new places to work, meet, and innovate around the city.

the goal: *help employees achieve their highest level of performance and efficiency, no matter where they are, and use the time gained to devote to non-work activities.*

non-work activities that support well-being

COMMUNITY/ AMENITY INTEGRATORS

For those who live far from their office location, the reduction of time-related stress is of paramount importance, and finding time to engage the community is a particular challenge. Creating dynamic places that support connection and interaction near home, paired with services that address daily needs and activities from grocery shopping to dry cleaning, is an opportunity to improve the experience and give time back to those living in suburban locations.

the goal: *less time spent commuting and running errands; more time spent with family, friends, or doing other non-work activities that support well-being.*

unwind while being exposed to new ideas

IMMERSIVE LEISURE HUBS

Busy urban workers often struggle to incorporate leisure into their hectic daily lives, while also feeling crunched to stay abreast of the newest trends. This concept focuses on the integration of amenities and services that enable workers to shift easily from work mode to more play-focused activities. Conveniently located inside or near a commuter hub or terminal station, it capitalizes on areas with concentrated consumer activity, and leverages partnerships to create experimental places infused with the newest developments and trends.

the goal: *create an experiential and experimental space for workers to quickly unwind while being exposed to new ideas and products of interest.*

PERSPECTIVES

With nearly 38 million people, Tokyo tops the United Nations' ranking of the world's most populous cities, followed by Delhi, Shanghai, Mexico City, São Paulo, and Mumbai.

– United Nations Department of Economic and Social Affairs, Population Division

WHAT'S NEXT

We plan to continue developing these prototype concepts for the next generation of third places using actual and potential projects, collaborating with major real estate developers, and conducting more in-depth research on potential users. These will feed more detailed design scenarios and proposals.

Emerging Work Styles

Can individual work survive in the "collaborative" workplace?

WHAT WE DID

We conducted both primary and secondary research to understand the nature of, and challenges to, individual work with a particular focus on open-office environments. We targeted software developers as our primary study group and one comprised of focus-oriented, knowledge-based workers. In partnership with a major technology company, we conducted interviews, focus groups, surveys, observational studies, and acoustic measurements to gather information about the conditions that prevent and enable individual work.

From our findings, we developed focus task typologies and work style profiles to define common work modes and areas of frustration in the workplace. We used these typologies, in light of current research on individual and collaborative work and their impacts on employee performance and experience, to develop a series of recommendations—from design strategies to behavior and cultural shifts—to improve employees' ability to focus.

EFFECTIVE FOCUS INVOLVES:
managing individual preferences and cognitive style, collaboration and team dynamics, organizational culture and policies, and the environment and circumstances in which one works.

THE CONTEXT

As organizations become more distributed, more collaborative, and more outsourced, the ways we work and connect are changing. The workplace had, and has, no choice but to evolve to meet new demands and realities. But even as companies and the workplace evolve, **the ability to focus at work has never been more essential for knowledge workers and for companies looking to compete in the global marketplace.** Workers who are able to successfully focus in their workplace report significantly higher levels of engagement than those who cannot.

Yet the ability to complete one's individual work is, in the minds of many, under siege in the workplace. Why? Many of today's workspaces are often built explicitly in pursuit of collaboration, efficiency, and flexibility—all top-of-mind issues for real estate managers and executives, and rightly so. At their worst, these same spaces compromise quiet "heads down" work, and ultimately employee productivity. But this isn't always the case: our prior research also shows that the right balance between focus and collaboration leads to greater innovation and higher performance overall. Understanding the behavioral, organizational, and spatial requirements to achieve this balance was a driving force of our investigation.

"Speech is the most disturbing type of sound because it is directly understood in the brain's working memory."

– Valtteri Hongisto, Acoustician,
Finland Institute of Occupational Health

THE RESULTS

DISTRACTION IS UNIVERSAL.

One of the biggest challenges to effective focus work is distraction, and the primary sources of distraction in the workplace are interruptions by coworkers and overheard conversations. These factors can be a significant detriment to workplace satisfaction, particularly when out of an employee's control.

Addressing distraction doesn't necessarily mean making it quieter, however—developer interview results showed a marked split between those preferring quiet, private spaces and those who work better in "buzzy" environments.

ONE PERSON'S DISTRACTION IS ANOTHER'S INTERACTION.

Noise isn't always bad. Some impromptu interruptions by coworkers are highly productive in terms of overall team performance, even if they undermine a certain amount of individual performance in the process. Similarly, overheard conversations—among team members and in the right context—can speed decision making and problem-solving on team projects.

MANAGING DISTRACTION REQUIRES DISCIPLINE.

What constitutes a distraction, and how disruptive that distraction is, varies—acceptable levels of distraction often relate more to individual preference or expectation than to the specifics of environments or noise levels. And many work process interruptions are self-imposed—upwards of 44 percent according to a study out of UC Irvine, noting employees' tendency to switch tasks frequently throughout the day (and particularly those in open plan environments).

WHAT THIS MEANS

SUPPORT INDIVIDUAL, TEAM, AND ORGANIZATIONAL WORK PROCESSES.

Finding effective strategies for improving people's ability to focus in the workplace requires taking into account not only the physical environment and workplace setting, but also team dynamics, work styles, and organizational culture. Workplace design must align process, culture, policy, and management for employees to perform at their best.

SOMETIMES, GROUP PERFORMANCE SHOULD TRUMP THE INDIVIDUAL.

Some distraction ultimately becomes productive interaction, and employees who work in teams know it. Help them filter out unproductive distraction and know when and how to accommodate the productive kind.

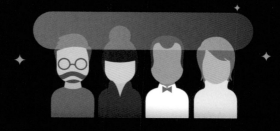

EMPOWER EMPLOYEES TO MATCH PROCESS TO PLACE.

Working effectively as an individual and team requires discipline and choice. Spaces and policies that support making these decisions are imperative. Employees know intuitively when they are open to interaction or distraction and when they're not—let them communicate among themselves and make their own plan.

WHAT'S NEXT

Undisciplined collaboration can be a significant hindrance to individual focused work. As future work trends predict that knowledge workers will increasingly adopt agile and flexible work styles, understanding the impact of disorganized collaboration will become more valuable to our clients.

We are exploring opportunities for user autonomy in design solutions that can apply to diverse client needs. We are also studying how focus and individual effectiveness are directly impacted by team efficiency and collaborative behaviors. We believe that when the team collaborates efficiently, there are fewer distractions and interruptions in the workplace, improving the ability to focus and, ultimately, employee productivity.

Appendix

2016

Gensler publishes Research Catalogue, Volume 2.

Gensler Research receives 173 proposals for research funding, the most in the program's history.

The Gensler Research Catalogue, Volume 1, wins Graphis Annual Design Competition Merit Award.

2015

Gensler researchers participate in the Robot Petting Zoo at SXSW, showcasing their Mobile Unmanned Printing Platform (MUPP) prototype.

Gensler's Legal Innovation Lab wins the Association of Legal Administrators' IDEA (innovation, development, engagement, and advancement) Award.

The "London Underline" concept, developed as part of The Future of Metro Transport research, wins the award for Best Conceptual Project at the London Planning Awards.

2014

Gensler publishes its inaugural Research Catalogue, Volume 1, which wins People's Choice in the 2014 Gensler Design Excellence Awards.

2013

Gensler Research expands its global footprint, funding projects in China, India, and Latin America.

Gensler Research convenes a SXSWedu panel on campus design and student learning.

2012

Gensler is invited to present research on innovation, education, and workplace design at the Harvard Learning Innovation Laboratory.

Gensler's research into "hackable buildings" wins NAIOP Office Building of the Future competition, the only entry focused on building reuse.

2011

Gensler Research establishes a formalized RFP and review process, open to all staff, dramatically expanding project breadth.

Yearly Research Process

Call for Proposals → Grant Awards → Progress Reviews → Peer Reviews → Final Reviews

2009

Gensler's research program is rolled out to all practice areas, funding projects ranging from the student experience to building envelope performance.

2008

Gensler's new Workplace Performance Index™ (WPI) survey tool receives trademark status.

Gensler Los Angeles launches four high-profile research projects focused on building performance and sustainability, growing the program significantly in both scope and scale.

Gensler's 2008 U.S. and U.K. Workplace Surveys find a direct connection between workplace design and business performance.

2007

Gensler establishes a formal research program to support investigations outside day-to-day client work.

2005

Gensler publishes its first Workplace Survey in the U.K.

How We Research at Gensler

At Gensler, everyone has the opportunity to be a researcher—that's just one of the ways our research program is unique. Every project is led by design practitioners embedded in our offices and practices around the world. Why is this important? Because it means our researchers are not only investigators, but doers, who can quickly integrate the new knowledge and insights they forge through their research efforts into the work they do with clients every day. By aligning research with practice in this way, we accelerate learning and innovation to maximize the value design delivers.

This distributed research network is built upon a platform of strong leadership coupled with in-house research expertise that ensures every project is carried out with the rigor required for research to be truly successful. Through our formal review process, we connect our research teams with experts and thought leaders who ask tough questions and help projects stay on track and on point. To aid in their efforts, our teams frequently partner with leading universities around the globe, which helps us advance our research and knowledge in a wide range of topic areas.

Our research program and processes have been developed and refined over the past 10 years, and are the foundation upon which this publication and the insights it contains are built. The program has grown exponentially since its founding, making the publication and sharing of our findings all the more imperative. Our focus remains on providing opportunities for our professionals to create new knowledge and make a positive contribution to the world through research-based design. As our research continues to evolve, we look forward to sharing the new opportunities and insights that unfold.

Christine Barber
Director of Research

About Gensler

Gensler is widely recognized as the world's leading collaborative design firm, not just the largest. Our architects, designers, planners, and consultants partner with clients across the globe on over 3,000 projects every year. Our clients are remarkably diverse: large and small, private and public, for-profit and not-for-profit. We help them grow, sustain, and transform; whatever it takes to embrace their future.·

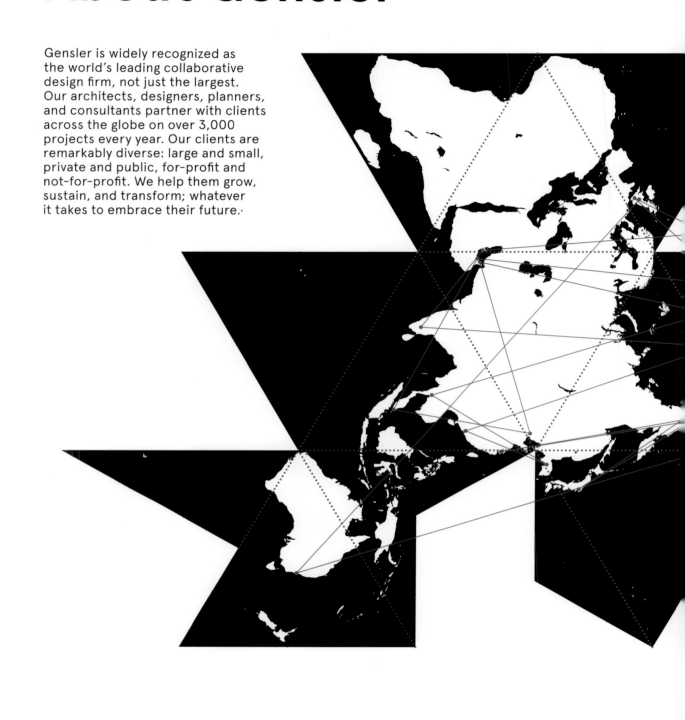

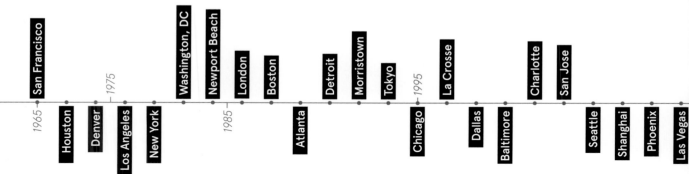

San Francisco · Houston · Denver · 1975 · Los Angeles · New York · Washington, DC · Newport Beach · 1985 · London · Boston · Atlanta · Detroit · Morristown · Tokyo · Chicago · 1995 · La Crosse · Dallas · Baltimore · Charlotte · San Jose · Seattle · Shanghai · Phoenix · Las Vegas

1965

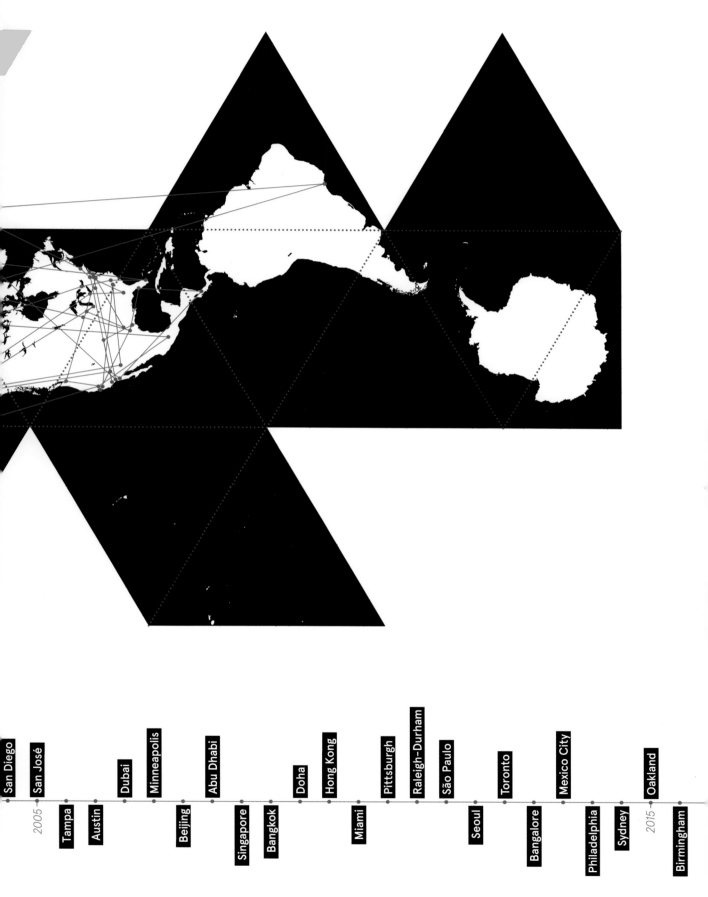

San Diego
San José
Tampa
Austin
Dubai
Minneapolis
Beijing
Abu Dhabi
Singapore
Bangkok
Doha
Hong Kong
Miami
Pittsburgh
Raleigh–Durham
São Paulo
Seoul
Toronto
Bangalore
Mexico City
Philadelphia
Sydney
Oakland
Birmingham

2005

2015

Bibliography

10 Hack the City

Vey, Jennifer. *Building from Strength: Creating Opportunity in Greater Baltimore's Next Economy*. The Brookings Institution, 2012.

16 Manhattan's Next Hot Neighborhood

East Midtown Rezoning. New York: Department of City Planning, 2015.

20 Curating the Right Mix

China National Human Development Report 2013: Sustainable and Liveable Cities: Toward Ecological Civilization. UNDP China and the Institute for Urban and Environmental Studies, Chinese Academy of Social Sciences. China Publishing Group Corporation / China Translation & Publishing Corporation, 2013.

"How Public Art Affects Real Estate Values." *Butler Burgher Group*. Febraury 25, 2015. http://bbgres.com/how-public-art-affects-real-estate-values/.

"Public Transportation Boosts Property Values." *Realtor. org*. June 16, 2014. http://www.realtor.org/articles/public-transportation-boosts-property-values.

Wolf, K. L. "Economics and Public Value of Urban Forests." *Urban Agriculture Magazine*, Special Issue on Urban and Periurban Forestry, no. 13 (2004): 31–33.

World Urbanization Prospects, the 2014 Revision. Population Division, United Nations Department of Economic and Social Affairs. June 21, 2016. https://esa.un.org/unpd/wup/.

24 Impact through Design

Energy Efficiency Retrofits for Commercial and Public Buildings. Chicago: Navigant Research, 2014.

Jacques, Carole. "Driven by Higher Rents and Values, Green Buildings Market Grows to $260 Billion." *Lux Research*. October 29, 2014. http://www.luxresearchinc.com/newsand-events/press-releases/read/driven-higher-rents-and-values-greenbuildings-market-grows-260.

Muyskens, John, Dan Keating, and Samuel Granados, "Mapping How the United States Generates its Electricity," *The Washington Post*, July 31, 2015. https://www.washingtonpost.com/graphics/national/power-plants/.

"Number of private and commercial motor vehicle registrations in the U.S. in 2014, by state." *Statista*. 2014. http://www.statista.com/statistics/191011/registered-privateand-commercial-us-motor-vehicles-by-state-2009/.

Reducing the Carbon Footprint of the Built Environment: A Roadmap for Action after COP21. Washington, DC: The American Institute of Architects, 2015.

Transition to Sustainable Buildings: Strategies and Opportunities to 2050. Paris: International Energy Agency, 2013.

30 Downtown Tech Boom

"Compass Global Startup Ecosystem Ranking 2015." *Compass*. July 27, 2015. http://blog.compass.co/the-2015-global-startup-ecosystem-ranking-is-live/.

"Employment by Industry Data." *State of California Employment Development Department*. May 2016. http://www.labormarketinfo.edd.ca.gov/data/employment-by-industry.html.

"Major Areas, Current Employment Estimates." *New York State Department of Labor*. June 21, 2016. https://www.labor.ny.gov/stats/lscesmaj.shtm.

36 Alignment for Impact

Wilson, Woodrow. "Address of President Wilson at Swarthmore College." Swarthmore College, Swarthmore, PA, October 25, 1913.

40 Making Global Business Work

"Managing government relations for the future: McKinsey Global Survey results." *McKinsey & Company*. February 2011. http://www.mckinsey.com/industries/public-sector/our-insights/managing-government-relations-for-the-future-mckinsey-global-survey-results.

State-Owned Enterprises: Catalysts for public value creation? PwC, 2015.

46 Rethinking Public Transit

"Facts and Figures." *Transport for London*. June 21, 2016. https://tfl.gov.uk/corporate/publications-and-reports/facts-and-figures?intcmp=28704.

Macguire, Eoghan. "Could London's disused train tunnels be transformed into cycle highways?" *CNN*. February 11, 2015. http://www.cnn.com/2015/02/11/travel/london-underground-cycle-tunnels/.

Roy, Cyprien. "The London Underline Could Be City's Next Great Project." *Architect*, February 9, 2015. http://www.architectmagazine.com/design/urbanism-planning/the-london-underline-could-be-citys-next-great-project_o

52 Airports without Waiting?

Airport Cities World Conference and Exhibition 2012. San Francisco International Airport: April, 2012.

56 Navigating Olympic Tokyo

Creating the Future: The Long-Term Vision for Tokyo. Tokyo Metropolitan Government, 2014.

Matsutani, Minoru. "Olympic Games expected to provide economic stimulus." *The Japan Times*. September 10, 2014. http://www.japantimes.co.jp/news/2014/09/10/business/economy-business/olympic-games-expected-provide-economic-stimulus/#.V3PcIusrLg5.

62 Measuring Urban Experience

Lynch, Kevin. *The Image of the City*. MIT Press, 1960.

68 Fuel Cells Now

Assessment of the Distributed Generation Market Potential for Solid Oxide Fuel Cells. National Energy Technology Laboratory, September 29, 2013.

Copeland, Claudia. *Energy-Water Nexus: The Energy Sector's Water Use*. Congressional Research Service, January 3, 2014.

Curtin, Sandra, and Jennifer Gangi. *The Business Case for Fuel Cells 2013: Reliability, Resiliency & Savings*. Fuel Cells 2000, 2013.

Curtin, Sandra, and Jennifer Gangi. *Fuel Cells Technologies Market Report 2014*. U.S. Department of Energy, 2014.

Fuel Cell Handbook (Seventh Edition). EG&G Technical Services, Inc., November 2004.

Kubert, Charles. *Fuel Cell Technology: A Clean, Reliable Source of Power*. Clean Energy States Alliance, May 2010.

Mielke, Erik, Laura Diaz Anadon, and Venkatesh Narayanamurti. *Water Consumption of Energy Resource Extraction, Processing, and Conversion*. Energy Technology Innovation Policy Research Group, Belfer Center for Science and International Affairs, and Harvard Kennedy School of Government, October 2010.

The Fuel Cell Industry Review 2012. Fuel Cell Today, 2012.

Wilson, Wendy, Travis Leipzig, and Bevan Griffiths-Sattenspiel. *Burning Our Rivers: The Water Footprint of Electricity*. The River Network, April 2012.

78 The Prefab City

Aitchison, Mathew. "20 shades of beige: Lessons from Japanese prefab housing." *Urban Design Australia Blog*. October 7, 2014. https://urbandesignaustralia.wordpress.com/2014/10/07/20-shades-of-beige-lessons-from-japanese-prefab-housing/.

Architecture for Manufacturing and Assembly (AfMA), Gensler, 2015.

Garrison, James and Aaron Tweedie. *Modular Architecture Manual*. Kullman Buildings Corp, 2008.

Prefabrication and Modularization: Increasing Productivity in the Construction Industry. McGraw-Hill Construction, 2011.

Quale, John, Matthew J. Eckelman, Kyle W. Williams, Greg Sloditskie, and Julie B. Zimmerman. "Construction Matters: Comparing Environmental Impacts of Building Modular and Conventional Homes in the United States." *Journal of Industrial Ecology* 16, no. 2 (2012): 243-253.

86 The Post-Book Librarian?

The State of America's Libraries Report 2015. American Library Association, April 2015.

90 Libraries Are for Studying

Robb, Alice. "92 Percent of College Students Prefer Reading Print Books to E-Readers." *The Republic,* January 14, 2015. http://www.newrepublic.com/article/120765/naomi-barons-words-onscreen-fate-reading-digital-world.

96 Remaking Student Living

Academic Libraries at a Crossroads. Gensler, 2015.

Changing Course. Gensler, 2012.

Fabris, Peter. "6 trends steering today's college residence halls." *Building Design + Construction*. November 7, 2014. http://www.bdcnetwork.com/6-trends-steering-todays-college-residence-halls.

102 A High-Performance Place for Learning

"About." *XQ The Super School Project*. June 21, 2016. http://xqsuperschool.org/about.

Doorley, Scott and Scott Witthoft. *Make Space: How to Set the Stage for Creative Collaboration*. New Jersey: John Wiley & Sons, Inc., 2012.

108 Graphic Learners

"Designing a Path to College + Career." *Publicolor*. June 21, 2016.

State of America's Schools: The Path to Winning Again in Education. Gallup, April 2014.

122 A Breath of Fresh Air

"Ambient (outdoor) air quality and health." *World Health Organization*. March 2014. http://www.who.int/mediacentre/factsheets/fs313/en/

Urbinato, David. "London's Historic 'Pea-Soupers.'" *US Environmental Protection Agency, EPA Journal*. Summer 1994. https://www.epa.gov/aboutepa/londons-historic-pea-soupers.

Wong, Edward. "China Exports Pollution to U.S., Study Finds." *The New York Times*. January 20, 2014. http://www.nytimes.com/2014/01/21/world/asia/china-also-exports-pollution-to-western-us-study-finds.html?_r=0.

126 An Easier Hospital

Berger, Craig. *Wayfinding: Designing and Implementing Graphic Navigational Systems*. Rockport Publishers, 2009.

Hogan, Dennis. *Wayfinding in the Built Environment*. Cooperative Research Centre for Construction Innovation, 2004.

Klippel, Alexander. *Wayfinding Choremes: Conceptualizing Wayfinding and Route Direction Elements*. SFB/TR 8 Monographs, 2003.

Kozhevnikov, Maria, Stephen Kosslyn, and Jennifer Shephard. "Spatial versus object visualizers: A new characterization of visual cognitive style." *Memory & Cognition* 33, no. 4 (2005): 710-726.

Landro, Laura. "A Cure for Hospital Design." *The Wall Street Journal*. February 3, 2014. http://www.wsj.com/articles/SB10001424052702303743604579355202979035492

Lorenz, Bernhard, Hans Jürgen Ohlbach, and Edgar-Philipp Stoffel. "A hybrid spatial model for representing indoor environments." In *Web and Wireless Geographical Information Systems*. Springer Berlin Heidelberg, 2006.

Lynch, Kevin. *The Image of the City*. MIT Press, 1960.

Montello, Daniel R., and Corina Sas. "Human factors of wayfinding in navigation." (2006): 2003-2008.

Salmi, Patricia. "Wayfinding design: Hidden barriers to universal access." Implications 5, no. 8 (2007): 1-6.

132 The Hospital Left Behind

"Announced Hospital Mergers and Acquisitions, 1998-2014." *TrendWatch Chartbook 2015*. The American Hospital Association, 2015.

Chung, A. P., M. Gaynor, and S. Richards-Shubik. *Subsidies and Structure: The Lasting Impact of the Hill-Burton Program on the Hospital Industry*. University of Illinois, December 27, 2012.

Walsh, T. "Telehealth Industry Trends 2016." *The Advisory Board Company*. February 29, 2016. https://www.advisory.com/research/market-innovation-center/resources/2015/telehealth-industry-trends.

Yanci, J., M. Wolford, and P. Young. *What Hospital Executives Should Be Considering in Mergers and Acquisitions*. Dixon Hughes Goodman, 2013.

140 Emotional Consumerism in India

Bijapurkar, Rama. *We Are Like That Only: Understanding the Logic of Consumer India*. India: Penguin Books, 2009.

Bijapurkar, Rama. *Winning in the Indian Market: Understanding the Transformation of Consumer India*. Singapore: John Wiley & Sons (Asia), 2007

India Retail Report 2015. India Retail Forum, 2015.

144 Consumer Multiplicity in China

Doctoroff, Tom. What Chinese Want: Culture, Communism, and China's Modern Consumer. St. Martin's Press, 2012.

150 Brands Go Global

"Consolidated FDI Policy." *Department of Industrial Policy & Promotion, Government of India Ministry of Commerce & Industry*. 2015. http://dipp.nic.in/English/Investor/FDI_Policies/FDI_policy.aspx.

"Mainland China entering new era of luxury cooldown, finds Bain & Company's 2013 'China luxury goods market study.'" *Bain & Company*. December 16, 2013. http://www.bain.com/about/press/press-releases/mainland-china-entering-new-era-of-luxury-cooldown.aspx.

Nardelli, Alberto. "Global middle class nears one billion mark." *The Guardian*, September 24, 2014. http://www.theguardian.com/news/datablog/2014/sep/24/global-middle-class-nears-one-billion-mark.

"The 2014 Global Retail Development Index." *A. T. Kearney*. 2014. http://www.atkearney.com/consumer-products-retail/global-retail-development-index.

Bibliography

156 Experience Reigns

Discovering WOW – A Study of Great Retail Shopping Experiences in North America. Verde Group, Wharton University of Pennsylvania, and Retail Council of Canada, February 2009.

Klaus, Philipp and Stan Maklan. "Towards a Better Measure of Customer Experience," *International Journal of Market Research* 55, no. 2 (2011): 227–246.

Magids, Scott, Alan Zorfas & Daniel Leemon. "The New Science of Customer Emotions," *Harvard Business Review.* November 2015. https://hbr.org/2015/11/the-new-science-of-customer-emotions.

Teixeira, Jorge, Lia Patricio, Nuno J. Nunes, Leonel Nobrega, Raymond P. Fisk, and Larry Constantine. "Customer Experience Modeling: From Customer Experience to Service Design," *Journal of Service Management* 23, no. 3 (2012): 362–376.

162 Experiential ROI

Andersson, Maria, Sara Palmblad, and Tajana Prevedan. *Atmospheric Effects on Hedonic and Utilitarian Customers.* Linnaeus University School of Business and Economics, 2012.

Bitner, Mary Jo. "Servicescapes: The Impact of Physical Surroundings on Customers and Employees." *Journal of Marketing* 56 (April 1991): 57–71.

Watermark Consulting 2015 Customer Experience ROI Study. Watermark Consulting, 2015. http://watermarkconsult.net/CX-ROI

Maklan, S. and Klaus, Ph. "Customer Experience: Are We Measuring the Right Things," *International Journal of Market Research* 53, no. 6 (2011): 771–792.

Petermans, A., W. Janssens, and K. Van Cleempoel. "A Holistic Framework for Conceptualizing Customer Experiences in Retail Environments." *International Journal of Design.* August 13, 2013. http://ijdesign.org/ojs/index.php/IJDesign/article/view/1185/576.

Plevoets, B., A. Petermans, and K. Van Cleempoel. *Developing a theoretical framework for understanding (staged) authentic retail settings in relation to the current experience economy.* PHL University College and Hasselt University, 2010.

168 #Winning the Fan Engagement Game

Lewis, Michael and Manish Tripathi. "Sports Analytics Research Blog." *Emory University.* June 21, 2016. https://scholarblogs.emory.edu/esma/.

Yi, Joseph. "The Value Of The Loyal Fan." *Sports Networker.* January 1, 2015. http://www.sportsnetworker.com/2011/01/25/value-sports-loyal-fan/.

174 Beyond Boutique

Balekjian, Cristina and Lara Sarheim. *Boutique Hotels Segment: The Challenge of Standing Out from the Crowd.* London: HVS, 2011.

"Demand for Independent upscale hotels." *Boutique and Lifestyle Lodging Association.* June 20, 2016. http://www.blla.org/news-room/.

Gevelber, Lisa and Oliver Heckmann. "Travel Trends: 4 Mobile Moments Changing the Consumer Journey." *think with Google.* November 2015. https://www.thinkwithgoogle.com/articles/travel-trends-4-mobile-moments-changing-consumer-journey.html.

Jang, Minseok. *Boutique Hotels Become Branded: The Impact on the Non-Branded Boutique Segment.* Independent Lodging Congress, 2014.

Mangla, Ismat Sarah. "Major Hotel Brands Compete For Space In The Boutique Hotel Trend." *International Business Times.* January 23, 2015. http://www.ibtimes.com/major-hotel-brands-compete-space-boutique-hotel-trend-1793168.

182 Design for Active Aging

Birrer, Richard B. and Sathya P. Vemuri. "Depression in Later Life: A Diagnostic and Therapeutic Challenge." *American Family Physician.* May 15, 2004. http://www.aafp.org/afp/2004/0515/p2375.html.

Hannon, Kerry. "For Many Older Americans, an Enterprising Path." *The New York Times*, February 7, 2014. http://www.nytimes.com/2014/02/08/your-money/for-many-older-americans-an-entrepreneurial-path.html.

McIlwain, John K. "The Surprisingly Simple Amenities that Help Urban Residents Age in Place." *Urban Land.* December 7, 2011. http://urbanland.uli.org/economy-markets-trends/the-surprisingly-simple-amenities-that-help-urban-residents-age-in-place/.

"Population Estimates." *United States Census Bureau.* June 23, 2016. http://www.census.gov/popest/.

"USC Emeriti Center Sponsors Apartment for Life Design Book." *University of Southern California, Emeriti Center.* June 23, 2016. https://emeriti.usc.edu/news/usc-emeriti-center-sponsors-apartment-for-life-design-book/.

Zickuhr, Kathryn and Mary Madden. "Older Adults and Internet Use," *Pew Research Center,* June 6, 2012. Retrieved from http://www.pewinternet.org/2012/06/06/older-adults-and-internet-use/.

190 U.S. Workplace Survey 2016

Adkins, Amy. *Majority of U.S. Employees Not Engaged Despite Gains in 2014.* Gallup, January 28, 2015.

Galvan, Veronica V, Rosa S. Vassal, and Matthew T. Golley. "The Effects of Cell Phone Conversations on the Attention and Memory of Bystanders." *PLOS One Journal.* March 13, 2013.

Kim, Jungsoo and Richard de Dear. "Workspace Satisfaction: the privacy-communication trade-off in open-plan offices." *Journal of Environmental Psychology* 36 (2013): 18–26.

"Measuring Productivity." *Centerline, Newsletter of the Center for the Built Environment at the University of California, Berkeley.* Summer 2012.

Neuner, Jeremy. "40% of America's workforce will be freelancers by 2020." *Quartz*, March 20, 2013.

Quenqua, Douglas. "Cellphones as Modern Irritant." *The New York Times.* March 13, 2015. http://well.blogs.nytimes.com/2013/03/13/study-adds-to-evidence-of-cellphone-distraction/?_r=0.

"Workplace Stress on the Rise with 83% of Americans Frazzled by Something at work." *2013 Work Stress Survey.* Harris Interactive on behalf of Everest College, 2013.

194 U.K. Workplace Survey 2016

Allen, Grahame. *Recession and recovery.* House of Commons Library Research, 2010.

International Comparisons of Productivity - Final Estimates 2014, Office for National Statistics, February 2016. Retrieved from: https://www.ons.gov.uk/economy/economicoutputandproductivity/productivitymeasures.

"UK Labour Market: February 2016." *Office for National Statistics.* February 2016. http://www.ons.gov.uk/employmentandlabourmarket/peopleinwork/employmentandemployeetypes/bulletins/uklabourmarket/february2016.

Working Remotely. YouGov, May 2015.

198 Asia Workplace Survey 2016

State of the Global Workplace: Employee Engagement Insights for Business Leaders Worldwide. Gallup, 2013.

204 The Indian Workplace

Guha, Ramachandra. *India after Gandhi: The History of the World's Largest Democracy.* Harper Perennial, 2008.

"India's New HR Challenge: Managing a Multigenerational Workforce." *Knowledge@Wharton.* February 14, 2014. http://knowledge.wharton.upenn.edu/article/indias-new-hr-challenge-managing-multigenerational-workforce/.

208 Legal Innovation Lab

Smith, Jennifer. "Law Firms Say Good-Bye Office, Hello Cubicle." *The Wall Street Journal*, July 15, 2012. http://www.wsj.com/articles/SB1000142 4052702303612804577528940291670100.

212 City / Building / Desk

Koolhaas, Rem. "Typical Plan." *SMLXL.* Boston: Monacelli Press, 1999.

Maas, Winy. "The Continuous Interior." *FARMAX: Excursions on Density.* 010 Uitgeverij, June 1998.

The Future of Office Work, Vol. 1: How We Got Here. Gensler, 2015.

220 For the Love of Purpose

"2015 State of the Nonprofit Sector Survey." *Nonprofit Finance Fund.* 2015. http://survey.nonprofitfinancefund.org.

2015 UST Nonprofit Employee Engagement & Retention Report. UST. 2015.

Baumeister, Roy, Kathleen D. Vohs, et al. "Some Key Differences between a Happy Life and a Meaningful Life." *Journal of Positive Psychology.* January 15, 2013.

Connecting People and Purpose. Great Places to Work, 2016.

Garton, Eric and Michael C. Mankins. "Engaging Your Employees Is Good, but Don't Stop There." *Harvard Business Review.* December 9, 2015. https://hbr.org/2015/12/engaging-your-employees-is-good-but-dont-stop-there.

Ryan, Richard M. and Edward L. Deci. "Intrinsic and Extrinsic Motivations: Classic Definitions and New Directions." *Academic Press.* 2000. http://ac.els-cdn.com/S0361476X99910202/1-s2.0-S0361476X99910202-main.pdf?_tid=cf7231a2-eaf4-11e5-b7fc-00000aacb362&acdnat=1458077467_088c59a37ac0bac05e2967687e098a76.

Schwartz, Barry. *Why We Work.* TED Books/Simon & Schuster, 2015.

224 Trading on Stress

Carney, Dana R., Amy J.C. Cuddy, and Andy J. Yap. "Power Posing: Brief Nonverbal Displays Affect Neuroendocrine Levels and Risk Tolerance." *Psychological Science* 21, no. 10 (2010).

Coates, John. *The Hour between Dog and Wolf: Risk Taking, Gut Feelings and the Biology of Boom and Bust.* New York: Penguin Press, 2012.

Fenton-O'Creevy, Mark. "It's clouds' illusions I recall… trading and the illusion of control." *Emotional Finance.* May 26, 2013. http://emotionalfinance.net/2013/05/26/trading-and-the-illusion-of-control/.

Greenspan, Alan. *The Map and the Territory: Risk, Human Nature, and the Future of Forecasting.* New York: Penguin Press, 2013.

Kahneman, Daniel. *Thinking, Fast and Slow.* New York: Farrar, Straus and Giroux, 2011.

Langer, Ellen J. "The Illusion of Control." *Journal of Personality and Psychology* 32, no. 2 (1975).

Lewis, Michael. "The Wolf Hunters of Wall Street." *The New York Times Magazine*, March 31, 2014. http://www.nytimes.com/2014/04/06/magazine/flash-boys-michael-lewis.html?_r=0.

Sternberg, Esther M. *Healing Spaces: The Science of Place and Well-Being.* Cambridge: Belknap Press, 2009.

Yap, Andy J., Abbie S. Wazlawek, Brian J. Lucas, Amy J.C. Cuddy, and Dana R. Carney. "The Ergonomics of Dishonesty: The Effect of Incidental Posture on Stealing, Cheating, and Traffic Violations." *Psychological Science* 24, no. 11 (2013).

230 Live + Work + Play in Tokyo

China's Spaces in between. Gensler, 2014.

Gen Y and the World of Work. Hays Recruiting Experts Worldwide, 2013.

Industry and Employment in Tokyo, a Graphic Overview 2015. Bureau of Industrial and Labor Affairs, Tokyo Metropolitan Government, 2015.

The Future of Office Work. Gensler, 2013.

Tokyo Daikaizo Map 2020. Nikkei Architecture, 2015.

234 Emerging Work Styles

Centerline, Summer. *The Holy Grail of Measuring Workplace Productivity.* Center for the Built Environment, 2012.

Craig, David. "It Doesn't Matter Whether or Not You Like Your Open Office." *Fast Company.* January 23, 2014. http://www.fastcoexist.com/3025052/it-doesnt-matter-whetheror-not-you-like-your-open-office.

Hongisto, Valtteri, Annu Haapakangas, andMiia Haka. "Task Performance and Speech Intelligibility—A Model to Promote Noise Control Actions in Open Offices." *Performance.* Foxwoods, CT: 9th International Congress on Noise as a Public Health Problem, 2008.

Kim, Jungsoo and Richard de Dear. "Workspace Satisfaction: The Privacy-communication Trade-off in Open-Plan Offices." *Journal of Environmental Psychology* 36, (2013): 18–26.

Lee, So Young and Jay L. Brand. "Effects of Control over Office Workspace on Perceptions of the Work Environment and Work Outcomes." *Journal of Environmental Psychology* 25, no. 3 (2005): 323–333.

Tierney, John. "Open offices prompt pleas for workplace quiet." *The Seattle Times.* May 19, 2012. http://www.seattletimes.com/nation-world/open-offices-prompt-pleas-for-workplace-quiet/.

"Too Many Interruptions at Work?" *Gallup Business Journal.* June 8, 2008. http://businessjournal.gallup.com/content/23146/too-manyinterruptions-work.aspx

Index

Acknowledgments

Editorial

Editor
Christine Barber

Managing Editor
Tim Pittman

Creative Director
Wesley Meyer

Lead Designer
Minjung Lee

Design Team
Gretchen Bustillos
Macaulay Campbell
Jamie Carusi
Vincenzo Centinaro
Miriam Diaz
Renee Dunn
Stephen Edmond
Brian Erlinder
Pierce Fisher
Julie Guirl
Rolando Gumler
Saybel Guzman
Laura Latham
Sabrina Mason
Joe Morgan
Ngoc Ngo
Mina Noorbakhsh
Beth Novitsky
Thomas Oesterhus
Emily Shields
Fabiano Vincenzi
Danny Wehbe

Editorial Board
Maddy Burke-Vigeland
Andy Cohen
Mark Coleman
Dian Duvall
William Hooper
Diane Hoskins
Tom Ito
Irwin Miller
Ian Mulcahey
John Parman
Janet Pogue McLaurin
Duncan Swinhoe
Rives Taylor
Gervais Tompkin
Li Wen

Contributing Editors
Nick Bryan
Clark Rendall

Additional Contributors
Bryan Burkhart
Kevin Craft
David De Leon
Laura Gralnick
Hey J Min
Meghan Moran
Holly Murphy
Zsuzsa Nagy
Rika Putri
Lainie Ransom
Sophie Reid
Oscar Saylor
Mandy Stehouwer

Research Teams

Team members are identified at the beginning of each chapter.

Image Credits

All images credited to Gensler unless otherwise noted.

Peter Adams / Photolibrary / Getty Images, 143
F. Affonso, "Bedroom" icon, thenounproject.com, 98-99
Tayseer AL-Hamad / Moment / Getty Images, 143
Andi Andreas / Moment Select / Getty Images, 145
Scott E Barbour / Stone / Getty Images, 147
Chris Barrett, 226-227
Akash Bhattacharya / Moment / Getty Images, 140
Louise Burnett, 50-51, 178-179
Stephen Edmond, 174-175
Filipe Frazao / Shutterstock, 152
Future Rail Transit Network, LACTC Annual Report (1983), 212
Shai Gil, 208
Chris Grosse, 132-133
Heidi Hampton, 118-119
Honeywell ad (1981), 212
John Harper / Corbis Documentary / Getty Images, 142
Brendan Jackson, 14-15
jaap, "Moving" icon, thenounproject.com, 98-99
John Lund / Blend Images / Getty Images, 140
Ashley Marsh, 106-107

Wesley Meyer, 100-101, 256-257
Irwin Miller, 156-157
Win Mixter, 156-157
David O'Brien, 156-157
pcruciatti / Shutterstock, 152
Radio Shack ad (1987), 213
Garrett Rowland, 190-191
Miriam Safi, 156-157
Jasper Sanidad, 192-193
Bonnie Sen Photography, 64
Shaw Walker ad (1980), 212
Elysee Shen / Moment / Getty Images, 146
Tetra Images / Getty Images, 224-225
Tam Tran, 72-73
My Linh Truong, 216
Images by Tang Ming Tung / Moment / Getty Images, 144
VasukiRao / iStock.com, 152
Kent Weakley / Shutterstock, 176
"Reading" icon, Gerald Wildmoser, thenounproject.com, 98-99
Captain Zhu, 156-157, 160-161